A **HUMOROUS** and **UNFLINCHING** account of
learning to **LIVE AGAIN** with **SUDDEN DISABILITY**

looking up

D1387774

TIM RUSHBY-SMITH

First published in Great Britain in 2008 by
Virgin Books Ltd
Thames Wharf Studios
Rainville Road
London
W6 9HA

ISBN 978-0-7535-1386-6

The Random House Group Limited supports The Forest Stewardship
Council (FSC), the leading international forest certification
organisation. All our titles that are printed on Greenpeace
approved FSC certified paper carry the FSC logo.
Our paper procurement policy can be found at
www.rbooks.co.uk/environment

Typeset by Phoenix Photosetting, Chatham, Kent
Printed and bound in Great Britain by
CPI Bookmarque, Croydon CR90 4TD

1 3 5 7 9 10 8 6 4 2

For Penny and Rosalie

1

Where to begin? Well, that's easy. I am lying on the roof of an old garage at the bottom of a garden. I am under a tree, looking up at the branches and the grey sky beyond, and I am confused as to what has just happened. I was working in the tree, six metres up and attached by rope and harness, preparing to come down after 45 minutes of climbing and pruning. Now I am on my back on a garage roof, and I can't feel my legs. So much for 'slow motion' – the accident is over before I even begin to work out what is happening.

I shout out to my wife, Penny, who is in the garden calling to me, and trying to get through a tangle of shrubs to see me. She is five months pregnant. Out of the corner of her eye, she has just seen me fall and, until hearing my voice, had presumed me dead. It is 1 April 2005, I am 36 years old, and suddenly my life has concertinaed so that all the happy times and periods of gentle contentedness have disappeared into the folds, and my history has become 36 years of stumbling from catastrophe to disaster, as if I am locked into a very inefficient subconscious suicide pact.

There is a voice in my head. It is my voice, and it is saying, 'Well, you've really gone and fucked it this time.'

Outside, my voice is saying, 'Penny, I'm sorry. I'm sorry. Pen, Pen, it hurts. I'm sorry. It hurts so much.'

Now, what's weird here is that I remember saying 'it hurts', but somehow I have no recollection of the pain. I remember thinking, 'it's going to hurt any minute now', and trying to put the pain off for as long as possible. I also remember howling like a banshee, so it must have hurt, but all I can remember is my legs feeling as if they are in a 'tuck' position, and I am unable to move them. I'm sure I can feel them, but they refuse to respond.

The 'thwup thwup' of the helicopter blades of the air ambulance cuts through the sound of vigorous spring birdsong that Penny has been getting me to concentrate on to keep me distracted. She has just scaled a six-foot-high fence into the adjoining garden, and is standing on their compost heap in order to be able to see me.

'Can you hear the birds? It sounds like a robin. Isn't it a beautiful spring morning?'

'I'm so sorry, Pen! Aww it really hurts! I can't feel my legs! Pen? Pen? I'm so sorry!'

'It's OK. It's OK. The ambulance is on its way.'

Penny is terrified that I will lose consciousness, so she keeps up a constant line of inane conversation, which is helping her to keep her own panic at bay, that sense of facing something monumental – the moment when you know that the world is turning, and the events before you are totally out of your control. She keeps her focus, and every time I try and lift my head, she shouts at me to keep still, and changes the subject. She gets me to talk about Australia, where she is from, and where we were on holiday less than a week ago.

The first emergency service to arrive on the scene is the police. Penny explains that we are landscapers and that this is our client's garden. She shows one of the officers where to climb over the fence that she has scaled in her pregnant state, and the policeman adds to my bewilderment by asking me for my name and address.

Within twenty minutes I am joined by a paramedic, who has very bravely climbed onto the roof (which is of dubious structural integrity and most likely made of asbestos), and she has answered my pleas by shooting me full of I don't know what, but nor do I know much of anything now. The world drifts in and out of focus and the light filtered through the branches becomes brighter and more colourful, and voices around me swirl in and out, and I think: this is it, I'm dying.

I'm dying. Except I'm not just thinking it, and the paramedic laughs and she says, 'You're not dying,' which comes as something of a relief, and so begins a two-week period under the influence of very strong drugs.

As I drift in and out of consciousness, I am put onto a backboard and someone tells me that they have to move me, and that they are sorry but it is going to hurt. I hear a voice inside my head telling me to scream, so I do, but it feels as if I am doing so merely to be polite and do what is expected of me, rather than because of any pain. I glimpse my brother among the various faces that drift past, and I have a very vague sense of confusion as to why he's here. I lose consciousness, and wake up in a hospital bed with a neck brace on.

From the outside, Penny has given me a more reliable account of what happens during this time. The paramedics arrive on the scene with an air of calm and friendly efficiency. The policeman is shooed back down into the garden, and after a brief discussion, the lightest paramedic climbs onto the roof so that she can assess me. Some firemen appear in the adjoining garden. As they are cutting off my clothes and harness, and Penny starts shivering with cold, fear and adrenalin, a familiar face appears over the shed roof. It is my brother, Chris. Penny is so confused at seeing him there that she forgets to ask how or why. It turns out that the neighbour is the mother of a good friend of Chris's, who knew that we were doing some work next door, and she telephoned him straight away. His presence is a huge help in preventing Penny from feeling alone. She also asks him if he could phone our mother, as the very thought of having to break the news makes Penny feel sick. He graciously agrees, but it is obvious from the look of concern on his face that he knows that it is going to be a terrible call to have to make.

I am lifted off the roof by the fire brigade using a sort of emergency platform that is extended from the back of a fire engine and delicately threaded through the branches of the trees. All in all, there are about eighteen people involved, and the whole neighbourhood has come out to watch. The London Air Ambulance lands in a nearby park, and I am taken first by the platform into a car park, and then on by ambulance to the entrance to the park, before being taken to the helicopter by gurney along a very bumpy path (more screaming, apparently), all the time accompanied by Penny. As we near the air ambulance, there is a man and a boy with a video camera, filming our approach. Penny shouts at them, and the paramedics ask them more politely to put the camera away. No doubt they are hoping to sell the clips to the world's media, and are disappointed that it's all just for some bloke who's fallen out of a tree.

Although it is against medical advice for Penny to travel in an unpressurised cabin during pregnancy, the choice is an hour by road or four minutes in the air, of which only about 30 seconds is at an 'unadvisable altitude' and the air ambulance crew can see that there is no way that she is going to be left behind, so they take her along too. I am carefully loaded on board, the various monitors and masks attached, bags of equipment loaded, Penny loaded and joined by two paramedics. They are ready to go when Penny spots a bumblebee that has landed on one of the paramedics' bags and is coming along for the ride. She points out the stowaway, and the pilot immediately calls a halt to take-off while one of the paramedics lifts the bag out before ushering the bumblebee away, amid jokes about bees flying onto noses of helicopter pilots. The remaining passengers are secured, doors closed and we are all flown across London to the Royal London Hospital in Whitechapel.

Once there, I am taken to the emergency room, where I am greeted by a group of about ten medics in scrubs and masks. Penny is ushered out to the waiting room to be quizzed further by the determined PC from the garden, and to fill out various hospital admission forms. Everyone comments on the date: 1 April.

Eventually Chris arrives, and Penny excuses herself to make her first call. Instinctively she wants to have a friend there as well as my family, so it is our close friend Graham who has his lunch interrupted, immediately senses the seriousness of the situation, and leaves work at once for the hospital. Penny is invited in to see me again, as the assessments have been completed. This time I look like something from a science-fiction film. I am naked on a bed, surrounded entirely by an inflatable transparent plastic bubble, with only my head poking out at one end.

One of the medical team explains: 'We're going to take an MRI scan to assess the damage, but we suspect a spinal-cord injury. In the meantime we are giving him large doses of steroids to try and minimise the damage.'

Penny returns to the waiting room, where Chris hugs her as she begins to cry for the first time, sobbing, 'I hate feeling this much out of control.'

My mother, Uli, arrives with my stepfather Eugene, followed soon after by Graham. They all pace the waiting room in a hot, stifling silence.

Eventually one of the doctors arrives. He is direct and serious, but comes across as open and approachable. At no time does he give them false hope as he reveals the results of the MRI scan.

'It's very serious. Tim has what looks like a complete severing of the spinal cord.'

He pauses, then, 'He won't walk again.'

Penny swears under her breath in an otherwise silent room. She can see my mother wiping tears away.

Less than four hours after my fall, the neck brace is removed and a young doctor comes in for the 'give it to me straight, doc' routine. He is very good, tells me I won't walk again, and pats me self-consciously on the shoulder. I feel sorry for him, and almost apologise for putting him through all of this. It must be the large amounts of morphine, but I feel as if I am playing this part in a film, and I'm trying to impart the right amount of emotional gravitas, but it's hard work, and I just want to yell 'cut' and take a break so I can work out my motivation.

I make upbeat comments to friends and family about life in a wheelchair, as if the adjustment will be effortless. Or rather, the film version of me says all these things. I cry some, but even this seems as if I am moved by the plight of someone else.

At one point in the afternoon, Penny joins my mother by the window, looking down at the courtyard below. She wants to tell her that she isn't going anywhere, and that she is still going to love me, despite the massive changes that are evidently going to occur in our life together. In the end, all she can say is, 'You know, I just love him so much.' It is enough.

In the evening, Penny is joined at my bedside by one of the female paramedics. She unclips my silver necklace from round her neck where she put it for safekeeping, and says, 'My shift has just ended and I've been wondering how you're doing, big fella.'

Eventually everyone leaves, and I find myself lying flat on my back, able only to move my arms and swivel my head. I do a quick inventory. Absolutely nothing going on from the waist down. No movement in my legs, no sensation in my genitals. Now this is something that hasn't occurred to me until this point, and there is a shock of realisation, although it, too, feels far removed, like a distant memory of something sad. Through the drug haze, I try and replay the events of the day. I struggle to explain what happened, what went wrong. The medication pulls me away from concentration and leaves me drifting.

Meanwhile, Penny has been thinking about the baby on and off all day, but she hasn't felt much movement. She asks one of the nurses on the ward if there is anyone she could see.

They suggest that she goes down to obstetrics or A & E, as it is now out of hours. Then one of the other nurses overhears, and ushers Penny to a neighbouring bed that is empty and pulls the curtain around. Penny's blood pressure is fine and the nurse assures her that she can hear a tiny heartbeat. She tells the nurse how relieved she is. 'We only had an ultrasound at the beginning of the week, where we saw the baby waving back at us on the screen. It was supposed to be me providing the big event of the year. Getting all the attention. And now,' she rolls her eyes, 'typical male, Tim goes and upstages me.'

She is offered a high-backed upholstered chair by my bedside to stay the night in, but she is so uncomfortable that at 11 p.m. she whispers goodnight, and goes home with our friend Neil, who is a consultant anaesthetist. Over the next few months he provides us with valued support and a bit of inside information that makes the medical world we have just become a part of less intimidating. Neil and his wife put Penny up so that she doesn't have to go home, and they sit up until the early hours discussing the day, before Penny eventually drags herself up to bed, where she cries herself to sleep.

For me, the night is punctuated by 'turning'. Turning takes the form of a group of three nurses rolling me over onto alternate sides in order to prevent pressure sores developing. Normally, if you lie in one position for a long time, you get discomfort in the form of cramp, or pins and needles. This is a signal to the brain, warning that the pressure on one spot is starving the skin and the epidermis of blood. The blood is needed to wash out the build-up of toxins, and to provide oxygen. No blood, and the cells in the area begin to break down, which can eventually lead to a pressure sore.

Although the nurses are very careful, the turning process is extremely painful, with hands grabbing at me from all sides as they try to keep my spine immobile while turning me over. Along with the shock and pain, my tears bring the added distress of visits from a nurse who insists on talking to me about God and 'our Lord Jesus Christ'. My rabid atheism has certainly not been tamed by my situation. If I am to find 'redemption', it is not now, and certainly not by being preached to by someone who is clearly taking advantage of a captive audience.

The next day starts with tears, tea and Ready Brek through a straw, as I can barely turn my head, and my arm movements are heavily restricted by pain. I receive a visit from a professor. He is the head of the neurological team at the hospital, and the visit involves looking at X-rays, lots of sage chin-stroking and various minions hanging around like needy kids round the teacher in a primary-school playground.

The professor explains that he is going to operate on me on 6 April, so that he can have his own team working with him. He plans to insert a fixation in order to stabilise my spine.

And so, I drift in and out of lucidity, hear tales from nurses about previous patients with spinal injuries, people who had been told they would never walk again, who have come back to visit the ward walking (a miracle, of course).

Meanwhile, Penny has the awful telephone calls to make. Her parents are at a wedding in Melbourne, but once Penny's brother has contacted them, they leave straight away to return home to Sydney. My father eventually gets a signal on his telephone in a remote area of France where he is on holiday with his wife Margaret, only to find that he has seventeen missed calls from Chris. Having tried unsuccessfully to return the calls, he telephones me on my mobile to see if I know what the emergency is, and so I get to tell him myself. I'm not even sure exactly what I tell him, as I am drifting in and out of lucidity, but I manage to get the main details across.

Penny spends much of the day on the fire escape to get a signal and some privacy to make all the difficult calls. She quickly learns to get across early that I am alive, but 'seriously injured'.

I receive visits from friends and family. Penny gets text

messages all day. They offer help and comfort in whatever way they can. Friends buy me an electric fan, as there is a mini-heatwave and the ward is fiercely hot. I'm given a digital radio as well but, most valuable of all, I get a seemingly constant stream of visitors. I lie in bed holding court, naked except for a white sheet that just accentuates my Australian tan, my feet even bearing the white lines earned by living for a month in flip-flops.

Through the confusion of shock and medication I play my role with élan, all brave face and witty remarks, but I'm drifting, on the point of drowning, and when I do come up for air all I can do is cry.

Things get a bit disjointed from here. I have surgery to stabilise my spine with a titanium fixation on 6 April. The surgery takes around six hours. Penny waits at home for several hours with friends and family, and then begins to phone the hospital at regular intervals. Unable to get any news, she phones Neil, who rings the hospital and finds out that I have been moved to recovery. Penny comes to the hospital, and waits for several more hours in the patient lounge, watching random television: a BBC special about Frank Gardner, the Middle East correspondent who suffered a spinal-cord injury after being shot in the back. The documentary includes footage of him walking in callipers at Stanmore spinal unit.

Eventually I come round and Penny is called as I am wheeled back to the ward. The surgery is described as having gone 'pretty well', although they couldn't fully realign one of my vertebrae and had to leave it, as surgery had taken longer than expected and I was 'losing too much blood', according to the rather vague account that Penny receives from one of the junior members of the professor's team, which includes a series of hand gestures to accompany the erudite explanation, 'Well, it was like that, we've got it to there, but it should be like that.' After a pause, he adds, 'It's complete.'

Without further explanation, he walks off.

Fortunately, Scott Cairns (the senior house officer) takes the time to get all the films out and explain to Penny and my mother how my spine has been 'fixed', and where the screws and rods have been inserted.

Meanwhile I am put on a patient-controlled analgesia (PCA) machine, where I get to press a button when it hurts and the machine administers a dose of morphine into my IV line. Yummy.

At first I am fairly out of it, and everything feels like it's under control. The pain-management team visit me, like pushers with clipboards, and tell me that I can have as much medication as I need and that there is no reason why I should feel any pain. I speak into a borrowed Dictaphone a few times and I feel confident of the incisive perception of my observations. The following is a transcript: '…strange thoughts and ramblings. I've just thought of all these women standing around talking about a charity for fathers who are missing during childbirth, and it's someone to come and eat your biscuits for you. I don't know if that's my subconscious saying that my main role in childbirth is to eat biscuits. But, er… just the tagline is, "Who's going to come and eat your biscuits for you?"'

At this point in the recording, there is a bleep of the PCA machine, and a rare moment of lucidity, when I suggest that this observation may have been triggered by the fact that 'the drugs are being handed out with a trowel at the moment'. There's more of the same. A lot more of the same, and also a few observations that suggest I am starting to assimilate what has happened to me. Only I'm not, on account of the morphine I am feeding myself at the touch of a button.

Then the morphine stops. I don't know this at first. The machine is still bleeping cheerfully when I press my little green button, but the pain seems to be getting worse. The dosage is upped, but still the pain worsens. Finally, I am screaming and in tears and the ward sister gets really furious with the pain-management doctor, who realises that the PCA machine is malfunctioning and finally, after 24 hours of excruciating pain, the pain doctor concludes that I need something much stronger than the PCA now, and she stands around with several other doctors discussing what a good idea she's had, and I scream, 'Just give me the fucking stuff!'

She looks around, rather flustered at the rude intrusion, the group of doctors breaks up, and someone is sent for the drugs trolley. I am given a small capsule of something very, very strong and I gradually drift away from the pain which, although still there, feels remote and imprecise.

From now on, my stay at the Royal London is punctuated at regular intervals by large doses of Oramorph, a kind of liquid morphine, which becomes virtually my only 'food', other than the odd piece of melon and occasional coffee which I insist on sending visitors out on long and confusing missions to procure on the rare occasions of coherence.

Most of my time is spent passing through consciousness, sometimes contented, in a warm blanket of painlessness, at other times filled with sadness and overcome with tears, but weeping for the pain that those around me must be feeling. The visits remain upbeat, but it is not hard to see the concern etched on people's faces in the pauses in our incoherent conversations.

I sleep a lot, and the edges between my dreams and reality become almost seamless. I am aware of my brother and stepdad visiting me, but I am unable to acknowledge their presence, especially as they are sitting at a grand piano, which they have somehow smuggled onto the ward. The ward that now resembles the library of a stately home. Every now and then there is a long beep and one of the staff will call out, 'Breathe, Tim, breathe,' as I am on so much medication by now that my respiratory rate keeps slowing down so far that the monitor starts to bleep in alarm.

I 'wake up' to find that reality is actually a dream that I remembered from several weeks before the accident, and that I am living in a shipping container in a shanty town in a third world country. I can't speak the language, *and* I am an amputee from the waist down. Cute. It takes about five minutes to rebuild the Royal London Hospital around me again, and get back to what is still a pretty depressing reality. The ward changes. From the grand library, it becomes bright and airy, half glass and empty, except for my bed and the nursing staff. Next, I am in a huge queue of hospital beds stretching out for miles.

In time, I become a little more coherent. The bed I am in is designed to prevent pressure sores, and I am no longer being turned. I can raise the head of the bed so that I am able to 'sit' up, supported by an air mattress that thrums away, day and night, creating a warm and fuzzy background noise that suits my warm and fuzzy medication.

Friends come in a regular stream, most talking about stem-cell research, as this seems to be the biggest internet hit when trying to find out anything about spinal-cord injury. There is lots of positive talk of breakthroughs in the field, and exciting possibilities. I listen with detached interest, and make encouraging noises. However, there is also one friend who comes in and sees me who has an interesting 'think outside of the box' take on the whole thing. In a lull in our mundane conversation, he looks up and says, 'You know, with nanotechnologies developing so fast, it will only be a matter of time before you'll be able to get some kind of exoskeleton that you can strap onto your legs, and use to walk run leap huge buildings.'

I have a plaster cast taken in order to make a full torso brace, which will support my back when I sit up properly, and plans are afoot either to move me to a spinal unit, or to carry out my rehabilitation within the Royal London, where I would be the only spinal patient going through rehab. There is discussion about several spinal units, and I hear the name

Stoke Mandeville mentioned, which triggers a strange sense of familiarity. I reach for a childhood memory and realise that this is probably the first time I have heard those two words unaccompanied by the name Jimmy Savile. It sounds strange, like hearing a long conversation exclusively about Ernie Wise.

One of the professor's team, the senior house officer Scott (again), who turns out to be a Tottenham Hotspur fan, finds out about my lifelong Arsenal obsession and, as well as distracting me with football banter, he takes the time to show me my X-rays, and explain about the spinal cord and the damage I have sustained.

'The nerves leave the spinal cord in bundles through each vertebra. They then travel down to the areas that they serve. In your case, the nerves are damaged where the last thoracic and the first lumbar vertebrae meet.'

He shows me a chart, a sensory 'map' of the nervous system. It is an image of a man with horizontal lines marked across his entire body, each section marked with a letter and number denoting the vertebra that relates to the nerves.

'The thing is,' he continues, 'after a trauma like yours, the nervous system can go into what's called spinal shock, which is a temporary defensive reaction, and means that it isn't possible to do a definitive assessment of your neurological condition until things have settled down.'

'How long?' I ask.

'About five weeks in some cases.' He pauses. 'Although, to be honest, looking at the damage to your spinal cord, it looks like it's about ninety-five per cent severed. The likelihood of you regaining any sensation in extremely remote.'

By taking the time and being fully open, he begins my understanding of the full implications of my injury. For the first time, I feel like I am being included in my treatment, and I realise how important this is.

* * *

As time goes on I become more aware of some of the other patients around me on the neurological ward. There's a patient opposite me called Barry, who I can just about see from my prone position, and who turns out to be another Tottenham fan. Together we demonstrate the importance of football as a male language in order to reach out, without looking like you are actually reaching out, if you see what I mean. Anyway, while he's helping me, picking up call buttons and whatever else that I drop in the night, unbeknown to me, Penny has been helping him by doing a bit of shopping, and I make him a gift of one of the several pairs of earplugs I have obtained (never go to hospital without them is my advice, especially if you are in the bed next to me, by all accounts). I find out later, when I receive a touching letter and a signed picture of the whole Arsenal team, that Barry is actually a golfing partner of George Graham, the former manager of both Tottenham and Arsenal.

To my right is a man of about twenty-something who has suffered some sort of neurological trauma that has affected his long-term memory, but seems otherwise fit and well. He is a student, and often receives visits from friends and classmates. The trouble is, he has no idea who they are. Every morning when he wakes up I hear him have the same conversation with the staff nurse.

'Good morning, can you please tell me why I am in hospital?'

'Yes,' comes the reply. 'You have a neurological problem which is affecting your memory.'

'I see, I see. And, who am I, please?'

It is difficult to listen to, especially when his friends visit, and they lose patience after he asks them the same question about how he knows them for the nth time, and their answers become less gentle and more mocking. I can imagine that it will not be long before he stops receiving visits, and I think of his life lost somewhere, perhaps never to be continued. I begin to understand just how important it is that my physical impairment hasn't compromised who I am, and I get a bit of an insight into just what must have gone through Penny's mind between seeing me fall and hearing me talk.

More days and nights pass, and I haven't had a bowel movement since the accident, although the urine bag attached to the indwelling catheter that is attached to me is being emptied frequently. So frequently that one of the staff nurses asks if I can go easy on the fluids, following a day when I pass over eight litres of urine. Morphine makes you thirsty. And it constipates.

Another week begins with the news that a bed has been found for me at Stoke Mandeville, and I am to be moved on Thursday (thirteen days after the accident). Then I am told that there isn't a bed for me, but that they have accepted me in principle, and that they have a 'bed meeting' every Friday. Sounds cosy until I realise that this simply means a meeting where they discuss how many beds are available, rather than some kind of pyjama party.

Between her daily visits, Penny spends her time talking to our accountant, the Health and Safety Executive, and making the last few difficult telephone calls to friends who haven't yet heard. Our friends and family rally round, and ensure that we don't have any immediate financial worries, and I feel as if I have a large net protecting me from day-to-day worries and allowing me to concentrate on what is happening to me. Penny also spends time trying to find information on the internet, as do all of our friends, and when she comes to see me she nods and listens intently as I tell her the latest bit of information I have gleaned, not revealing that she knows it already.

Friday comes around, and the word is that I have a bed, and I will be moved up to Stoke Mandeville on Monday. In the meantime I am moved into a side room, which feels like such luxury, despite the non-functioning television and the peeling paint. In the morning the ward sister, having asked Penny if I usually wear a beard, comes in and gives me a shave, a gesture of great kindness that makes me feel a little stronger about facing the day, as the morning is the hardest part of the day, waking up and finding that it is all still real. I still haven't seen myself in a mirror, but Penny tells me that one of the things that she finds really bewildering is that I still look so healthy.

In the afternoon the physiotherapists at the Royal London put me in the new, made-to-measure fibreglass waistcoat, and I manage to sit up on the end of the bed. The sense of achievement leaves me weeping. I feel like Douglas Bader in *Reach for the Sky*. By this time I am being given morphine twice a day, and on demand every two hours if required, so I actually think that I am Douglas Bader in *Reach for the Sky*.

The weekend comes and goes, punctuated by visits of family and friends, all impressed at my bravery and sanguine cheerfulness. It is easy to play this role, all the time insulated by the detachment offered by the medication. The only thing that punctures my protective layer is when I insist Penny brings in the photographs from our recent trip to Australia. We got back at the weekend, and I had the accident on the following Friday, not even long enough to get the photos printed.

The opening few are images of me and a friend on the beach in Melbourne, charging around kicking a football (Aussie rules). We attempted to stage epic catches and scenes of sporting brilliance, clowning around on the beach, jumping and running and eventually hurling ourselves into the ocean. The impact of these images is unavoidable, and I quickly decide to defer the picture show until some other time. This decision is enough for the heavy, red-velvet pharmaceutical curtain to close again.

As the amount of morphine administered is increased, so are the doses of laxative, but without effect. On the Sunday, I notice a hard lump in my abdomen, and I am sent for an X-ray, dropped by the porters onto a hard stretcher with profuse apologies for the intense pain caused, wheeled over painful lumps and bumps down a corridor that looks so old that I am expecting any minute to pass a top-hatted Dickensian character called Mr Bumblesnatch or some such. The X-ray reveals the lump to be 'nothing'. The cause is constipation.

Monday arrives and no sign of my transfer. The ward sister phones the bed manager and she is told that I will be moved on Monday *or* Tuesday.

My parents come and visit, and it is as if I am full to overflowing with the pain and sadness of my situation, and at last I cry properly, uncontrollably. I cry about my condition and because I am terrified, but I also cry at the pain that my situation is causing to those closest to me, and it is this that I find most difficult to bear.

The lump in my abdomen is still there, and is joined by another. On Monday night, things take a turn for the worse. Chronic or compacted constipation can cause the sufferer to dry retch as the system backs right up, and the body tries anything to rid itself of waste products. It also causes a pain that the morphine cannot touch.

I get no sleep whatsoever that night, between the dry retching and two further trips to X-ray to confirm that it is 'just constipation'. By Monday morning I am in a very bad way. The ward sister arrives on the early shift, and takes over, performing what is delightfully referred to as a 'manual evacuation' every hour for three hours until the pain subsides. Just as she gets me comfortable, she is shocked to find an ambulance crew on the ward to pick me up for the journey to Stoke Mandeville. She and Penny have fifteen minutes to get me dressed and pack up my various goods and chattels (which one accumulates surprisingly fast in hospital), before I am transferred onto a stretcher with a discreet handful of pills for the journey, and we head off through the hospital and across the car park, conducting teary farewells with the wonderful ward sister and promising triumphant return visits after rehabilitation.

* * *

So off we go to Stoke Mandeville hospital or, more accurately, the National Spinal Injuries Centre. I am still whacked out on morphine for the journey up, and the ambulance ride is pretty uneventful. Penny travels with me, and we both feel that the move to a spinal unit is a positive step, although the prospect of being 40 miles from home in Hackney is difficult to face, especially as we aren't sure how much longer Pen will be able cope with all the travelling as her bump grows ever larger.

When we arrive at the spinal unit, my only view is the ceiling, except for a brief glimpse of someone in a wheelchair going past at high speed, which triggers a vague sense of there being a future, a thought that causes a lump in my throat. It is the closest thing to relief that I have felt so far. We emerge from the lift and the spinal unit has an atmosphere of peace and calm control compared to the chaos of the Royal London. This is not the only contrast, as I am given somewhat different treatment.

I am put into a normal bed, instead of the airbed that I have been in since the operation. I am not allowed to sit up, as they treat all patients as spinally unstable on arrival until they have verified the fixation for themselves, and often they decide to redo the surgery. I meet my consultant, Dr J, for the first time. He strides into the room, making strong eye contact as he shakes my hand, and introduces himself in a soft, calm voice. I feel an incredible sense of strength and reassurance from such a small gesture. He is the first senior doctor I have seen who has made direct physical contact in this way and, possibly due to his many years of experience in dealing with spinal patients, he makes me feel like I am at the centre of things, and important in the decision process. It's difficult to explain, but I'm sure it's his habit of speaking to the patient first, before talking to all the other relatives, friends or staff who may be in the room. He tells me that I am 'on Stoke Mandeville time' now, and that I have to start thinking of things in terms of weeks rather than days, a concept that I accept with a grin, but which becomes a painful frustration in time.

My most immediate problems are identified, namely the compacted constipation and my drug habit, and I am taken off the morphine. Not weaned off, taken off. No more.

2

And so I begin the worst two days of my life. Cold sweats, pain in my back and insomnia are all indications of how insulated I had been from the physical reality of the injury I have sustained. I have attacks of nausea punctuated with more bouts of dry heaving as my body tries to clear itself. The retching is loud and very painful, and produces nothing but a small amount of bile and extremely sore stomach muscles and throat. Then there is the psychological impact. The fact that I have been on such large amounts of opiates since the accident means that I have also been insulated from the full psychological implications of what has happened.

On Tuesday it all caves in on me at once, and I am a real mess. I feel the worst kind of claustrophobia at being trapped inside my own body. Any attempt to move my legs, or even to move in bed leads to a lurching panic attack, as my brain reacts to the lack of response from my body. I become distraught that I can't 'wake up' from what is happening. In my mind, I run a parallel life, the one where I don't fall from the tree, and I imagine what I am doing instead of lying in a hospital bed unable to move. I try with all my will to jump from this world into that, but it doesn't work and the panic rises again and turns into cold dread. I look at Penny holding my hand and looking so calm, as if pregnancy has made her indestructible, wrapped her in a warm, living shield and the thought of what she's going through is enough to reduce me to a howling, sobbing mess.

I feel almost resentful that I can't even consider giving up, as I have a wife who loves me, a family who love me, and I am three months away from being a father for the first time, something that had filled me with nervous excitement before the accident. It was a part of my justification for the whole tree-surgery thing.

Although Penny and I are both artists, this has never been a reliable source of income, and for the last three years we had run our own garden-design and construction business. Now that Pen wasn't going to be working for a while as parenthood takes over, I thought that if I train for tree surgery, I can always get a bit of other work to help to support us. I remember seeing a tree-climbing competition at Westonbirt arboretum, and we were both thrilled and inspired by the sight. Having previously spent some fifteen or so years working as a telephone engineer and regularly climbing telegraph poles, I knew that I enjoyed working up high and, coupled with my love of trees and the outdoors, it seemed a perfect combination to make a successful arborist.

I think back to a long walk in the bush and a conversation I had with Leon, my father-in-law, when we were in Australia just a couple of weeks ago. He is a furniture maker with a passion for timber, and we talked about trees and timber and careers, and I sensed that I had found something that I loved and could even make a living at. Especially something that would be in demand if we moved to Australia, an intention that we have held for some time. But somehow something always comes up. Or falls down. But when we're there, it's really clear that we can do it, and I can see a life for us there.

Instead I find myself staring at nothing, completely unable to move or speak or think. While Penny has been allowed to stay over in one of the relatives' rooms provided by the hospital for the first couple of nights, it is clear that this has just been a very temporary measure, and that it is time for her to return to London in order to keep our life ticking over, and for a change of clothes. Fortunately, I have the presence of mind on the Wednesday afternoon to ask to see someone from the psychology team, as I feel that I am sliding out of control. The day is also punctuated with a visit by the hospital chaplain.

Speaking softly, she asks me, 'Would you like someone to come in and see you from time to time for prayer, a chat, or even just to sit with you?'

I explain that I am an atheist, trying to sound earnest myself, as if I were explaining that I was a Methodist or a Catholic.

'That's absolutely fine. *No* problem. We're still happy to come and talk if you think it could help.'

I say that I would like that, although I'm not sure why, and I never hear from her again.

This is now the second time that I have been approached by people who would claim to be doing His work on earth, and after she leaves I have a little rummage through some of the more obscure boxes in the back of my mind. Conversations with God? Conversations about God? An internal dialogue, perhaps. When one is lying in a hospital bed as the result of a near-fatal accident, it is probably inevitable that, as an atheist, I find myself wondering if my rather vocal anti-God (well, more anti-organised religion, and if I'm honest, the organised is a relatively recent caveat) opinions have led me to this situation. I'd certainly have to admire the Big Fellow's sense of humour.

On Thursday I wake up and stare at the wall, unable to acknowledge anyone who comes in to see me. I feel as if I can avoid all of the hurt and panic as long as I don't move or speak or think. A member of the catering staff comes in to take my order for lunch, although I haven't eaten anything for two days. I don't even acknowledge her presence. She leaves, and soon after I am joined by a student nurse who is so concerned by my 'closed down' behaviour that she returns with a staff nurse.

She asks me directly, 'Tim, are you all right?' and I realise that she is not going to let me get away with the silent treatment.

I manage to utter, 'Help me.'

But the nursing staff on the ward have already recognised that this is an urgent situation, and instead of waiting for my scheduled appointment on Monday, a psychologist is summoned from the first European conference on the Psychology of Spinal Cord Injury, which happens to be taking place at Stoke Mandeville the week of my admission.

Dianne, the psychologist, arrives to see me, and the first thing that she has to deal with is my utter panic, which is causing me to hyperventilate as I attempt to crawl out of the hospital bed. She explains how important it is for me to consciously take control of my breathing in order to combat the fight or flight response that a panic attack induces, as by slowing the breathing down the body sends a message back to the brain to say that there is no imminent danger, and I can begin to wrest control back.

Once I have stopped huffing and puffing like a demented wolf, I pour forth lists. A list of all the things that I will never be able to do again, a list of all the things I will never be able to do for the first time, a list of all the things I will now be unable to do with my child, a list of all the emotional aspects which I can't come to terms with, and she says, 'Don't. It's too big for you to deal with now, while you're still unwell, and so recently injured. There is a "cod" psychology phrase that actually holds some truth in situations like yours. It's "fake it until you can make it".'

This totally wrong-foots me, as the message seems to be denial is good. But it helps, and it is true. Lying on your back staring at the ceiling of a hospital room for two weeks is far too much of the wrong kind of time to come to terms with anything, let alone a huge life-changing event. So I don't. Or rather I try not to as best as I can. In a way, she tells me it's OK not to think. I have to fill my head with white noise. Listen to music, read a book, or watch TV.

I am joined in the afternoon by Penny, and I lose it a bit again, although now I don't feel quite so out of control, as I have accepted that I can't begin to accept anything yet. While I have been busy falling apart, Penny has been busy ploughing through forms for various benefits with the help of Graham, who has worked in local government for many years, but is still shocked by the complexity of the bureaucracy involved.

My father arrives for a visit and stays the whole afternoon, obviously impressed with the spinal unit, which is probably due in no small way to the comparison with the Royal London. The next visitor is a timely one. A wonderfully mumsy Australian woman called Marion introduces herself as my discharge co-ordinator and makes Penny promise that she won't fill out any more forms, because that's what the discharge co-ordinator does. She strikes the perfect tone, and reassures us that we are in the best spinal unit 'in the world', which is why she came to work here, and that there is a department, her department, which is there to negotiate all the paperwork and pitfalls to do with getting out of here and going home. Marion also imparts a somewhat peculiar gem of wisdom. She tells us that having a spinal-cord injury doesn't change who you are fundamentally. 'For example, if you were an arsehole before your accident,' she says in a conspiratorial whisper, 'you are likely to be an arsehole after.'

The whisper tells me that:

a) somewhere on the ward there is an arsehole who has just had a spinal-cord injury, and

b) it isn't me.

Soon after, Jackie comes to visit us. Jackie works for the Spinal Injuries Association, the SIA. I immediately decide to cancel my membership of the ISA (International Society of Arboriculturalists) and join the SIA while quietly wondering what the AIS might be, as I am bound to end up a member eventually.

Jackie is the first person in a wheelchair that I have spoken to since my accident. She looks at me and smiles and, without saying anything, I know that she has been through something similar to what I am going through. That feeling is indescribable. Well, maybe not, maybe it's called empathy, but it is a huge lift for me.

She tells me about her experience. 'I had my injury when I seventeen, in a fall from a climbing wall. As this was 25 years ago, there were very few operations carried out then, and I was put on twelve weeks of bed rest, which was the way that spinal injuries were treated.'

I think about my struggle with being flat on my back for two weeks.

Jackie then tells us, 'Since then, I learned how to ride a horse again, learned to drive, got married, had two children, raised them, got divorced, and I have recently discovered skiing.' In other words, she has led a full and active, 'normal' life.

After she leaves, my father says, 'Well, what a wonderful lady. So positive and lively.' I realise that we all need a positive role model at this stage. Someone to represent the future. In suffering a spinal-cord injury and becoming paralysed, I have lost many things. Not only have I lost the use of my legs, I have become impotent, and lost control of my bladder and bowels. But I have also lost all of the versions of my future that I had imagined for myself. None of them involved me in a wheelchair, and the loss of this future, as well as the way that I have been whisked away from the past (I left the house in the morning like any other day, and weeks later I am on my back in hospital), makes the meeting with Jackie hugely important. Seeing someone who has got on with her life after just such an injury helps me to start the construction of an image of life beyond the hospital, something I have not even begun to do up to this point.

So I start my rehabilitation. On the Friday I meet the head of the psychology department, Dr K, and he casually swats away all of my concerns with a bit of 'cognitive thinking' delivered in a warm Irish brogue. Very encouraging stuff at first. After convincing me that a wheelchair is merely a functional device to get from A to B (although his comparison to wearing glasses as another functional 'device' seems somewhat insensitive), and that using catheters and suppositories is merely a question of getting used to new methods – 'No one really likes going to the toilet or even talking about it, and we do it in private. The only difference is that you'll do things a bit differently' – he deals with my concerns about parenting. I inevitably talk about images of kick-abouts in the park, and he poses the question, 'But what's really important about being a parent? Sure, there will be some things that you can't do, but a loving environment is much more important than kicking a ball in the park.'

On more immediate matters, he deals with my frustration at being on bed rest, and how I feel that I need to be up in order to set and achieve goals. He tells me that I need to set my challenge as 'to be on bed rest'. This is my first target. He then suggests using autohypnosis to help relaxation and avoid panic attacks, and presents me with a CD he has recorded for the purpose. After he leaves, I put the CD on, sceptically expecting to hear a recording of him gently saying, 'Ah shure bot you'll be foine,' repeatedly, but it actually turns out to be quite useful as a great help for relaxation, especially last thing at night.

Television turns out to be less useful as 'white noise'. Every time I turn on the BBC, the programme is preceded by a link showing three guys in wheelchairs dancing on a basketball court, Channel 4 is in the middle of a Fred Astaire season, and ITV is showing *Strictly Come Dance Fever On Ice*, or some such nonsense every night.

Bed rest is tough. It stretches out in front of me like a prison sentence, without being given a specific or even vague idea as to when I will be allowed to get up. However, I do make an interesting discovery. I find out that my left testicle, which has up to now been as sensationless as the rest of my 'below the waist' area, has now gained some sensation. It is a painful discovery, as I find this out by trapping it between my thighs, but at least it demonstrates that there is still a connection of some kind between my brain and a point below my injury. While I am quick to acknowledge that this newfound sensation will not aid me to walk or drive a car, it still feels symbolically important. I consider *My Left Testicle* as a possible title for any memoir that I may write in the future.

I manage to start reading again, which is a huge boost to my time-killing arsenal. The breakthrough is *Cloud Atlas*, a book of such ambitious scope written with such skill as to be able to draw me from my hospital bed into another world. A world of different times, different realities that are all connected. It almost feels written for just this circumstance.

I rediscover music. I'm listening to 6music on a small digital radio when they play a session by Rufus Wainwright, and his song 'Pretty Things' reduces me to tears. I know that I am crying for my plight, but crying over someone else's story frees me up, and instead of trying to suppress the tears for fear of losing control and sliding into a full-blown anxiety attack, I let go and wallow in a heaving, weeping mess for three minutes. Over the following weeks, I use this 'music therapy' often, in particular rediscovering my extensive Tom Waits collection, which I have always used as a background when I am painting, but which now takes on another, even more personal aspect. Penny translates my list of demands onto an iPod, which I have received as a gift from her brothers, sent over with Penny's mother Ginny, who arrives from Australia two weeks after the accident to stay with Penny. Her visit is a great emotional support to me, preventing me from imagining Pen going home to an empty house.

I manage to keep my own side room, as I am informed that my urine has tested positive for MRSA. This means that although I don't have an infection or pose an immediate risk to myself, I am considered infectious, and must be kept away from other, non-MRSA patients, for fear that my bugs get into their wounds, or something along those lines.

The frustration of bed rest is further compounded by

delays in my visit to radiology for an MRI scan before any decision can be made about whether I can sit up, or if I need to go
under the knife again. The scan is rescheduled three times and
the frustration is worsened by the lack of information, which
causes me to spend three days in expectation, only for it to be
dashed each time by the shift change, which denotes the end
of the working day. I struggle to be as comfortable as possible,
but it is so difficult to get used to lying on one side for three
hours, before being rolled over by three nurses. As soon as I am
turned, I feel uncomfortable, or remember that my water or a
book or my radio is now behind me, and I feel foolish buzzing
for a member of staff to come and retrieve it for me.

In this I am grateful for the help of a young student nurse
called Isat, who seems to 'adopt' me and decides to look out
for me a bit, making sure that I get my choice of meals, and
coming in for a quick chat or to see if I need anything. It could
be that she does this for all the patients, but I don't think she
could have the time, and I feel that my openness and honesty
helps her to get a bit of an understanding of what a patient
goes through after spinal-cord injury.

I finally have the scan on Friday, and I am assured that
one of the consultants will look at the image this afternoon
and give me the decision. After several hours, I ask again, and
I am told that the consultant is now in a meeting, and won't be
looking at my scans today. My frustration builds.

The next day is a Saturday, but due to my complaining I
receive a visit from Dr B, one of the surgical team who looks
at my films and explains that the fixation installed by the team
at the Royal London will need to be replaced, and that a bone
graft will be done at the same time in order to fuse my T12/
L1 vertebrae. In the meantime, the existing fixation is unstable
and I shouldn't even sit up. This comes as a huge blow, and
I thank the doctor for coming in to see me, before breaking
down yet again.

Somehow I cope. I have to. Every night I tell myself that

I have got through another day, even though I don't know how many more I will spend flat out in bed. People visit and tell me how amazing I am for dealing with it all so well, and being so brave. But I don't have a choice. I can't take a day off, or give in. It just is, and it's in my face every waking minute of every day so that I can't do anything *but* cope.

My mind is not very supportive. One night I go to sleep, but wake up soon after, as my legs are tingling. I feel myself sliding of the bed and, in a panic, I try and put my right leg out to stop myself from landing on the floor. To my utter astonishment, my right leg responds, then my left, and now I am standing up. I try a few tentative steps, as I can feel the excitement building up. I start to shout for a nurse, and I walk briskly out into the corridor, where I find the ward sister.

'This is real, right? Tell me I'm not dreaming.'

'No, Tim, you're not dreaming,' she replies, grinning excitedly.

'This *is* real.'

'Quick, get Dr J on the phone. I must speak to him.'

I watch as she picks up the handset and dials the number. And then I begin to feel things slipping from my grasp, and a sense that this isn't happening to me, but I am trying really hard to keep the story running. And all of a sudden I am awake, and the same four flecks of brown paint are on the ceiling above me, next to the same strip-light glowing dimly with the night-light on. And I am crushed. Pushed lower by false hope created by my own subconscious. What a bastard I am.

In my view of the spinal unit, the four flecks of paint (I hope it's paint…) and a strip-light are accompanied by a set of three windows with a pot plant and a vase of flowers on the window-sill (both of which came with me), and a miniature 'anglepoise' television. To my right is an air line, a respiratory mask (in a plastic bag) and a suction device with a scary-looking plastic pot attached (scary because of its size – I'm guessing about three pints – and the fact that it's transparent, which means that all

I can think about is how unpleasant three pints of gunk suctioned from any part of a patient would look in a transparent pot. This unpleasant thought highlights the degree of boredom that makes up most of the time between the rushes of outright panic). I do get the occasional view and sound of a couple of magpies and on one occasion I even see a group of Canada geese fly overhead. On visits Eugene describes the courtyard garden below the window for me and then other parts of the hospital, and I begin to build up a picture of the world beyond these four walls.

I have an assessment by a physiotherapist to determine the full extent of my paralysis. During the assessment, I find it pretty much impossible to remember to keep repositioning my 'modesty', as I don't feel it move. Just to clarify what may appear a bizarre euphemism, the 'modesty' in question is in reality an extra pillowcase that all patients are given to, well, preserve their modesty, as patients are naked in bed to reduce the risk of pressure sores from clothing. The physio keeps pointing out that my modesty has slipped, and I become quite blasé, seeing as nudity has never been a particular anxiety of mine, especially in a clinical environment, and it is only later that it dawns on me that the staff may not want to have to look at my excessively relaxed 'modesty' either. The light-hearted nature of the assessment drains away as each unsuccessful attempt to move my feet, ankles and legs serves to compound the desperation of my situation, and I realise that when I was in full panic I made an unconscious decision that trying to move my legs just worsened the anxiety, so I simply stopped trying. By the time we are finished I am in tears again and I have to start the slow rebuilding process all over again. The result of the assessment is a confirmation that I am diagnosed as what's known in medical circles as 'T12 complete'.

OK, books or internet out, people. You'll need to know this. The C6, T12, L1 stuff refers to the vertebrae in the back, and is used to define the level of spinal-cord injury. C stands for cervical (neck), T for thoracic (the ones with ribs on) and L for lumbar. So I am described as T12 complete, which means that the last level of sensation that I have is in the nerves that leave my spine at the level of my twelfth thoracic vertebra. The 'complete' does not mean that my spinal cord has been completely severed, but rather that I have no pockets of sensation or movement below the T12 level. The now-famous left testicle does not count, apparently.

The higher up the spinal cord you go, the more of your body is likely to be impaired, so someone who has damage at the cervical or 'C' level is likely to be tetraplegic, which means that there will be some impairment to all four limbs.

Every day I hear talk of going 'downstairs': it all starts when you go downstairs. The spinal unit is organised into five wards. Upstairs is St Andrew's, which is an acute ward, and where most new admissions begin. There is also St Patrick's, which is for readmissions, but readmission isn't really discussed when you are first admitted. Downstairs there are two rehabilitation wards called St George's and St David's and, finally, there is St Joseph's, which is where the patients practise independence before they are discharged.

I have no idea what being downstairs will entail, I just know that it will involve activity, and up here involves no more than being able to help with my bed bath, or change the channel on the miniature television suspended above my bed. The TV control has a reproduction of Jimmy Savile's signature on it in gold. It is a signature I recognise well, as I remember getting his autograph in the BBC canteen when I was about eight years old. Little did I know, etc.

Friends visit me over the weekend, often arriving looking rather pale after passing a patient with a higher-level spinal-cord injury on a ventilator and unable to move from the neck down. Comments like, 'You were pretty lucky, really. That guy down the hall is paralysed from the neck down.' I find it strange when someone *walks* into the spinal unit to see me, paralysed from the waist down, only to tell me how lucky I am. It is, I'm sure, said out of a sense of relief that they find me looking relatively well, and so they feel able to confide in me their feelings about the people in the unit who are 'really' ill.

Another response that I get from several friends, especially those that I only speak to on the telephone, is to talk to me about the 'tragedy' of my accident and subsequent situation, especially as Penny is pregnant. The trouble is, this response leaves me with nowhere to go after the phone conversation. I understand that people are wrestling to even comprehend the severity of my injury and the long-term implications, but I find myself almost consoling people in order that they are able to conceive of a future for me, for us. Otherwise their sombre sympathies and 'good innings'-type platitudes leave me with nothing.

I spend a lot of time thinking about control. In particular, how much control I really have over my life. I feel as if someone has yanked the reins from my hand.

I think about aspirations, about people who are successful, have a good job, a family, a nice car, a nice house and yet feel unsatisfied, unhappy: the Reginald Perrin syndrome. I'm thinking this because of all the simple pleasures that I didn't get to relish before they were taken from me, but also because I now feel that we don't have anything near the amount of control over our life and happiness that we think we do. I chose to climb that tree, and all the others previously, but the spinal unit is full of patients who have sustained injuries as a result of everything from car crashes through to slipping over in the shower. I'm not fatalistic in any way. Well, maybe a bit. It's not that things are predestined to happen, but more that we have to convince ourselves that we are in control of things in order to function, so when things go sideways on us, it's a bit of a mindfuck. Or something like that.

I have a good friend B, a recovering alcoholic who has

been sober for twelve years. His wife was in a car accident two years before they met, an accident that left her partner dead and her immobile in hospital in a 'halo' head brace for several weeks. They have a young son who has a rare but profound genetic disorder called Angelman Syndrome, which means that he will need constant care throughout his life. When B comes to see me, he asks, 'How are you feeling? When I heard about the accident, I thought about your being confronted with this huge event, and having to be still, lying on your back, and I got quite emotional.'

'It's the worst thing in many ways,' I explain. 'Suddenly having your whole life come to an abrupt stop, and having to stare at the ceiling all day.'

'I remember when I heard about my boy. It was overwhelming. And trying to find some kind of acceptance, that's the most difficult thing.'

I tell him about the parallel life, the one I can't jump into.

B often goes to Buddhist meditation retreats, and I feel that his experiences combined with his outlook now mean that he can understand what I am going through emotionally, somehow. I think he can identify with the 'leaf in a hurricane' feeling.

As the week continues, I feel more and more disheartened, wondering why the work done at the Royal London is not considered to be 'fit for purpose' by the National Spinal Injuries Centre, London is the largest conurbation in the land, and the most likely scenario in the event of spinal-cord injury is that the patient would be taken by air ambulance, which lands at the Royal London. It stands to reason that there must be more SCIs coming through their doors than anywhere else in the country, so why does their work not come up to the standards of the national centre of excellence for SCI?

Then one day I hear Dr J outside my door, talking to

one of his juniors, and I dispatch my stepfather Eugene out to intercede on my behalf, and request an audience, explaining how I had been told that I was on bed rest awaiting further surgery some time towards the end of April, and that I was wondering if I would be able to sit up by 9 May, as that is my birthday. A bit of a kerfuffle ensues, and Dr J storms into my room, asking who had told me that I needed further surgery. I explain what Dr B said.

Dr J's reply is, 'It is like my mother used to say, I should rub chilli on his lips for telling such lies. I have made no such decision, and it is my decision to make. In fact, I will tell Sister that as of tomorrow you are to start sitting up.'

I try to hold back the tears (yet again) of relief and gratitude, and I ask, 'So I don't need further surgery?'

'I have not made a final decision,' he replies, 'but you can certainly begin to get up. I will tell you my decision next week.'

He makes some witty remark that I instantly forget, as I am filled with excitement at the prospect of not being flat on my back any more, and he turns on his heel and leaves the room.

After he has left, I can't help but wonder what would have happened if Eugene hadn't collared him in the corridor, but I don't have much time to ponder this before the ward sister comes to see me to tell me that I can start to sit up, and also that I am to be moved into another room, to share with a patient called Mark. I have seen Mark on my travels in a bed to the X-ray and MRI scans, and we have reciprocally nodded. He looks very ill. He has a tracheotomy and a tube for breathing. We are both MRSA positive, so we get to share a room, but at least I am sitting up. I can see my feet. They look very far away.

In the afternoon, I receive an even more auspicious visit. While I am discussing the exciting news from Dr J, I detect a hint of cigar in the air, and then he is upon us.

'Good morning. Good morning.'

For it is he. Sir Jim. Sir Jimmy. A knight in shining shell suit.

He says, 'Now then. Now then.'

He calls me young man. He makes suggestive remarks to the female staff. I ask for his autograph for the second time in my life, only this time for a friend of mine who is a consultant anaesthetist and who does a very enthusiastic Sir Jim impression, which probably has some profound influence on his patients' subconscious.

But this time the man of gold jewellery declines; instead he offers to pose for a picture. Luckily I have a friend visiting who is ready with cameraphone to capture me and Sir Jimmy, thumbs aloft.

That night, Penny sends this image around the world in a group email, and for many of our friends and family it is their first glimpse of me since my accident. For many, it is also their first glimpse of Jimmy Savile. There I am, grinning like a lunatic, accompanied by possibly the most bizarre-looking man on the planet. Especially if you have no idea who he is.

Since my arrival at Stoke, I have developed a great respect for Jimmy Savile's commitment to the place. The spinal unit was built with the large amount of money that he raised with all his charity work, and he is still very involved, raising money and making decisions on how it is spent. It would have been easy for him to walk away from the place (unlike most of the patients, ho ho). Despite my great respect for him, on his subsequent visits to the ward I pretend to be asleep.

I begin to get to know my room-mate Mark in the evening. We have a conversation during which we are both facing the same wall, divided by curtains, monitors and side tables full of personal possessions. Mark is in his twenties, a motorcyclist and fan of 'happy hardcore', a particularly fast and exuberant form of dance music (thankfully he has a Walkman rather than a hi-fi.). Mark was on his motorcycle driving along a dual carriageway when someone pulled out across his lane, and he hit the side of the car at speed, compressing several vertebrae in his neck. He has already spent many weeks in intensive care, and has been very close to death. Mark is now tetraplegic (tetraplegia used to be called quadriplegia, and still is in Australia and the US), and still has a tracheotomy, which he no longer uses to breathe, but which is used regularly to draw mucus out of his throat. Because of the high level of his SCI Mark has problems coughing and clearing his throat, as the muscles around the diaphragm are also paralysed, meaning that he can't 'push' on his lungs. In order to counter this and to keep his airway clear, the staff perform a procedure called assisted coughing, which means that they push on his chest while he clears his throat. This isn't too bad, but when the pump is used to drain his throat he finds it very unpleasant, as do I (I'm not good with mucus, sputum or vomit – in fact anything that even hints at being the product of regurgitation, which obviously doesn't bode well for parenthood).

The difficulty with sharing a room with Mark is that it makes me self-conscious as I continue with my lachrymose self-pitying conversations, knowing that there is the possibility that my pain at the loss of the use of my legs is being inadvertently overheard by someone who can barely breathe for himself. This is not something that we discuss, and I reach the conclusion that rather than attempt to take solace in the 'always someone worse off than you' model, which requires that the participant settles with their lot, I need to develop a degree of emotional tunnel vision, as I find little comfort in the knowledge that other people have had their lives even more soundly fucked over than mine.

3

The next day I am filled with excitement as I get helped into some easy clothing, have a urine bag attached to my catheter and strapped to my leg, and receive a visit from Marieke, my South African physiotherapist, who introduces me to a mighty steed called the Breezy. She also introduces an instrument of torture called a binder. The binder is actually something like an elastic corset secured with Velcro, and makes me feel like William Shatner in his *TJ Hooker* days, but it apparently helps to stop all my blood rushing down to my ankles when I sit up which could cause me to faint, as the muscles in my legs are now unable to help to pump the blood back uphill.

To mount the Breezy (a wheelchair, if you haven't guessed), I have to be lifted out of bed by two nurses and a hoist. Remember those old *Ivanhoe*-type knights-in-armour movies? That's me being loaded on the horse for the joust. It feels exciting just to be leaving the bed behind, although the sensation of sitting is a mixture of pain from my back and woozy instability. Once the initial light-headedness subsides, I set off for my first wheelchair push with Penny by my side and I feel elation at being a body moving through space again after so much inertia. The pushing and steering seems to come naturally to me, although any bump or corner leaves me clutching the armrests on the chair with a sense of panic at my complete lack of balance. Undeterred, however, we set off, headed for the door out onto the roof walkway that I have watched from my room for the last two weeks. I just want to be outside, as four weeks inside have left me feeling pretty itchy, and I head as swiftly as I can for daylight and the fresh air that tastes so sweet and real. I grab Penny, hold her round belly and cry with relief, to feel the fresh air on my skin, to be able to hug

Penny, even from a seated position, rather than holding her hand from a bed.

The buoyancy lasts, and I feel OK to be upright, so Pen takes me for a tour of the establishment, which up to now has only existed for me as a series of ceiling panels between the ward and the X-ray department, the descriptions of visitors, and the odd glimpse out of windows.

First, we go into the relatives' room, which has an adjoining kitchen for relatives to prepare food for patients, and a large television in the lounge area for all the downtime spent waiting. It feels like an achievement, to be seeing it myself rather than having it described to me.

We leave the ward and go out to the lifts, one of which is operated by a movement sensor so that it can be operated by patients who do not have the dexterity to press the buttons. We take the lift to 'downstairs', from where I get to see the legendary staircase that has been the first topic of conversation with pretty much every visitor I've had since arriving at Stoke. The décor bears all the hallmarks of Sir Jimmy, with a stunning multi-coloured floral chandelier and, at the bottom of the stairs, a multi-layered plastic flower display to match. Moving on, I finally get a sense of the rest of the spinal unit. We visit Jimmy's Café, named after the great man himself. The other exciting thing about Jimmy's is that once a patient is mobile, they may take their hospital meals in the café environment, and interact with other patients.

We also take a quick peek at the rehabilitation wards that will be my next target, once I am ready and a bed is available. I am surprised to find them to be much like the wards upstairs, only with fewer staff, and more patients in wheelchairs or walking with frames. The main difference is that the upstairs ward is an acute ward, and down here many beds are empty, as the patients are mobile.

After a couple of hours, I am exhausted and rather light-headed, so I am returned to my bed with the aid of the hoist, and I shed my clothes with much help and a deal of swearing before returning to the 'modesty' look. I am absolutely drained and exhausted, but for the first time since my arrival at Stoke, I feel a real sense of progress. Penny has found some bed-and-breakfast accommodation in the area so that she doesn't have to make the long drive from east London too often, and she stays with me until late in the evening and we talk and laugh and I even manage not to cry.

The following day I am champing at the bit, eager to 'get up' as soon as possible, still full of elation at the success of the previous day, and with much prompting, the nursing staff haul me up in the hoist and plop me in the chair and off I go, only today it's different, and not just because Penny's not with me. I feel crushed. Imagine learning to ride a bicycle. Now imagine getting on that bicycle and being told that you have to ride it every waking moment for the rest of your life. I find an empty corridor in the psychology department, as it happens (now then, now then), and I slump into self-absorbed panic once again. It isn't long before I am noticed, and I end up talking to Dr K again. He still talks as if delivering well-worn platitudes, but much of what he says makes sense with time. He describes my spinal-cord injury as taking up most of my life right now, but in time, although it will obviously still be there, the rest of my life will come back into focus, and the injury will make up less of the total. Or something like that. He also tells me that he thinks I will push the boundaries of the spinal unit during my rehabilitation. Anyway, my keel is evened, and I head back to the ward feeling a little more normal again except, well, except for this rather unpleasant smell which seems to have pervaded the entire hospital, as it is the same wherever I go. Suffice to say on my return hoist, I discover that it is me. I have soiled myself.

Bowel function is a rather sticky subject (poor choice of phrase?), but I feel we should just get it out there, and all try to get a feel for it (I'll stop now, I promise). When I suffered my injury, my bowels went into something approaching shock, and as I was then shot through with so much morphine, effectively everything ground to a halt. On arrival at Stoke, I was put on a strong laxative and a fibre booster in order to try and get my bowels functioning again. The bowel continues to work after SCI through peristalsis, which means that although I cannot feel it, or control my rectum, the digestive process itself will continue, albeit somewhat slower. (Because it is slower, the body reabsorbs more water from the stool, which is why constipation can often be a long-term problem for people with spinal-cord injury.)

One of the first steps in rehabilitation is to try and train the bowel into a routine. This means that all patients are given two glycerine suppositories at 5 a.m. and what is charmingly called a manual evacuation at 6 a.m. The idea is that the glycerine acts as a mild irritant as well as a lubricant, and this causes the bowel to move of its own accord. During the hour in between, patients lie on something that at first I thought was called an Ink Co. sheet, which appears to be made of recycled paper fibres (hence the Ink Co. – a newspaper reference, perhaps?) and is very absorbent. In actual fact they are, of course, called inco sheets, inco being short for incontinence. It takes the body some time to get used to this new regime, especially, if, like me, the body is used to a cup of strong coffee and breakfast before 'the earth moves', as it were. My approach to this morning routine on the ward is to try to remain as asleep as possible, except for a quick lunge for the air freshener, so that by the time I wake up for breakfast at about 8.30 a.m. it seems like a rather unpleasant dream. Obviously I can't feel any of these 'intrusions', but it is unsettling all the same, especially as it is a reminder of some of the things that I will have to learn to do by myself.

While we are on the subject of waste products, there is also a set of new skills to be mastered around the emptying of my bladder. The bag that is strapped to my leg is connected by a short length of plastic pipe to an 'indwelling catheter', the first of which was fitted at the Royal London when I was first admitted and still completely ga-ga on whatever I was shot full of on the garage roof. (Incidentally, this is the number one suspect for the MRSA issue, as it has only been found in my urine. One has to bear in mind that about one-third of the population carry MRSA in the community anyway with no ill effects.)

Now that I am mobile, my indwelling catheter is attached to a bag on my leg that is smaller than the one attached to the bed and I have to make sure that I empty it regularly. This involves a trip into the sluice room, a place where all the patients' waste products are disposed of. The sluice into which everything goes is mounted on the wall at just above knee height, and on my first visit I almost tip myself out of the chair backwards as I struggle to get my foot onto the edge of it in order to drain the beach-ball-sized bag of urine strapped to my calf. It is a bit of a disaster, as half of the urine leaves via my trouser leg and shoe, and I am trying to dry my clothing with paper towels when another patient whizzes in, nods briefly and goes over to the rack of plastic bottles and jugs on the wall behind me, chooses a suitable vessel, puts it on the floor and drains his leg bag without moving his leg. I feel like I have had the merest glimpse at what I am up against in this game, and I return to my bed to change, damper, smellier, but wiser.

I receive a visit from my friend James with whom I have been going to watch Arsenal for over twenty years. He came to see me at the Royal London, but I hardly remember who came when and said what, so it is good to see him now that I am at least a little more coherent. James tells me how he contacted Arsenal immediately after I was injured to see if they would be able to send me a signed shirt, what with me having had a season ticket for fifteen years and all. He was put through to the promotions department, who told him that the players only signed one shirt a day, but if he sent the shirt into them, they would put it in the pile.

Interestingly, another friend of mine also contacted Arsenal, only his demands were altogether more ambitious, requesting that the club:

a) provide me with a complementary season ticket, and/or

b) send the players to visit me in hospital.

The response he got was a parcel containing a signed shirt, with a letter saying,

'We trust that this will be satisfactory.' In other words, leave us alone. Stuart, the friend in question, works for a well-known national charity, and one wonders whether his email address may have had something to do with the response, but either way, I have ended up with a signed Arsenal shirt to accompany the photograph sent to me by Barry, the man from the bed opposite me when I was in the Royal London.

I show my treasures to James, who shows a mixture of relief and disappointment.

'On the plus side,' I say, 'you got me the huge electric fan with remote control, which is a damn sight more useful.'

I reach my birthday with a sense of optimism, as I was told on admission that I may be able to sit up in bed on my birthday. The day has arrived and I am out of bed, in a wheelchair. Penny brings my family, our best china and a tablecloth, and we are able to sit together for tea, cake and laughter in the relatives' room, although tempered with a melancholy that is lurking just around the corner, as I struggle to keep a lid on all the negative thoughts and comparisons that remain my closest and most despised companions.

The comparisons lurk in every corner, waiting for any sign that I may be happy or enjoying myself, and then they strike. For example, there is a football match on in the evening. Not between patients, obviously, although the mental image of a football pitch and 22 people in wheelchairs looking awkwardly at the ball does make me smile. The match in question is between Arsenal and local rivals Tottenham Hotspur, and even though I don't share the kind of blood-curdling rivalry of many fans, I still get excited at the prospect of a highly competitive match. A bit of banter and prediction with other patients and staff, and I make sure that I am back in bed to watch the game on the JimmyTelly (the small TV on an anglepoise arm). The build-up over the afternoon makes me feel like I am tapping into a pre-injury pleasure and reclaiming a small part of my life.

As soon as the match kicks off, all of this excitement and optimism is shattered, as I am confronted by 22 overpaid young athletes running, turning, jumping, diving and generally waving their legs in the air as if mocking me, and at the same time seemingly oblivious of their good fortune to be able to do this. It dawns on me that a large part of my football viewing pleasure in the past has been based on the fact that I was able to play myself, albeit to a very low standard, and just as everyone thinks they are an excellent driver, so everyone who plays football watches others with a critical eye. I end up turning the TV off and retreating into my head. It is beginning to dawn on me that as a result of my injury, I am definitely never going to get the call from Arsene Wenger looking for a new centre-half. The whole sport thing is a huge hole, something that I feel I will have to learn to live without.

Better news comes the following morning. Now that I am 'up', the decision is made for me to be moved downstairs onto one of the rehabilitation wards, and so for the second of many occasions, I am packed up straight away, the photographs and cards come down off the pinboard, the clothes come out of the locker, and the various radios and phone chargers are unplugged, and we head down to my new home on St George's ward.

Once again, my MRSA status has its privileges, and I am given my own side room. I feel as if I have made progress, although there is an undoubted anxiety that comes from going back to feeling new and vulnerable, which reminds me of the move from primary to secondary school. Patients are pootling around in wheelchairs, going between their various appointments for rehabilitation therapies.

Many of the routines remain the same as up on St Andrew's ward. The 'Jolly trolley' comes around three times a day, dispensing medication to all the patients. By now I am taking diclofenac (a powerful anti-inflammatory for my back) three times a day, and lansoprazole (to protect my stomach from the risk of developing an ulcer caused by the diclofenac) in the morning, along with Detrusitol, which apparently keeps my bladder flaccid, thus making it possible for me to have an indwelling catheter. I am still turned by two nurses every three hours or so until sleep time, when I have to make a decision whether I want to spend the night on my back or my side, my legs arranged and propped with a variety of pillows into a neutral position so that the ligaments and tendons don't become shortened from lack of stretching, a problem that can occur when people with paralysis are on prolonged bed rest.

One thing does gradually change. I begin to get a pins and needles sensation in both my legs, particularly towards the end of the day. It isn't wholly unpleasant to start with, but in time it starts to become a little uncomfortable, and I raise this with Dr J, who enigmatically (this appears to be his only setting) tells me that I 'mustn't let the pain win', and prescribes amitriptyline to be introduced into my evening medication, as it can cause drowsiness when taken for the first few times. I am not sure what letting 'the pain win' actually entails. Do I admit defeat? Does this mean that the pain gets some kind of trophy, and goes off for a series of public appearances, culminating in pain's photograph appearing on a cereal packet? As I have no intention of letting this happen, I gleefully gobble up the little yellow pill in the evening, and have a very solid night's sleep.

When morning comes, I wake up (or at least I think I wake up) to find myself under water. Having opened my eyes, I find that keeping them that way is a bit of a struggle, and I can't really be arsed to do anything else. This is what is sometimes referred to as a drugs hangover, in this case caused by the amitriptyline. The word hangover implies that:

a) you had a good time the night before, and
b) you only have yourself to blame, should have drunk more water/ taken a multivitamin/ swallowed a raw egg/ eaten monkey testicles, etc.

Neither of these apply, and I wonder whether this is going to be a regular side effect. Happily, one of the nurses tells me that this is not the case, and that I should feel normal again in a day or two.

Eventually I gain a modicum of energy and, undeterred by my submariner's view of the world, I get on with the challenge of getting up and at 'em. First comes the daily bed bath, much of which I now try to do myself – certainly my arms, armpits, chest, washboard stomach (the morphine diet knocks the shit out of Atkins. Only trouble is, you end up needing someone to knock the shit out of you … may have to work on the strap-line for that one), and down as far as my rather forlorn genitals. Now this is an interesting one, and I'm sure a point of curiosity to many more inquisitive minds. Now that I am paralysed from the waist down, does handling my … well, myself, does it feel like I am handling someone else's … self? Answer, I'm not sure, having not tried it. Now by way of a better answer, it does feel strange, but only in the way that feeling your own hand or foot or any other appendage feels strange when it has gone to sleep. It still feels like me somehow, and my brain struggles to work out where my hand stops feeling, and my legs or penis or whatever is supposed to start feeling. I'm not sure if that makes any sense, but that's the best I can come up with.

After the wash comes the shave, a strong symbol of 'looking after myself' and I am hoisted into my chariot. Once in my chair, I get a visit from my occupational therapist, who happens to be profoundly deaf and lip-reads. The role of the occupational-health team in my rehabilitation is fairly limited in comparison to someone who is tetraplegic (referred to as a tetra in the spinal-injury world). With a tetra, occupational therapists spend a lot of time mobilising their hands, and making splints for them in order to stop the tendons from shortening, or in some cases, where the patient has movement in the wrist but no grip, splinting the hands closed so that tilting the hand back at the wrist causes the fingers to close, thus providing slightly more function than would otherwise be achieved. But for me, the OT department will help with becoming independent enough to be able to get dressed, cook a meal, and even to drive again, as well as help with my blue badge parking entitlement and other paperwork.

It becomes a very busy day, as I am presented with a green timetable card showing the various appointments I am to attend as part of my rehabilitation. Penny arrives shortly after lunch, and we head off to the physiotherapy gym for my first proper look at the place where I shall be spending two hours every weekday. It bears only a passing resemblance to any gym I have used in the past. There are exercise bikes and crash mats and giant gym balls, and even the odd dumbbell, but the most obvious difference is the abundance of 'plinths' or low, upholstered benches, and tilt tables, which are similarly upholstered, but are motorised, and can be tilted from horizontal to vertical, with the patient strapped to them, in a scene reminiscent of *Frankenstein*. It is, of course, with these that we start. Selina, the physio who has been assigned to me, lines my wheelchair up alongside one of the tables, which is in a horizontal position, and she removes one of my most beloved armrests and holds up a plywood board about 20 cm wide and 60 cm long.

'This is a sliding board,' she announces and then shoves one end of the plank under my backside to bridge the gap between the wheelchair and the tilt table. Next comes the tricky bit, as I have to try and lean forward into a tuck position, before sliding myself across the board and onto the table. Selina helps me with this, saying, 'You'll be able to do this on your own in no time.'

I feel a degree of reassurance, although the experience is still pretty terrifying, as I feel as though I haven't just been cut off at the waist, but that the bottom half of my torso has been tapered to a point. To my relief, Selina helps me to lie on the bench and uses various Velcro straps to secure me to the table, before hitting the button on the remote control attached to the bench, causing it to tilt gradually up to an angle of about 45 degrees, and handing me the controls so that I can increase the angle when I feel comfortable. My patience is virtually non-existent with the prospect of resuming a vertical position for the first time in a month and in no time I am upright.

I survey the room around me, which is filled with other patients and physiotherapists engaged in what appears at first glance to be a series of wrestling bouts, some involving pieces of home-made equipment, while another patient sits in a wheelchair looking on, tapping his foot impatiently, obviously waiting to be tagged into the action. In reality, there are several patients being 'stretched' in order to keep their muscles, tendons and ligaments from shortening due to inactivity, while other patients are being helped in balance exercises, and 'transfers', the different techniques for getting from one place, i.e., wheelchair, to another, i.e., bed. The patient tapping his foot is my first encounter with spasm, which is caused by a short-circuit in the spinal cord.

It is not long before my upright position has an effect and I start to feel decidedly queasy and light-headed, so I recline again. The feeling is due to my blood rushing to my feet, even though I am wearing the 'Shatner' again. Selina assures me that this will pass in time, as my vascular system adjusts and constricts to keep the pressure more even, and the other muscle groups in my body take over more of the work of pumping the blood around.

It is a constant source of wonder to me that the human body can make this kind of adjustment. If we cast back through the mists of time and imagine life as a hunter-gatherer, a fall from a tree (while foraging for nuts and berries) causing damage to the spinal cord would result in certain death, if not from the shock of the accident, then certainly as a result of being on the menu for a passing sabre-tooth tiger. And yet, now that medical intervention allows us to survive such a trauma, the body is able to adapt to the change in circumstances. The digestive function continues through peristalsis, the vascular system recalibrates to cope without the action of the largest muscle groups in the body, and the trunk muscles are able to take on the job of balancing.

We finish the session on the tilt table and I am transferred (via the sliding board again) onto a plinth. As I slide onto the plinth I clutch the edge for stability, but Selina prises my fingers off, and slides me over until my legs are also on the plinth, before kneeling on the plinth behind me, and getting me to lean back. It's difficult to convey the feeling of utter helplessness as I try and sit upright. It feels a bit like trying to stand on a football. Now that my buttocks and thigh muscles no longer work, I don't have a 'base' to make the micro-adjustments necessary to keep me balanced. I have to learn to balance my top half using the muscles in my stomach and my back. It can only be akin to learning to sit up as a baby, and as that is beyond the memory of most people, including myself, it's an unhelpful comparison. Also, as a baby, I didn't have to cope with the added difficulty of a brain saying, 'Come on, you can do this. It's just sitting up, right? What's the matter with you? Are you doing it on purpose? You are, aren't you? Oh, honestly, sometimes I wonder why I bother, I really do. And another thing. Call this an internal dialogue? There's only one voice here. What have you got to say for yourself, hmm?'

Although my sitting is not quite there, I do manage to roll myself over. All I need to do is stay and play dead, and I'm fully trained. I try to take solace in the famous saying from the *Way* of Lao-Tzu: 'A journey of a thousand miles begins with a single step.'

At which point my internal voice sniggers, 'Well, that's you fucked, then isn't it?'

I feel overwhelmed at the magnitude of the task ahead of me. There's more lying in wait, because after about five minutes of sitting, I start to get a really savage, sharp pain from my lower back. The session comes to an end, and Selina asks, 'Do you have a key worker, yet?'

It is obvious from my look of bewilderment that I probably do not. Realising my confusion, she explains, 'Your key worker is the therapist or nurse that you go to as a first point of contact to discuss your rehabilitation. Every few weeks, you have a goal-planning meeting, attended by your named nurse, your physio, psychologist, occupational therapist and a doctor from your consultant's team. In the meeting, we discuss and set long-term goals as well as more immediate short-term goals for your rehabilitation programme. I'll be your key worker, if you like.'

Key worker duly appointed, we get ready to leave the gym, when a shock confronts me. On re-entering the wheelchair, I turn and see myself in a full-length mirror for the first time since the accident. I have lost about two stone in weight, and my clothes resemble pyjamas, which is not surprising, as relative to the 'modesty' outfit of bed rest, what used to look like pyjamas does feel like proper clothes, and seeing as getting into a pair of baggy checked drawstring trousers feels like the equivalent of putting on a corset and a wetsuit combined (although quite why one would combine a corset and a wetsuit will remain a mystery, I fear), it is for practical reasons that I have adopted the 'sleeping surfer' look. Strangely, the wheelchair doesn't look out of place, partly because there are so many other people in wheelchairs, but also because I just look as if I am sitting down, ready to leap to my feet. I look away before I ruin this illusion by trying to stand. Still, self-image adjustments aside, it has been a good day, as I am now 'rehabilitating'. I have something to push against.

By the next day, I realise that the something is pushing back. I wake up to an excruciating lumbar pain, which seems to be 'just one of those things'. The muscles that I have protected so judiciously throughout my working life with safe lifting techniques, and then rested for four weeks, having had someone cut through a few for good measure, are now being called upon to do all the work that my buttocks used to do (and what buttocks they were – they stuck out and I was proud of them). As it is the gluteus maximus that enabled Homo erectus to be, well, erect, it is the development of this muscle that enabled one of the most important evolutionary leaps in our physical development. And seeing as my arse used to stick out by a country mile, I considered myself to be a little further along in evolutionary terms than some of the more buttock-deficient among us. I'm worried that this is taking us dangerously into the world of eugenics and phrenology and other extremely dubious pseudo-sciences, so let's just say that I was attached to my arse. Obviously I still am attached to my arse, but it has already become a shadow of its former self. Still, it should make buying trousers easier.

Along with my arse shrinking, I have a fabulous six-pack, the only problem being that it's appeared just at the time in my life when it is necessary to inject anticoagulant just under the skin on my tummy every night for six weeks, and a bit of flab would make things a lot more comfortable.

Thursday is a 'stand by your beds' day, as Thursday is Dr J's ward round. He blesses me with his presence for an intimate one to one with myself, himself, two or three junior doctors, the ward sister and maybe a couple of the nursing staff for good measure. He asks me how I am getting on. I have no idea, as my mind has gone completely blank, as it always does when he marches into my life. We discuss my pain, he ups the dose of little yellow pills, tells me that the lumbar pain should settle down – I mustn't let it win, of course. He also explains that he still hasn't made a decision about further surgery, as he wants to talk to Professor Kluger before he makes a decision. Prof Kluger is the top knife at the spinal unit. There is even a fixation used to stabilise spinal fractures that is called a 'Kluger' fixation.

The fact that Dr J is consulting so widely gives me some reassurance that he isn't taking the decision lightly. Still, it is a fear in the back of my mind, but he assures me that he will only perform further surgery if it is absolutely necessary, and that if I do have to go under the knife again, the post-operative experience will be much better that the first time when I was in trauma. He then makes a jovial quip, and while we all turn and chuckle to each other like a sycophantic chorus in a Gilbert and Sullivan production, he turns and leaves the room. Damn, he's good.

4

As my mobility improves, I spend more time away from my bed. I start to attend a course of lectures that are put on in the patient education room. I am looking forward to getting some kind of qualification at the end of it, perhaps a scroll, or the letters SCI after my name, but with time this hope is dashed. The room is spacious by some standards, but not once there are half a dozen patients in it. We become a living version of those square puzzles where you have to slide the pieces around just to get one moved. The lectures themselves cover a large variety of subjects, from coping strategies to bladder and bowel management (everything seems to be about bladder and bowel management), skin care, housing and transport, sexuality and relationships, etc.

The first lecture is more of an introduction, and is hosted by Dianne, my psychologist. I feel a little uncomfortable at first, but soon warm to the opportunity to discuss people's preconceptions about what we will face when we are discharged. We talk about coping strategies, breaking down negative thoughts and other scenarios where 'cognitive thinking' can be employed. This seems to be the cornerstone of much of the help from the psychology team. I can see the usefulness of this, but at the moment it seems like an intellectual exercise, as I often forget to employ it when I am sinking.

One advantage of the group scenario is that I soon realise that we are all dealing with the same basic issues, only some of us are coping better than others. It turns out that my enthusiasm for 'forthright' (and at times overly colourful) discussions on the workings of the bladder and bowel is not shared by everyone. Here I encounter not just social taboos, but a reluctance in some people to face these issues, as to do so means to begin to accept the permanence of their condition. This may sound strange, but then most patients have not had the same clear-cut experience that I have had so far.

The effect of spinal shock means that some people, particularly those with neck injuries, have been completely paralysed from the neck down initially, but then begin to recover some or even all sensation and movement in the rest of their body. In my case, my symptoms have not changed from the immediate aftermath of my accident to now. I don't know if this is easier or harder. Easier because I know what I have to work with from the word go, or harder because there has been nothing to give me hope, which may have helped to get through the initial emotional shock (better than morphine, anyway).

My brother Chris comes up to see me with his partner Sarah and their little daughter Jessica, who is fourteen months old, and I watch the constant battle they have keeping everything out of her mouth. I feel like I'm looking through a window into the future, only if our child inherits anything from their father, then we will have the extra task of trying to keep things out of their nose, as this was apparently a habit of mine when I was very little.

Chris brings me a new pair of shoes for my birthday, which may at first glance appear to be a rather sick joke, as I'm not exactly going to be walking anywhere, but is very useful, as I can no longer wear any of my old shoes because my feet swell as the day goes on, and I wouldn't be able to feel if my shoes were pinching. As well as losing the use of my shoe collection, socks have to be worn inside out to prevent the seams pressing on my toes, and I can't wear any jeans or trousers with buttons, flaps or studs on the backside, as they can cause marks on my skin that could then develop into pressure sores. Prompted by this information, my mother-in-law Ginny enthusiastically attacks a pair of my combat trousers, and cuts off every popper button, including those on the side pockets, front pockets, back pockets and anywhere else where there could have been one, and I am left with something resembling combat fishnets.

On the subject of shoes, Chris has the burden of looking after the shoes I was wearing when I had the accident, the only articles of clothing that weren't cut to shreds by the emergency services, although the laces went. The shoes are virtually new, as I bought them in Australia, trying on dozens of pairs to find some that were really comfortable. I don't want to see them, but somehow don't want them to be thrown away either. Chris's burden also includes liaising with the health and safety officer who has been given the task of investigating what happened, as it constitutes an industrial accident. My climbing equipment has been sent off for specialist testing, although the site wasn't 'forensically preserved', as the priority was to get me off the roof and into the air ambulance, and I believe they may even have used the rope that was still attached to the tree for extra security against the risk of falling through the roof. I'm glad I was of service.

My dear brother's responsibilities don't end there. The friend's mother who lives next door to where I had the accident holds a special lunch and fundraising auction, with lots including a signed script from *EastEnders* (which I must confess I don't watch) and a football signed by the entire Tottenham team (oh, the irony).

Chris attended as my 'representative', and he tells me how people were coming up to him and offering their sympathies at such a difficult time, and he started to feel rather uncomfortable, as if he were at a funeral, and he felt like saying, 'He's not dead, you know. I'm going to see him tomorrow.' I love him for this, because he understands that I have to move on from here: it doesn't just stop. That being said, I'm extremely grateful for the money that has been raised for us, and we put it in the fighting fund, along with some generous contributions from fundraising initiated by family and friends. I find the generosity overwhelming at times. While I appreciate that people can feel helpless when they hear news of such an accident, a bit of pragmatic financial help is invaluable, especially as we were running our own business. Penny has had to sack me, so that I'm not responsible for my own sick pay, which I haven't been getting. I think I should have got myself unionised, but as a company director I would have had to deal with myself in negotiations, and I'm an awkward bugger sometimes, so instead I've given myself the bullet. You think you know someone...

Family and close friends drop money on us in a very matter-of-fact way. One very close family friend, who wants to help financially, visits me and she talks about how an event like this sends ripples through the lives of those around you. It is a nice image, somehow, and it makes me feel like I am part of a wider world. To be missed by people makes me feel that there is a strength I can tap into, people we can lean on. I also get cards and letters from an aunt and cousins in Canada that I have met only once or twice in my life, and I am deeply touched, especially when one of my cousins reports that she will be singing a healing song for me with the Native Indian singing group that she is a part of. If ever my instinctive nose for mysticism should be twitching it is now, but instead I find strength in the thought that someone so distant has been moved to offer help, even if it is just symbolic.

The other big change in my day has been the discovery of an internet café in Jimmy's, and suddenly I am connected to all my friends and family again. My relentless openness about all of the changes I am trying to assimilate takes hold immediately, and it occurs to me that emails are not just a great way of keeping people informed, but that if I am frank, they may also be useful in avoiding potentially embarrassing situations after I am discharged. This dovetails neatly with an innate desire to make people squirm whenever possible. I find as I write the first missive that my openness doesn't automatically include my darker emotional thoughts. The thought of dropping that kind of load into an email to people on the other side of the world seems unfair, and I decide that I will keep it for quiet reflection and the occasional 'live gig' (invite only).

5

13 May 2005

Hello, all ...

A quick dispatch from the world of wheels.

I've received various bits and bobs in the post recently. This has been very uplifting. Getting post first thing in the morning really makes my day.

There's nothing quite like snail-mail, so keep the letters (and huge parcels. Go wild, people) coming. Big thanks for the stuff from overseas.

Physio has slowed down dramatically this week after last week's jubilant 'how hard can it be?' approach – the reply came back (from my back): bloody hard.

For those who don't know, I've been moved down onto St George's ward, which is a rehab ward. I've also learned today that they will not be redoing my fixation, but will monitor it during my rehabilitation with a view to removing it as soon as is practical. This means that they think that my body will repair the break in my spine sufficiently well, even though the L1 vertebra is not fully realigned.

Keep smiling. I am, honest.

The morning routine still involves a cast of thousands, but now the bed bath is replaced with a shower. And not a 'St Andrew's shower', where I was occasionally rolled onto a blue plastic tray attached to a trolley, before being wheeled into the shower room, hosed down, soaped up and hosed down again by two nurses. It was a real treat after being in bed for three weeks, but down here on St George's we are talking a proper shower, sitting on a seat and clutching the grab-rail for dear life, having first checked that my bits and pieces haven't dropped through the hole in the seat when I transferred out of my wheelchair (the limited sensation in my left testicle doesn't always act as a reliable reminder that 'things' aren't being afforded the correct level of respect and attention). The hole in the seat is not for removing appendages, although the rather sharp edge of the vinyl cover might suggest it is, but rather it is for cleaning yourself thoroughly, and thinking about it too much is generally not such a good thing, although I suppose it's no different to sharing a toilet. In fact it's better in that there are copious amounts of soapy water involved. Still…

Where the nursing staff up on the acute ward included quite a large contingent of nurses from the Philippines, the staff on my new ward includes a number of Spaniards who came over to work in the NHS in the 1970s after the death of General Franco. There is also a nursing auxiliary from Portugal, staff from Mauritius, the Philippines, Ireland, South Africa, Zimbabwe and even Buckinghamshire. I feel that I get on well with all the staff, especially the ward sister, Liz, who is keen for me to get through my rehabilitation and be with Penny at the birth. In fact, in our first meeting she tells me that she will kick me out regardless come the date of delivery, so I had better get on with it.

Liz comes to my aid on several occasions, most notably on the road to self-catheterisation, which sounds like a less well-known book by George Orwell, but is actually the method by which I will manage my bladder in the future. Yes, my friends, we are on to the first big B of self-caring (the second big B is bowel, and I will warn you of its appearance later). The idea behind self-catheterisation is to give the patient more independence and also reduce the risk of infection, by sticking a tube up your urethra (by whichever route you have; male catheters are considerably longer than female ones, obviously) and into the bladder when it needs to be emptied, rather than having an indwelling catheter permanently in place and acting as a bug motorway straight into the bladder.

The real difficulty in self-catheterising is mastering the process of putting a catheter in without compromising its sterile status while at the same time having to train the sphincter (the valve of the bladder) that letting this tube in is a good idea. The type of catheter that I am given comes individually packed in long foil packets filled with a sterile, water-based lubricant. Getting the long, lubricated tube from the packet and into the end of my penis while wearing a sterile glove on one hand (for handling the catheter) and my other hand handling... well, handling, is an exercise in dexterity that I feel ill-prepared for, and on several occasions I have to give up because the catheter has come into contact with everything in the room except my penis.

Having finally managed to get one of the suckers up the end of my end, it hits a solid, unyielding barrier and I have no idea how hard to push, as I have heard of people bleeding a bit when they first get used to the procedure or, rather, the sphincter gets used to it, and although I cannot feel anything, there is a strong self-preservation instinct that says sticking a tube up your cock until you bleed is basically a bad idea, and one to be avoided at all costs. Now I'm sure there are some people who may disagree with this, and they no doubt have websites devoted to their strange practices, but for me it is a huge source of anxiety when I am unable to carry out catheterisation unaided.

Intimidated but undeterred, I struggle on with the procedure. I try coughing, which is supposed to help, but to no avail. I pull on my penis to straighten my urethra (not *that* old excuse) and poke and coax and cajole until after a couple of days of this the inevitable happens, and I wake up feeling like shit. I mean really bad. Not only do I feel achy and nauseous, but it feels as if someone is stabbing my legs with a cattle prod, as belts of hot, shocking pain fire every 30 seconds or so.

A quick once-over by the nursing staff, and the conclusion is that I have a bladder infection. This is pretty common, as a good sterile technique takes a while to perfect, and hospitals are chock full of germs just waiting to get into the nearest bladder and have some fun.

My temperature has shot up, and I am put back onto an indwelling catheter with a bed-bag, which rapidly fills up with the most cloudy wee that I've ever seen – although to be fair, I'm not putting myself forward as an expert with years of experience, or anything. But it *is* extremely cloudy. A sample of the offending/offensive urine is taken and sent off to the path-lab for testing, while back on the ward my day goes from bad to worse.

One of the staff nurses comes in to tell me that I am to be moved out of my side room into a bay with five other patients, four of whom are on ventilators. This means 'Psh-te-koof-psh te-koof' like Ivor the Engine all day and all night, times four.

The news is more than I can take, and I feel so lousy that I return to a previous incarnation, that of bummed-out former morphine addict who just can't take it any more, and I put my foot down. No, not literally, obviously. But I howl and wail and mention my heavily pregnant wife and how this room is the only privacy we get etc., etc.

And there she is. My saviour in a dark-blue uniform. Ward sister Liz comes in to talk to me. She consoles me. She listens, and then she says, 'Don't worry, darlin'. Leave it with me.'

Five minutes later she returns to tell me that one of the other patients has agreed to move instead, and I get to keep my side room. I weep. Again. What a wuss. Mind you, I am extremely grateful, because if I ignore the oxygen and suction pipes emerging from the wall above the bed and I really blur my eyes, I can lose the hospital and imagine I am in a cheap hotel in Bulgaria or somewhere.

Now that my accommodation issue has been dealt with, I can get back to the important business of feeling like shit. I try and wrap my shivering, sweating, aching body in the NHS blanket, but I get a surprise. Two nurses come into the room, feed me some paracetamol, whip off the bedding and produce an electric fan, which they aim at me as I shiver beneath my 'modesty'. As I gibber and chatter slightly more unintelligibly than usual, one of the staff nurses explains to me, 'Our first priority is always to get the patient's temperature under control because until this is done, the body can't begin to tackle the infection. If your temperature gets above forty degrees, then you will suffer serious tissue damage.'

This doesn't make me feel better about chattering my way through most of my teeth, while lying naked under a pillowcase with a storm-force ten blowing over me, but I know it's for good reason.

During the first day it becomes obvious how said bug got in there, as among the various bits and bobs in my urine bag floats a hair, which obviously hitched a ride on the blind side of one of the ever so sticky pre-lubricated catheters. With the discovery and departure of the offending 'carrier', I begin to feel somewhat better, and even manage to eat some of the food that Penny and her mum have made for me. And who knows, maybe tomorrow I'll be well enough to get up and perhaps go to hydrotherapy?

The next day arrives, and I feel like shit again. My temperature is back up, my sheets are off, and the north wind is blowing through my room again. All this is taking a large toll on my coping abilities, and I am thankful that Dianne from the psychology team still visits me on a regular basis. In my feverish state I tell her of my suspicion that Dr J only told me that I could be mobilised as a punishment for being an uppity patient, and that he knew that I would still need further surgery, but in the meantime I would cause myself a lot of pain. I think this is verging on delusional paranoia, but hey, let's not use 'labels'. To give myself a little credit, I do dismiss this notion as paranoia without the need for professional intervention.

I also have a recurring sense of dread, a sense that I'm not really dealing with things, and that all I am doing is clearing a very small space in the middle of a room that is precariously piled with nasty realities, just waiting to land on me. At other times I feel as if I'm sitting on the lid of a box that is going to burst open, releasing the full horror of my situation. A horror so profound as to make it insurmountable – if it's ever possible to 'surmount' a horror, that is. Dianne reassures me that this is all a natural response to the situation that I find myself in, and that managing to clear a bit of 'floor space' is progress in itself. As we get to the end of the session, she tells me that she has spent ten years working with people who are terminally ill. Her friends often ask her if she finds this work depressing.

'In fact it's just the opposite,' she tells me in her American accent which, coupled with her glasses, remind me of Dr Malfi in *The Sopranos*, 'I am constantly amazed and inspired by people's abilities to cope with the most desperate of situations.'

After Dianne leaves, I find myself thinking of Penny. How she describes that gap of a million moments between my fall in the corner of her eye and my subsequent scream, thinking that I was dead. The relief she felt when she heard me cry out her name has been enough to sustain her through all that has happened between then and now. On a number of occasions I have passed on Dianne's offer to talk to Penny, if she feels it would help. Penny usually looks at me with a slightly quizzical expression. In the end it is Eugene who ends up seeing Dianne to talk about his feelings over my accident and resultant disability, and it helps immeasurably.

Finally the bug is identified, and I'm put on a course of oral antibiotics rather than a drip, which is a relief, as all I can think of is when I can get up again and get on with my rehabilitation. I feel a bit like a wildebeest that knows that if it doesn't keep moving, a lion is sure to get it. I'm not sure what the lion is. I think it is just some kind of survival-instinct scenario. Every day I spend in bed I feel noticeably weaker and my frustration grows. It is Saturday tomorrow, and I can at least look forward to visitors who generously make the journey up from London to see me.

My friends have been magnificent in their support. From dealing with my drug-fuelled bravado and near lunacy in Ye Olde Royal Londonne, to my more depressed, less entertaining but at least more coherent state in Stoke Mandeville. Graham starts up a monthly collection from various anonymous friends to whom we will be forever in debt. The contributions are enough to enable us to rent a small flat in Aylesbury, where Penny and her mother Ginny set up base camp while they search for a flat in the area.

The trip up from London takes something over an hour by car, and those who brave the train have to get a cab from the station, so I feel grateful that many people make the effort. All that being said, for some inexplicable reason I can't help revelling in the discomfort I cause visitors by regaling them with tales of the new processes now involved in my bodily functions, and inviting them to stay in the room while I slip behind a curtain and wrestle with a catheter. Thinking about it, were the roles reversed, I think I would be heading off to Jimmy's for a cup of tea at the first mention of bladder, bowels or catheter, let alone the whip-snap of a surgical glove being donned. 'Nurse! Nurse! The lubrication, if you please!'

6

24 May 2005

OK ...
been a while, I know. Sorry 'bout that. Penny's packed up our bongos and moved up to Aylesbury. Having her around the corner is a HUGE plus for me. We see each other every day now, and I've only eaten one hospital meal in the last week! Heartfelt thanks to everyone who's making this possible.

I've got to go, as I've got a wheelchair skills lesson to get to. Wheelies and kerb negotiation at the moment, but in no time it will be bunny hops and staircase climbs f'sure! be lucky,

The antibiotics have a pretty swift effect, bolstered by a variety of extremely tasty food-based gifts that I am presented with over the course of the weekend by the postman as well as visitors, especially Ginny, who plays the supportive role in a very reassuring way for me. On visits, she often disappears to give Penny and me a bit of time on our own, and she gives me the security of knowing that Penny has someone there for her when I can't be. I am beginning to realise that Penny has to learn all about spinal-cord injury and how to live with it at the same time as me. Ginny also spends time on knitting and other grandparent-to-be activities, reminding me of the other big event coming up in our lives.

The weekends are particularly difficult, as there are no therapies, and those patients that are able manage to escape for a couple of days. I miss my old life – our old life – with a passion that makes my whole self hurt profoundly. I remember some advice I was given by Dr K during a particularly nasty attack of the what-ifs when I was still flat on my back. He said, 'Look, you can go on thinking about what might have happened, what went wrong, where you would be now and all of those things, but it's expensive. Emotionally expensive, and it's you who will have to pay. The deeper you go, the harder and more painful it is to get back.'

He's right of course. But it's like having the most tender wound and not being able to resist giving it a poke every now and then, just to see how much it hurts.

Chris, Sarah and Jessica come up to see us on Sunday. Jess pushes me around the ward in my wheelchair, much to the delight of the staff, and then we head outside, for it is a lovely spring afternoon. Around the back of the spinal unit, between the staff car park and the eye outpatients department (or 'Eyeout Patients', as the sign appears to say), we find a small square of grass with a bench and a tree to sit under. Pausing only for me to empty my leg bag in a convenient flowerbed, we have ourselves a picnic. I am free of the spinal unit, watching little Jessica roll around on the grass, and Penny and Sarah share pregnancy experiences. Having this pause, I start to unravel. I feel this crushing sense of loss and sadness and panic and helplessness, and I feel worse because I want my family to take away a positive view of how we are coping. It hurts to hurt them, but I can't help it any more. I cry and cry, and that just makes me feel worse, and everyone sits quietly, uncomfortably, my brother puts his hand on my shoulder, and Sarah and Penny's eyes moisten.

And then it stops. I remember Dr K's advice about the cost of all of this, and somehow I find a way of pulling myself back out of the hole, fighting my way back to some kind of equilibrium.

'Sorry, 'bout that.'

Chris shakes his head. 'It's fine, it's fine.'

Then Jessica tries to stand on her head, and makes me laugh, and I feel a tingle of excitement at the thought of my child playing with my brother's child, and I am transported back to our childhood together. All the time we shared making up games and doing foolish things. I remember the time that he fell out of a tree, breaking two planks of a rudimentary tree house with his back before falling a further ten feet onto the ground. All he did was hurt his right thumb. Go figure.

There are a great many incidents in my youth that start to take on a more scary aspect, especially my teenage years. But we were young and invincible. Except that, being in a spinal unit, I am now surrounded by those who didn't quite get away with it.

I was a Mod. My friends were Mods, and we all had scooters, which we hurtled around on, often illegally, and sometimes drunk. There was a running joke among our group of friends that we were never all on the road at the same time, because as soon as one of us got their scooter roadworthy, someone else would lose their licence or lose control on a corner, or hit a car and write their scooter off. I look back now on literally dozens of crashes between us, most fairly innocuous, often pretty stupid, but some of them could have been, well, life changing. Or ending.

There was one. There was a friend, a member of the same scooter club, but as the club was a loose meeting of people from north and south London who went to the same nightclubs and all-nighters, it was more a coming together of different groups of friends. He was someone I had spoken to a handful of times, and I liked him. I heard that he was riding his scooter, probably a little bit too fast, when a woman in a car pulled out of a side street, and he went straight over her car and into a lamppost head first. Apparently, he got to his feet, and berated her for the loss of his beloved Lambretta, but he died pretty soon after, having suffered a massive head injury inside his helmet.

His parents didn't get to go to a spinal unit or some other rehabilitation hospital, to grieve over his paralysis or loss of a limb. They had a big funeral, and we all rode our scooters behind the hearse, as they knew it was what their son had loved in his life. We all cried when they played his favourite Northern Soul song at the service, and then we all went to his house for a sandwich. I was on a friend's Vespa. My Lambretta had been written off the night before when someone pulled out on me in a van.

And yet … and yet. Through all of this, through all these times, it would never happen to me. Not me. Invincibility diminishes with age, but even so. Paralysis? From the waist down? No, not to me. And this is one of the things I struggle with. I still try and jump sideways into another life. One where I don't have the accident, or one where I only break my leg. But with all the other possible outcomes, there is one that I still don't see, one that I won't allow myself to see. The one where people play my favourite songs. And cry.

The patient education programme continues for those of us who want to attend. It's not compulsory, but I certainly find the information invaluable. The skin lecture is pretty grim. The intention is to explain how the skin works, why it is important to protect it, and what happens if you don't. The first two parts of this are educational and informative, but the final part reminds me of schoolchildren in a reference library, finding medical books and looking up the pictures of hideous injuries and diseases. We are treated to a slide show of some of the most horrendous images of sores and holes and ulcers on paralysed people. The problem is that if you can't feel a part of your body, you must look to find out if things are breaking down, but even so, the size and extent of the damage we are shown must surely point to psychological issues preventing the person from seeking medical intervention earlier, as it is far too severe to have simply been overlooked. There is one image that will haunt me for a very long time, of a patient who wore jeans that were too tight around his groin, although I can only assume that he wore them continuously for a couple of weeks. Where the jeans were creased, they had cut off the circulation to the skin, and the result was open sores either side of his genitals that went right into the pelvic bone.

While I appreciate that the lecture is designed to shock people into taking care of themselves, I'm not sure that the cavalcade of horror is really necessary. I get the message enough to make sure that I do my 'pressure relief' regularly. Pressure relief involves leaning forward or sideways in your chair for a minute or so every hour, in order to take the pressure off the skin directly under the ischial tuberosities, or bum-bones, to use the correct medical terminology. This allows the blood flow to increase in the skin, and prevent toxins from building up and the tissue breaking down. In this regard I am doubly fortunate. Firstly, I have very good skin, courtesy of my mother. It heals quickly, and has good circulation. Secondly, as the neuropathic pain provides me with acute discomfort most of the time, I will probably never sit still long enough to develop a pressure sore. I am also trying to build up my 'chair-miles' from four or five hours a day up to eight or so, the main barrier to this being the pain, which gets worse the longer I spend in the wheelchair.

At the same time as trying to spend more time in the chair, I attend my first wheelchair-skills class, which takes place in the archery gym. The archery gym is part of the original spinal unit, the first of its kind in the world, which was set up by Professor Ludwig Guttmann in 1944 to care for the many spinal-injury patients who came home when a second front was opened in the war in Europe. Guttmann was also the founder of the Stoke Mandeville games, which eventually became the Paralympics. This long hall, the cradle of the Paralympics, is an illustrious place to undertake any 'sporting' activity. The archery bit intrigues me as well, especially as I did some archery when I was at school, and it was something that I really enjoyed.

The wheelchair-skills sessions are run by the sports physio, Lou, who casually takes the anti-tips (small wheel on the back of the wheelchair to stop me going arse over 'tip'?) off and stands behind me while I try and balance on the back wheels only. This is a vital skill if I wish to get over rough ground or even up a kerb. There is a bit of me that enjoys the challenge of mastering a new vehicle and physical skill. So, geed up by this, I roll backwards, and then pull on the wheel rims. The front wheels come off the ground, and I lurch backwards, awash with adrenalin, only I am caught safely, and righted so that I can try again. The idea is to be able to keep the front wheels aloft through pulling and pushing on the push-rims, rather like a unicyclist pedalling back and forth. It reminds me of trying to master the 'bunny hop' on my mountain bike, a skill that took me a while to crack.

At wheelchair skills I meet another patient, Philip, who I remember seeing in his wheelchair up on St Andrews when I was still in bed. Some of the staff told me that I looked exactly like him. It turns out that this is because we both have dark hair, glasses and stubble. Philip was injured in March while on his honeymoon in Barbados when the balcony of his hotel room gave way, and he fell to the ground, causing his spinal-cord injury at T10/11/12. It is the first time that I have met another patient of a similar level as me, and he is great to talk to, as we get to compare notes. We have the same consultant, and he is a couple of months further along in his rehabilitation than me, so I get to see where I am headed. He also gives me some good advice.

'It's important to be a nuisance here, otherwise stuff sometimes just doesn't happen.'

I am reminded of the frustration of waiting for an MRI scan when I was first admitted.

I ask Philip about pain.

'Yeah, I'm in constant pain. My whole back and my legs.'

'What meds are you on? Dr J has mentioned a few that I could try.'

He scoffs. 'They weren't doing anything for me, and I just got so fed up with it all that I've stopped taking them.'

We go back to Jimmy's Café, and Philip introduces me to another T12, called Lee, who is further along still.

Lee is in the RAF. He was driving to work very early in the morning when he hit a patch of black ice on a bend. By chance, probably the only other car on the road at that time happened to be coming the other way and they collided head-on. The two people in the other car were unharmed. Lee was in a coma for several days, eventually waking to find that he was paralysed from the waist down. His father is in Jimmy's, and joins us for a chat. He explains how the doctors told him of Lee's condition first and were going to tell Lee, but he intervened.

'He's my boy, and if anyone's telling him, it's going to be me. So I told him and we had a bit of a cry, but then we got over it, and he got on with his rehab.'

Watching Lee and Philip makes me feel like the new boy. I don't feel as if I have even begun to process the full implications of my injury, either physically or in terms of its impact on my life's hopes and dreams.

The conversation moves on to consultants (we all share the enigmatic Dr J, who really is like that, and not just with me) and rehab. Talk turns to what can be achieved, and I find out that it is possible to go up a flight of stairs in a wheelchair if you are strong enough. I make a mental note to be strong enough, and add this to a wish-list of new skills that I have begun to assemble in my head, along with getting in and out of a car, getting off the floor and back into my wheelchair, climbing kerbs and, of course, back-wheel balancing, a skill that both Philip and Lee are proficient in, and it looks so much like cool showing-off that it pushes it straight to the top of the list.

It is such a joy to have this resource of shared experience, and after an hour spent chatting and joking, I return to my room feeling lifted, appreciating just what peer support can mean. However, something happens on the way. At some point, for no reason except that I am feeling happy, a darker side of my brain takes over, and an internal voice screams, 'And what exactly have you got to be so fucking happy about, all of a sudden?'

It feels as if the lid of the box full of panic and loss and pain and despair has loosened, and I have to spend the evening trying not to look inside. It is extremely sobering.

7

28 May 2005
Subject: Quickie

Here I am again, but briefly. What's been happening? What's the word in Jimmy's? Boredom. That's the big word this week. This place feels very small these days, and I'm desperate to improve my 'transfers' (e.g. from bed to wheelchair, to car, to hang-glider, etc.), so that I can escape for a couple of hours here and there. At least then I can get a change of scenery and a bit of privacy. Mind you, for the time being this will involve someone who is not seven months pregnant accompanying me so that I don't fall out or can at least be put back in the chair if I do.

Discovered new medium to express myself in yesterday, when I managed to wheel myself from my room into Jimmy's Café and back again with the valve open on my leg bag. I was in Jimmy's thinking: what's that patch of water down there? and dribbling wee all the way back to my room, before realising that I had also filled my shoe, and having to sheepishly ask the staff to clear up the intricate pattern in the corridor while I got changed. Oops. Ah well, at least I might still be able to write my name in the snow one day.

I find the whole NHS experience rather baffling, too. For those that don't know, the NHS provides me with the world's best specialist spinal-cord doctors, consultants, surgeons, psychologists, physiotherapists and nurses, but can't keep the floor clean, or provide a bit of fibre in the diet. It seems to be the small, fairly straightforward things that they fall down on, while the big stuff is met head on.

Wheelchair skills are coming on. Able to balance on
two wheels, providing there is someone behind me when
I launch. Need to work on my confidence with that, then
I should be flying up and down kerbs in no time. Hoping
to start archery next week, too. Good for the balance, you
see. It's not about fun, oh no, this is serious rehab. Yes
indeedy.

As far as side rooms go, I have really got lucky. My fairy god-
mother Liz has put me in a large side room opposite the
nurses' station on the ward. It has an en suite bathroom, which
is perhaps a generous description of 'my very own hospital
bathroom'. The best feature of all is a door out onto a paved
courtyard. The courtyard has a plaque at one end describing
it as the '*Daily Express* Charlotte's Courtyard for children' or
somesuch, and it consists of dark brick paving and raised beds,
overlooked by windows on all sides. It is strangely planted with
a mixture of mahonia and berberis, two of the most spiky and
unpleasant shrubs. I don't know who this Charlotte was, but
she was obviously seriously pissed off at children. One particularly good feature to the garden is that it is a haven for birds,
being cat-free, and occasionally populated by bored hospital
patients with too much time and sub-standard bread on and
in their hands. Strangely, the other patients rarely venture out
for very long, so I often have the courtyard to myself, except
for the abundance of windows that surround me. Among
the feathered visitors is a family of blackbirds who take up
residence under one of the spiky bushes, and they become a
regular feature of my trips outside. Three rather cautious fledglings occasionally emerge from under the bushes, before their
mother shoos them back in. They rather enjoy apples, which
is a good thing, as I am eating an awful lot of them after a
German friend of ours told us that in the hospice where her
mother works (in Germany), they don't use senna and lactulose
and all the other laxatives and fibre boosters that I am

prescribed nightly; instead they rely on a diet virtually exclusively made up of apples to shift any constipation.

As well as scoring with my room, I have a very good relationship with many of the staff, and their wealth of experience and gentle encouragement is very supportive. I begin to feel a hint of optimism as for the first time I contemplate the possibility of actually being at the birth of our child. There is a peculiar kind of connection going on too, as I feel in some ways as if I have been (painfully) reborn. Now, obviously, I haven't reached rock bottom and seen the light in the hope that a holiday in Lourdes is all the rehabilitation I need. The rebirth that I am talking about refers to having to start all over again. Learning how to sit up, how to move, how to avoid shitting and pissing myself. How to look after my skin, and avoid burning myself or getting frostbite, or catching my leg in a car door, table saw or combine harvester, seeing as I no longer have pain to act as a warning. Ominously, several members of staff have told me not to worry, because 'the body finds a way of letting you know when all is not well'. I think back to how the neuropathic pain in my legs worsened when I had the bladder infection, and wish that my body had chosen a more subtle method of communication, like a twitching eyebrow, or a vague sense of wistfulness. A craving for cress, perhaps.

Luckily, physiotherapy is still extremely painful, proving that my body is still content to use the usual channels some of the time at least. The staff reaction gives me the impression that this is not uncommon. Either that or they have become rather complacent about pain, and I would rather the former than the latter. Still, I press on, practising long sitting (legs out straight), short sitting (legs hanging over the edge of the plinth), throwing and catching a ball, which forces me to adjust my balance, and standing in a standing frame.

The standing frame is part a piece of furniture, part an important piece of British manufacturing history. It is called the Oswestry standing frame, Oswestry being the name of a spinal unit in the Midlands, presumably where the standing frame was invented. The Oswestry standing frame is made out of timber that has been given a deep glassy varnish, and has leather straps with sheepskin covers. It is made by a Welsh firm of cabinet-makers who have been in business since 1946 (perhaps a boom-time in the disability equipment business?), and consists of a frame that looks a bit like a lectern with straps attached at different heights, one to go around the back of the heels and one in front of the knees. With these in place, the user then grabs the frame and pulls himself into an upright position, lying stomach-down over the desk bit of the lectern, reaches behind and attaches a third strap behind his backside and then straightens up into a standing position.

The first few times I need a fair amount of assistance, but it feels good to be back up to my six-foot two-inches height, or maybe even taller these days (I have been presented with the notion that one can become taller after paraplegia, as gravity no longer operates on the spine in the same way, and all the joints get a bit more relaxed). The standing frame and area required to access it take up a lot of space, and once I am upright, the desk bit rather makes me feel like holding forth to an imaginary assembled multitude. This tendency results in the other users of the gym having to hear my opinions on any and everything, and I sense that one or two would throw things at me if only they could balance sufficiently well to do so, so I decide in future to bring a book.

The advantage in standing is primarily the effect on bone density. Because I am no longer putting any weight through my legs, the body decides that I no longer need to have all that calcium doing nothing, so it starts to reabsorb some of it. The results being:

1) I have an increased risk of developing osteoporosis in my legs. Which, bearing in mind I could break a bone and not know about it, could present me with all sorts of problems.

2) I have an increased risk of developing bladder and kidney stones. Which, bearing in mind that this would be above my lesion (break), would hurt like hell.

It is also good for my vascular system to have to pump uphill every once in a while, and straightening out like this stops my hip flexors from shortening. The hip flexors are a group of muscles that join the femur (thigh bone) onto the pelvis and lower back. We use these muscles to lift our knees, but also to arch the lower back when the pelvis is fixed or rotate the pelvis when the lower back is fixed. In other words, they are the sit/stand/knees up Mother Brown muscles, and when people become para/tetraplegic, the effect of sitting all day is that these muscles become shortened and it becomes increasingly difficult to straighten out properly, which can be a problem when sleeping or on other occasions when lying flat may be required (when being tied to a roof rack or placed in a coffin … all right, I'm struggling here).

As well as standing and balance, I spend a lot of time working on my transfer skills. Transferring involves lifting one's backside from one surface and placing it down on another, with a degree of control. This is particularly difficult, as just sitting feels like balancing on a football, let alone pushing up onto my hands. For my first attempt at a transfer, I summon a monumental effort, straining to lift my backside off the plinth and bending forwards, tucking my head in. Although I can't see anything but the floor, I'm sure that I can sense my arse rising majestically into the air. In reality it doesn't move an inch, and all that I achieve is a loud and sustained fart. This outburst is not uncommon during physiotherapy, or indeed any physical effort, as the constricting of the bowel caused by bending can force gas out. On some busy days, people passing the physiotherapy gym could be forgiven for thinking that it houses an incompetent brass band.

I try again, with slightly more success, but as soon as I get any height in the push, my pelvis starts to swing wildly back and forth and I have to time the release in order to avoid landing on the floor. I find it hard to imagine I will ever be able to get up from the floor into the wheelchair, and if I can't do that, then how much am I really going to be able to play with my child? At the moment, whenever I go outside, I feel removed from my surroundings, as if I am just an observer. What if I feel like this about parenthood?

As I reach the end of the day's physiotherapy session, Penny walks into the gym with smiles and encouragement, and I look at her, all bump and loveliness, and it makes me ache with a desire to stand up and wrap her in my arms, and protect her, keep her safe. This should be her time, when she can just be. I had it all planned in my head; looking after Penny was the best way that I could see of sharing the whole pregnancy. Instead, I am putting her through the wringer.

We leave the gym and head back to my room. My lower back is hot with pain, as every bend and turn feels like bone grating on bone. On the way back we bump into Jackie Bailey from the Spinal Injuries Association, and I ask if we can talk to her about parenthood. She agrees, and once back in my room, I put the kettle on (all mod cons, see?), and find some of the various exotic biscuits that everyone seems to have decided are the best cure for SCI.

Jackie is just the voice of reason I need as she talks about her experiences of parenthood. 'When my two were babies, they knew instinctively to stay still on my lap. I only realised this was unusual when I looked after my niece and she wriggled all over the place.' She pauses, and then laughs. 'The biggest problem,' she reveals, 'actually comes when they get a bit older and they want to play with your wheelchair while you're sat on the sofa, which is fine until they leave it out in the hall and go off and play with something else!' Jackie's openness and patient assurances leave me feeling much more confident that I can overcome the challenges of rehabilitation and be a real parent once the baby is born.

After Jackie leaves, I shut the door and show Penny how I can transfer onto the bed, managing without the chair sliding sideways from under me, or the pendulum effect causing me to career off down the room. Perhaps I am getting a little better at this. We lie on the bed together, no mean feat, considering our respective conditions. After a few minutes, I break the silence. 'I just feel so relieved after hearing Jackie talk about coping with parenthood.'

Penny smiles. 'It helps to be reminded that we won't be the first.'

Yet again she exudes a calm and a confidence in me, in us, that I find so warm and reassuring that it makes me feel foolish for having any anxieties about forthcoming parenthood. She tells me that her recent trip down to London made her feel guilty at being able to escape all of this. We have a cuddle. It feels so good just to hold her and her bump, and we thumb through a book of babies' names while the namee kicks the crap out of daddy, every movement making me shiver with wonder and impatient curiosity. Just who is in there? Will they like me?

Now that I have stopped navel-gazing, or rather transferred my gaze to her navel, Penny announces that she has some news for me. Before her mum Ginny returned to Australia for a recharge, they managed to find a more permanent base. A two-bedroom flat for rent just ten minutes' walk from the hospital, and we plan our first expedition to the car park and beyond…

8

3 June 2005

Evening all...

So, I hear you ask, what's the word on the street? Well, it's a tired old line about pain and more pain, with the enigmatic Dr J (for it is he) helping me along with encouragement like, 'You must fight it, you must keep busy, and you must not let it win.' Aw gee, ta for that ...

Got meself upgraded from the slicks I was whizzing around on, as they kept sliding sideways when I tried to get in or out of the chair. Very embarrassing, and not terribly practical. Instead, I've got a pair of wheels with an ancient set of pneumatic grey tyres on. The walls of the tyres have got cracks in them where the rubber has perished, and were it not for the absence of crayon marks and spokey-dokeys, I would swear they were the wheels off my first bicycle.

The only downside is that now, instead of sliding around corners like Tom and Jerry on a polished kitchen floor, I make the most awful rubbery squeaking noise every time I attempt to make any kind of movement.

Rehab in general is progressing pretty well. Realised that I'm learning the skills faster than my body is adapting to all the new movement, which is one of my pain issues that will hopefully improve in time.

Penny has found a new flat just down the road from the hospital. It's small but perfectly formed, and fully accessible by chair, which means that we're going to try for a 'car transfer' this weekend. Hopefully I can manage this without doing a 'John Paul II' on the car park tarmac, and

we can get a few hours of let's pretend to break up the
weekend.

Get the sense this place is too small? No!

Keep them wagons rollin'.

My occupational therapist introduces me to 'the workshop'.
'The workshop' is a small woodworking shop, just off the corridor to the archery gym. Here I find a softly spoken Geordie
called Mike and we start talking tools and wood and before
I know it an hour has gone, I'm on my second cup of tea and
lost in the familiar world of sawdust and splinters. I have spent
a fair amount of time working with wood, either building
decks and other wooden structures or carving and sculpting,
a medium I was introduced to by my father-in-law Leon, a
furniture maker of some repute, and it is his workshop that
I find myself thinking of. A workshop I was in just a week
before my accident. For an hour or so I feel normal again, able
to focus on tools and skills that have nothing to do with my
injury, my rehab. Except that this can be part of my rehab, a
chance to find ways to overcome the difficulties of woodworking with the help and experience of someone who works with
spinal-injured patients all the time, and can show me tricks
and solutions he has developed in the process. Or we can just
drink too much tea and yarn about this and that without actually getting much done, but just escaping into a piece of a
different world.

Sport has appeared all over my green appointment card, too.
Archery, table tennis, swimming. The archery is very good
exercise for core muscle stability, vital to balance in the wheelchair. Table tennis provides similar balance training, although
I have an image in my head. A table tennis table, two people
in wheelchairs, one ball. A short rally, followed by 'tick, tick,
tickaticka tut tuddle uddle uddle', as the ball comes to rest
directly under the middle of the table and the sports hall falls

silent except for the muffled grunts of two wheelchair users trying to reach under the table. So when I go for the first time, I am a little disappointed to find a hall full of four tables, about a million table tennis balls, and eager helpers picking them up using an ingenious device made out of a cardboard tube, a walking stick and a couple of elastic bands. Once collected, they are poured into buckets next to the players. The players themselves range in abilities. Some are paras, some tetras with the table tennis bats bandaged into their hands.

There is one player who stands out straight away. His name is Eddie. I take my place at a table and find that, having wasted a few hours on various table tennis tables in my life, I am in good shape to channel a bit of energy into some competitiveness, and I am immediately aware of a flash of interest from Eddie. Nothing is said, except by Lou, the sports physio, who comments that I have obviously played before. The session ends, and Eddie nods as he leaves, the three-spoked alloy wheels on his metallic purple wheelchair flashing in the light. And from then on, without anything being said, I play against Eddie in every table tennis session. He loves the competition, and so do I. He beats me easily at first, but then the margins close, although I never quite get the better of him, despite our games going on for hours, long after the session has officially finished.

Eddie is a 'delayed discharge' because his old flat isn't wheelchair accessible, and he has been in Stoke Mandeville for over a year. He 'lives' in one of the beds in a six-bed unit on St George's ward, his home consisting of a bedside cabinet and a curtain around the bed. Because he is considered 'rehabilitated' and is ready for discharge, he gets no physiotherapy any more, except for the use of the standing frame and the weights in the gym. I also discover that he, too, is an Arsenal fan, and so we stop for brief chats here and there, staying in the safe male domain of football talk. He is one of a group of young male patients, all late teens or early twenties, a mix of paras and low-level tetras who hang out together, and when I see them I wonder to myself if there is a better or worse time to suffer a spinal-cord injury.

If you are young you have the strength and stamina to adjust to the physical demands. But if you are young you may not have a long-term partner. You may never have children. You may have never had sex, even. And your financial future may be dependent on your family.

A spinal-cord injury for an older person can be devastating. They may not have the physical strength to transfer independently, or even push a wheelchair. But they may have better family support, and perhaps a bit more life experience to help cope with the emotional upheaval. Of course, in both cases I am only talking about the physical challenges of my injury, and this is an easy generalisation to make. The physical difficulties I am struggling with are completely different from someone who is tetraplegic.

As with so many aspects of spinal-cord injury, I tend to fall into the assumption that all the other patients are going through the same rehabilitation experience as me, but although we have far more in common with each other than we do with a 'non-injured' person, comparisons are not always that helpful. Conversations often start with, 'What level are you?' and, 'How did you have your accident?' But I soon realise that incomplete injuries can mean just about any combination, so that, for example, a C4 incomplete might be walking. Also, it's impossible to trade up or down, even hypothetically, as I can't really feel what it's like to have a higher-level injury, not being able to stay upright because you have no functioning stomach muscles, or not being able to tell if you are hungry. I also struggle to imagine being able to stand and walk but not steadily, as some of the muscles in your legs don't respond.

The second question is a bit tricky, too. I notice that people who have been injured for a long time don't tend to ask, although I can't imagine my own curiosity dwindling, until someone points out to me that there are occasionally patients in here as a result of injuries sustained in a failed suicide attempt. Imagine you have decided that you can't bear your life any more and you try and end it all, only to wake up in hospital, paralysed from the neck down. Not only are you still alive, but you have also lost the physical ability to try again. That would have to count as a bad day.

Friends come up to visit, and we decide to make the 'walk' to the flat that Penny and Ginny have found. This will be Penny's home, as well as our baby's if all goes according to plan (there was me expecting our child to be a salt-of-the-earth cockney-type, instead of which they will have a predisposition for hanging around under the statue in Aylesbury town centre, texting friends and drinking cider).

Escape committee assembled, we head off from the hospital, first negotiating the bristle-brush carpet between the two sets of sliding doors in the main entrance. This may not sound like much, but I suspect it is no coincidence that the 'pile' is aligned so that as soon as your wheels hit it you are propelled at a sharp ninety-degree angle into the wall of the vestibule. To think so many brave patients who have hit the rug at speed, full of optimism at the prospect of freedom, only to have their hopes (and toes) dashed against the bricks. To navigate this mat under your own power is certainly a rite of passage, and as I clear the outer doors, I am riding a tide of elation that takes me all the way up the shallow hill and on to the main road.

Through the grounds of the hospital, the going is pretty good, with shallow drop kerbs on junctions, and I am high on the excitement of being out of doors, especially out of those doors in particular. The challenge increases on the main road, however, as I have my first encounter with a cambered pavement, each push sending me into the grass verge, my right arm pushing, my left arm braking. Traffic thunders past at enough speed to create a noise over which no one can hear me from 'down here', and I get an inkling of what my life has become.

Crossing junctions is also fraught with danger. The first side road, and I cruise down the slope and across the road, before hitting the drop on the other side where road and pavement meet, and instead of flicking my front wheels and casually breezing up the slope, I bottom out and just about manage to keep my bottom from coming out of the chair. Folded in half at the middle and staring at my shoes, I feel the reassuring clutches of several friends who manage to right me and get me out of the road.

We press on, and after about half an hour we enter a peaceful square of newly built houses and flats, and Penny lets us in to the ground floor of one of the blocks. There is a very small lip at the threshold to the block, which I manage without problem, and another into the flat itself. Inside it feels small, because anything would feel small compared to the generous proportions of the spinal unit, but it is bright and cheerful. I feel unsettled at first, partly at seeing our familiar things in an unfamiliar setting, but it's not just that. There is something else, and I can't quite put my finger on it. That is, until everyone has sat down, and I realise I'm just not used to entering a room with my own piece of furniture attached. I still instinctively case the furniture, sizing up which looks like the most comfortable perch.

We have lunch, picnic style, among the boxes and furniture. I try out access to the rest of the flat, which I can make without too many multiple turns. The bathroom has a bath with a shower over it, but we have been assured by Selina, my physio, that in time I should be able to transfer onto something called a bathboard that straddles the bath to make a fixed seat under the shower. All that seems like an age away, but for now it is just nice being somewhere that isn't a hospital.

The afternoon comes and goes, and we eventually decide to strike out for the spinal unit along the now very intimidating east face of Stoke Mandeville Road. In a plucky effort, I manage about a third of the return journey before I finally surrender to the inevitable and allow our friend Stu to push me. It is an unnerving experience, and I feel something akin to motion sickness, because although Stu pushes me with a great deal of consideration and we have a nice chat along the way, I realise that I have become used to self-propulsion, and to be moving without controlling the direction or speed of travel makes me feel motion-sick.

We get back to the hospital and after everyone has left I transfer onto my bed, as I feel pretty worn out from the pushing, or at least my not insignificant contribution. My legs begin to buzz with pins and needles, as they have many times before, only this time it gets more intense and uncomfortable. It feels as if I have belts around both thighs being pulled tighter and tighter, making me squirm. Soon I am getting electrical jolts of pain down the outside of my left thigh. As the pain peaks every 30 seconds to a minute or so, I find it very difficult to sleep, and end up chasing the jolly trolley for a dose of temazepam, my prescribed rip-cord for when I am struggling to sleep. It takes longer to work this time than on previous occasions. I try to visualise the pain as bands that I can mentally slide down to my feet and off. It seems to work. Either that or the temazzy does.

In what has become a tradition, I have hydrotherapy following a drug-induced sleep that has left me feeling cheerful but a bit crap. I'm a bit sore, so I start my session in the jacuzzi attached to one end of the pool. The pool itself is about ten metres long, with an electric hoist to get patients in. The first time you are fitted with a large inflatable collar to make sure you don't sink head-first on entry, but from the first go I feel pretty comfortable, although the process of 'treading water' requires a lot of quite vigorous work with my arms.

After a few minutes in the bubbles, one of the two physios in the pool gives me a 'stretch' while I hold onto the side. The pool is a great place to stretch, as the warm water makes the muscles more relaxed, and after a bit of 'seaweeding', which involves being pulled along floating on my back waving my arms and legs from side to side (it feels great, believe me), I am attached via a waist belt to a bungee cord, the other end of which is fixed to one end of the pool, and I swim breaststroke up the pool, trying to get to the other end. Breaststroke without the legs is quite a different prospect from normal breaststroke. Instead of lifting the head on the leg kick, I have to swim one stroke forwards and one stroke up to get a breath. What I do discover is that I can hold my breath underwater for much longer, probably because the biggest muscles that use the most oxygen are no longer in use.

The best thing about hydro is getting out and being completely pain-free for about an hour afterwards. The worst thing is that I always manage to forget my shower gel, and I have to use whatever people have left behind, which seems to consist of one bottle of rose-scented bubble bath that leaves me smelling like Barbara Cartland looked.

Another new experience that comes in the aftermath of soothing, stretching and half-drowning, is getting dressed when slightly damp. The upshot of all of this is that trying to sit up on a paper-covered foam mattress and feed my legs through the correct openings in my clothing in the right order is nigh-on impossible, for no sooner is one leg into my shorts, than I fall backwards onto the pillow and my other leg leaves the bed, acting like a giant fly-paper and dragging paper sheets, clothing and anything else it has touched onto the damp floor, so that when I start again, my trousers are damp as well. Of course, once I have got the right limbs through the right holes, I have to lie down and sort of wriggle in order to get the clothing up over my hips.

This achieved, I sit up with a feeling of accomplishment, only to find that when I transfer back into my wheelchair I have half the paper towel and two of the bristly white hospital towels shoved down the back of my trousers, like an enormous bustle sporting the words 'hospital property'.

9

7 June 2005
Subject: Like a wheel within a wheel...

Hi, y'all.
Had my first wheelchair dream last night ... dreamt I had
a puncture and kept going around in circles ... not sure
what this means ... ahh, the windmills of my mind ...

Penny isn't quite the size of the Hindenburg yet, but
there's still eight weeks to go, so plenty of time yet. She's really looking terrific, and seems really well. I don't know how
she does it, but the girl has some serious inner strength.

I'm watching, stroking, singing to and being booted by
(cause and effect?) the bump every day now, which is such
a buzz. All the nurses think it's going to be a boy, but I think
it's because one stuck their neck out, and the rest followed.
Ah well, there's a fifty-fifty chance they'll be right.

I'm getting myself dressed in the morning these days,
which is an achievement I'm pretty proud of. It's not an inspiring sight, mind you. My big useless legs flapping about
all over the place, and when it comes to getting dressed, I
have to get my thigh-high (woof!) anti-thrombosis stockings on, which are seriously elasticated. One yank and my
knee flies past my ear, I lose balance and the stocking
flies off and ends up hanging off the light fitting. Still, I've
only got to wear them for another month, by which time,
I'll probably wear them out of choice ...

The morning after the wheelchair dream I feel strangely
changed. I am worried that I will lose the walking dreams. It
dawns on me that I may find one day that I have forgotten

what it feels like to walk, dance, run or jump. I feel acutely vulnerable all over again.

I am put on a new medication, gabapentin, to combat the neuropathic pain in my legs, which has been getting worse and often keeps me awake at night. The pain is caused by the damage to the nerves in my spinal cord, but I get a few different opinions from staff that I talk to.

a) Dr K (psychology) tells me that although it might feel like it's in my legs, the pain is just white noise in my nerves caused by the damage, and it is my brain that is interpreting this as pain, so it's important that I don't think of it as pain, as this can 'hard wire' the brain to view it as pain. All very good advice, except that it sure as hell feels like pain, so I guess that particular ship has sailed. In fact, I'm not sure just how that one works, seeing as it would have to feel like pain before it would occur to me that it could be interpreted as pain.

b) The physiotherapy response is simple. They just ignore the neuropathic pain, and only talk about the musculo-skeletal pain. There is some logic in this, as they are staying within their particular discipline, and the acupuncture that one of the physios administers has some limited success in that area, although it is somewhat hindered by the great big lumps of titanium that the good professor at the Royal London left with me. The big downside of the physiotherapy take on neu-ropathic pain is that it colours my mood, affects my sleep, and has a massive effect on how the rest of my rehabilitation goes. To be fair to Selina, she is sym-pathetic, but thinking back to my pre-injury days the idea of hurting where you can't feel would be pretty inconceivable.

c) Then, of course, there is the Dr J 'you mustn't let it win' approach, which at least acknowledges the pain as pain, but otherwise doesn't really get much further than to add yet another medication. Mind you, if it works, then great. I have long since given up on any wholesome concern about taking medication, my temple having been thoroughly desecrated recreationally, long before the medical need arose. Any medication short of morphine, that is. I think my rationale is that we're through the looking glass already, just being alive with such a profound injury.

d) I discover that there is a legacy from Dr Guttmann as far as attitudes to pain are concerned. Apparently, on ward rounds, he would ask patients, 'How is your rehabilitation going?'

The reply would come back, 'Well, I've got this really bad pain in my …'

At which point the good doctor would say, 'But how is your rehabilitation going?'

'Well, I'm nearly able to transfer, and I'm doing a bit of archery,' etc.

'Excellent. So I'll see you next week. Keep up the good work.'

The following week, 'How is your rehabilitation going?'

'Still a lot of pain, I was wondering if …'

'And how is your rehabilitation going?' etc.

After about three weeks, the patient gives up asking, and the pain has 'gone away'.

I start the gabapentin at night, and I am barely able to wake up the next morning. I feel stoned all day, as well. I have quite a good day as a result of the side effects, breezing around the hospital all chatty and smiley. My archery suffers a bit, though. I manage to hit the target, but my averages suffer, and I find it hard not to giggle after each shot. Louise finds this hugely entertaining, although she pays extra attention to make sure that I've fired all three arrows before she goes down to the targets to retrieve them.

That evening I get a visit from some friends and we sit in the evening sun, enjoying the sound of the blackbirds and we talk a bit about how I'm getting on and the adjustments I am having to make. Then someone drops the 'b' word, and, despite the gabapentin, I feel a jolt of sadness, as if something in the box of nasties in my head has woken up and is thumping on the lid. The 'b' word is 'brave'.

Many people have admired my 'bravery'. It's a hard compliment to take. Maybe the way I am dealing with it is seen as brave. Some patients are unable to engage with the reality of life after a spinal-cord injury, and the necessity of rehabilitation. What I find particularly difficult to deal with in my situation is that I have a head full of images of what I would be doing in the future, especially with the child we are having in two months' time. I find it difficult to disabuse myself of the idea that I'm going to walk out of this hospital and resume my life, with this whole experience as a bad episode. The reality is that everything has changed. My life has changed, and the way that I interact with the world around me has changed.

Bravery, to me, implies a voluntary thing. Throwing yourself on a grenade, pulling children out of the path of a runaway truck, that kind of thing. But I have no choice, nowhere to hide. If I don't get out of bed, if I try and jump into the parallel life in my head, to reclaim my images of the future, then the panic starts to build. It starts in my feet. I try and move them, and then my legs and then I start to be consumed by anxiety until I feel as if I am completely paralysed, and the fight to regain control is a long and difficult one. If I get up and move around, work at physiotherapy, stay moving, even if it is just finding excuses to do laps from the gym to my room via Jimmy's Café, then I feel like I can push the paralysis back down. On a good day I feel more of me works than doesn't. This isn't bravery, though. It's just humble survival.

As a result of this internal struggle, it is very difficult not to appear tactless towards able-bodied people who cannot conceive of just what it feels like to have a spinal-cord injury, but can only see it as 'the unthinkable'. Or, rather 'an unthinkable', as I could imagine myself pre-injury being unable to imagine what it feels like. It would be on the list along with getting cancer, going to prison, being an alcoholic, losing a loved one, or being abducted by aliens. Sometimes even staff in the unit can give the impression that spinal-cord injury is beyond their ken. One of the physios tells me about a previous patient. 'David's tetraplegic and he's just done a tandem skydive jump. You see, anything's possible.'

I rather cruelly respond, it not being one of my better, more optimistic days, 'So can I climb a ladder again, then?'

'Er, no.'

As far as I know, a tandem parachute jump requires giving consent, and then being strapped to someone who throws themselves (and their 'passenger') out of an aeroplane, then opens the parachute, and lands. Sure, it takes courage, but not a lot of dexterity or skill, and certainly does not demonstrate that 'anything is possible' after a spinal-cord injury. So there.

The following day I'm not stoned at all. My body must be getting used to the meds already. I miss the feeling that I had on the previous day, though. I go out in town with Penny for a bite to eat for lunch. I make it sound so casual, but this is straight off my list of goals from the last goal-planning meeting. The coconut matting in between the front doors poses little challenge, and my car transfer is just about passable, I make it into the passenger seat in one, although I am using a sliding board. And not just any sliding board, oh no. This one has been lovingly made for me by my brother out of a piece of solid oak, an offcut from a fancy kitchen he's building. Yes, I am sliding my bum across a bit of Lesley Garrett's kitchen worktop.

The outing is exciting, but I have a real feeling of vulnerability caused by every bumpy road or kerb. Aylesbury is pretty good for accessibility, I guess due to the proximity of the spinal unit, but it still feels like a big, bad world out there. I mentally push kerbs to the top of my list of wheelchair skills to master, with back-wheel balancing a close second, when I feel all of my fillings shake loose as the front castors rattle over the cobblestones.

It's not only wheelchair skills that are brought into sharp focus by our trip into town. I get more of a sense of what is in the box, a little peek inside. The box is what I feel like I'm sitting on. It's a box full of something emotionally huge and it threatens to burst open at some point in the future. I go past a bicycle shop, and I get a hint of what's in the box. No, it's not a bicycle, but rather any encounter with my old life, specifically the things I used to do which I no longer can. It feels like a stab of dark melancholy, and I close the lid as quickly as I can, for fear that it will overwhelm me.

Lunch is a real treat. We are given the table by the door, I suppose because it's more accessible, but in time this is something that I get rather bored of. I have a beer. I have a pizza. We have an hour of closeness, lost to the constant reminders of the spinal unit, and I discover how being around a table with someone can make me feel 'normal' again.

We go to the flat in Aylesbury for a cup of tea, and I bravely attempt a split-level transfer onto the sofa. I manage it without nose-diving onto the floor, which for me is a big success, and one that I intend to boast about at the next goal-planning meeting. It is very difficult to convey just how top-heavy I feel. It's also impossible to replicate the movements involved if you have legs that work, as it's impossible to switch them off. This is a point I often make to the physios when they effort-lessly demonstrate the techniques involved in several transfers. My suggestion that they have an epidural as part of training, in order to get a better sense of what's involved, receives an understandably frosty response.

When I attempt to get off the sofa, I realise that what

went down isn't necessarily going to come back up. After a couple of frankly pathetic attempts to get my arse off the sofa, the wheelchair begins to grow in size until it reaches Eiger-like proportions, and it is only with the help of the sliding board and a heavily pregnant woman that I manage to drag myself up the north face and land, panting and flustered in the security of the cushion on the summit. I decide to postpone my announcement at the next goal-planning meeting.

After a rest, we head back to the spinal unit via the super-market, and buy a cafetière for my room along with piles of fresh fruit and some decent muesli, in preparation for the next big challenge on my goal-planning list. Having gone out for lunch, I am going to be going in for lunch. If you get my meaning …

10

Alf. Alf is short for Alphonse? Alfred? I can't tell you. What I can tell you is that Alf is from Galicia in northern Spain, softly spoken, and has a calm, encouraging presence. Alf gets me up most mornings, and he encourages me to take over more and more of my own care, patiently explaining how I need to look after myself with little tips and pointers.

Alf explains to me how to stimulate my rectum using a gloved finger. He gets me to put my own suppositories in on the bed, get up, have a cup of coffee and then transfer on to the toilet. Then we wait. And wait. And wait. The glycerine acts as a lubricant, but is also a mild irritant, which stimulates the colon into action. Sometimes. After a reasonable wait of about half an hour, I take matters into my own hands, or take my own hand into the matter, and start the process with a lubed and gloved finger, and then gravity takes over. All this detail may seem unnecessary, but it is an important illustration of the kind of things (especially bodily functions) that we take so much for granted when we are able bodied. We learn to control our bladder and bowel functions at an age which we don't really remember in great detail for the rest of our lives, so it feels like it's a natural instinct. But if you watch a baby become a toddler and then a small child, you can see some of the skills that most spinal-cord-injury patients have to learn, and others that we have to find alternatives for, as part of our rehabilitation.

Alf is unflinching and open. There is no embarrassment, only encouragement. I ask him about the 400 pillows that I use to position myself when I go to bed at night, and he says, 'When you go home, you'll probably only need one to keep your knees from pressing together. Or maybe you'll have your wife's leg to rest yours on.'

It's a light-hearted remark with a little smile, but it's these that help to humanise everything. Instead of a lecture on the risks of pressure sores, it's a casual remark that gets the message across. Alf's relaxed and cheerful bedside manner puts me at sufficient ease that I find much of the rehabilitation process to be a positive experience, as it feels like progress towards independence rather than an underlining of my disability.

The spinal unit has many staff members who, like Alf, have years of experience and many are able to convey information and advice in an encouraging manner. This is one of the best resources and perhaps not fully appreciated, but when a patient is going through the rehabilitation process, and has no previous experience of spinal-cord injury, it is the staff who are able to provide the experience. When that experience is no longer enough, one seeks out other people who have been injured for longer and who can give you advice on living in the outside world, but when that time comes, it comes because you have outgrown the staff, and that is a testament to them.

Once emptied, showered and dressed, I devise a new version of *It's a Knockout*, as I try and negotiate the bumpy courtyard with a lap-tray containing a very full cup of coffee and my laptop. Not a good combo. The blackbirds come out to laugh, three young fledglings squawking as mum and dad hop back and forth with bits of apple and biscuit, as well as any passing insects.

The rest of the morning is taken up with table tennis (curse you, Eddie, you win again) and weights. The weights session involves various pieces of gym equipment and free weights, and is designed to develop the muscles needed for pushing around and transferring. I am fortunate that I was in pretty good shape before the accident. I had given up smoking three years before, my work involved laying paving, decking and grass, digging holes, planting and, obviously, climbing trees. I would finish the day feeling tired but satisfied. I was also playing football and Ultimate Frisbee (look it up on the net) regularly, and going to the gym. At 36 years old, I was aware that I wouldn't be able to continue with this very physical lifestyle for ever, and I was enjoying myself immensely. My physical fitness and strength helps in my rehabilitation, as it is easier to rebuild muscles that were strong before than to build them up from scratch.

However, psychologically it is very difficult to go from a lifestyle that was physical to a sudden stop. A month in bed is plenty of time to reflect on all of the things I would not be able to do again. I still think of walking down a country lane and seeing an unusual plant halfway up the verge. I stop and step over the ditch, climb the verge and take a look. I think of playing sport, reacting instinctively to the game. Or even a sunny weekend morning, dancing around the living room like a complete loon. All of these things I feel I've lost. I think it is best described as spontaneous movement, the ability to act compulsively, without condition.

A new perspective on movement comes in an inspiring afternoon organised by the Back-Up Trust, an organisation set up for a freestyle skier by his friends after he broke his neck practising moves on a trampoline. The 'back up' in question was originally finding a way to get him back up the mountain, and they still organise a lot of skiing trips, but they have diversified, and they now do skydiving (here we go again), water skiing, outdoor activity courses in the Lake District, all sorts of other derring-do, and advanced wheelchair skills, which they come around to spinal units to demonstrate. Lots of back-wheel balancing, slalom courses, kerb mounting, hopping around, and general showing off. The most inspiring thing for me is watching the trainers moving around as if the wheelchair is a seamless part of them.

The event is presented by a man called David Ball, who has been injured for about twelve years, and is in training for a fundraising push up Helvellyn, the highest peak in England. And there's me complaining about the camber on the pavement.

David comes across as relaxed, assured and, most importantly, at one with his chair. This is the most inspiring aspect of the afternoon for me. The other instructor is tetraplegic, and shows how he can get up and down kerbs, and it becomes obvious just how far us 'new lesions' have to go. I sign up for any information I can get. Back-Up encourages people to go on their multi-activity course within a year of discharge from hospital with the aim of 'enabling people with spinal cord injury to surpass their aspirations'.

Stirring stuff, and something that strikes a chord with me. A whole realm of new possibilities opens up and I finish the afternoon tired but inspired. At this stage I am content to avoid thinking about the logistics of getting out into the great outdoors again, but just the idea of being able to reconnect with those passions in my life is enough to make me feel buoyed. Yet again, it is the interaction with other spinal-cord injured people that gives me succour.

The following day is a bit of a comedown. It is a Saturday, and Penny has gone back to London to sort out our flat, as we have some friends who will be house-sitting for us. Weekends are difficult. On weekends there is no physiotherapy. On weekends, many patients go home. On weekends, there are a lot of visitors wandering around the spinal unit, looking for somewhere to sit, somewhere for the kids to play, or somewhere to smoke. On weekends I used to struggle just getting through a day when I first arrived here. Now things are a little different. I can write stuff. I can draw stuff on the paper that I have stuck on every bit of wall in my room. I can send emails. In these ways, I can feel like I am doing something creative. I can feel like I am making progress. Usually, I am merely making a mess, but as long as I feel like it's progress, it's all right.

The paper on the walls is quickly filled with charcoal drawings of figures crouching, sitting on circles or on the floor as I try and find a way of processing what has happened to me. It is all catharsis, along with the emails, which are very much glass half full and can leave me feeling flat. Our friend Nigel has sold me his old laptop for an embarrassingly small price, and I begin to write down some of the darker stuff.

The darker stuff always seems to fill my head when I brush my teeth at the end of the day. I usually have a half an hour of catch up and banter with the night staff, many of whom only work nights, but I can feel the sadness lurking there. I don't know why it creeps up on me then. Maybe it's just a point of reflection on the day. My mind starts to pick away at the fragile optimism that I have spent the day constructing. Like a tongue to the hole where a tooth has been pulled, or a childhood fingernail to a scab on a knee, it just worries away, thinking of things I'll never do again, or coming up with ever more inventive lists of things I'll never be able to do that I haven't got around to. Often these are things that I never had any intention of doing, but it's the finality that has the desired effect.

Getting into bed is a major undertaking. It involves preparation. I have to get a bed bag ready, so that I can transfer my catheter from the leg bag that I have been wearing all day. I have to make sure that I have a 'modesty' ready. I still find this an emotionally charged item to deploy, as every time I drape it over my penis, it feels as if I have just pronounced the old fellow dead.

Having collected the various items, I steer the wheelchair up to the side of the bed, reversing to ensure the front wheels are pointed forward to reduce the risk of the chair tipping during transfer. The next move is the transfer itself, the execution of which is entirely dependant on the kind of day I've had, as tiredness or a lack of concentration can make the process somewhat hazardous. So far, I've managed to avoid planting myself face first onto the lino, but there have been a few close calls, and there's nothing like a surge of adrenalin just as you go to bed to unsettle your sleeping habits.

Assuming I have landed OK, the process of undressing can now begin. The crucial knack with the trouser removal is to avoid flipping the tap on the leg bag beneath, and inadvertently peeing the bed before you've even undressed, especially as you get no feeling of wetness to alert you to this event.

Next come the stockings. 'Still wearing those stockings?' I hear you say. The stockings and the evening injections, both to prevent deep vein thrombosis, continue for the first six weeks after injury. They are as hard to get off as put on, even with the elasticated tops now stretched and saggy. It's definitely not my best look.

Once the underwear is removed, the modesty arranged (with a few solemn words said), and the leg bag attached to the catheter tube, it's merely a question of taking off my shirt without losing my balance and falling out of bed, and I'm ready to tackle the pillows.

I still have a lot of pillows. Six, in fact. It may seem excessive, especially with Alf's predictions for a future of a bed full of entwined (entangled?) legs, but they are not all for my head. The pillows are arranged to prevent the risk of pressure on areas where the bone is close to the skin, such as ankles, heels, and knees. Arranging them is a dark art, with each nurse having their own variations. I have developed a hybrid of two methods, which keeps me down to three pillows for the legs, instead of a more traditional four or even five.

Once in bed, the dark thoughts are still there, but I am usually tired enough (or drugged enough) to get off to sleep pretty quickly.

The next day sees my morning routine cut down to a sprightly two hours flat, which in the context of my rehabilitation is real progress, but doesn't give me a great deal of confidence that I will ever have time to be doing much more than 'managing my condition'.

Once I'm showered and dressed, and with the optimism of strong coffee coursing through my system, I make my own bed (whooooo!) and open the door to let the summer day in.

I tidy up a few things and then turn around to find two of the fledgling blackbirds in the room looking for biscuit crumbs. My sudden movement causes them to flee, nervously pooping everywhere.

As I follow the small birds out to the courtyard, my mobile phone rings. It's a classmate from the arboriculture course that I took last year.

'Hi, Tim. How are you doing? Are you going to the summer training course at college? It should be good.'

What do I say?

'Er. No. I take it you haven't heard?'

She sounds concerned. 'Heard what?'

I'd love to know what she's thinking, because whatever it is, I'm about to trump it.

'I've … um, well, I had an accident in April. I fell out of a tree, broke my back, and now I'm paralysed from the waist down.'

'Oh my God. Oh, I'm so sorry! Oh God!' I can hear unbridled panic in her voice.

'Look, really don't worry, I know it's a mind-fuck, but don't feel bad for calling, really.'

'I'm so sorry.'

I decide to give her an out, so she can get her head around it all. 'Just take care, OK?'

When I finish the call, I feel really low. I have been reminded again of my 'other' life.

The further I get from the accident, the more sketchy my other life becomes, and the easier it is to avoid, but every now and then, something (a phone call, perhaps?) comes along and drops me momentarily into my other life. The big problem is that spending time in my other life is still very expensive. It is emotionally very draining, and it leaves me with a huge yearning knot in the pit of my stomach, and a feeling of panic in my head.

It takes a big effort to talk myself down. I sit in the sun

and watch the birds flitting around, and I think of home. I miss our old life so much. Not just the mobility and relative freedom, but all of it, especially our home. The flat in Hackney, less than ten minutes walk from Hackney Marshes and the nature reserve. If I close my eyes I can picture the vast open skies over the flat marshes. Trains going back and forth on raised embankments. Herons flapping lazily overhead looking like rowers on a sky-blue lake. I try and put myself there sometimes in an effort to relax, but all my experiences there are conditional, of course. Walking, running, cycling, wading through waterlogged fields in winter. Reaching into bramble bushes in summer and picking the plumpest blackberries for summer puddings. I know, it's all turning a bit Hugh Farmer's Marketstall, but I suppose nostalgia kicks in pretty quickly when you know you aren't going to do something ever again. Then I think of David from Back-Up, and his upcoming mountain adventure. My first reaction was that he must be an ex-army fitness fanatic or something, but then I think, no, I could do that. I might not want to do exactly that, but I just have to start thinking about interacting with the great out-doors in a different way.

In the afternoon, Penny and I go to the flat and I manage to tick a few boxes. I open my exam results for my arboriculture exam, which I took back in February. God, how long ago that feels. Anyway, I got a 'distinction'. Big whoop. I can't see it really helping in the future, unless I go into teaching, and who's going to want to learn how to climb trees from someone who's fallen out of one?

Next, I manage to look through the holiday photos from our trip to Australia. When I tried to look at them in the Royal London it was too painful. Suffice to say they are still littered with images of me showing off the full range of leg move-ments, and the choking lump of sadness is there, but I am out of the hospital and the sun is shining, and just to be able to spend a few hours with Penny away from that environment is lift enough to be able to face it down this time.

After a late lunch, we lie down on the double bed, which feels enormous. It feels so good just to be able to lie down properly together. We kiss and caress, and sort of have sex. Or, rather, we take part in a sexual act. I enjoy it very much, and there is a strong and familiar desire in me, but the experience is also strange. It's not like resisting the urge for penetrative sex, which most males feel very strongly during foreplay, and the stirring that isn't in my loins is, strangely, somewhere else. In my head? I'm really not sure, but the experience is intensely pleasurable. Just the touching and stroking, feeling Penny's fingertips on my skin, is charged with a sort of intense emotional pleasure. To experience such intimacy again after so long apart comes as an emotional relief, as if we are winning back a small but important part of our old life. Encouragingly, I look forward to exploring this whole area a lot more in the future, but I'm also aware that Penny is going to have to learn about my 'new' body at the same time as I do. She describes her unease and confusion as to just what to do. I try and explain, to make suggestions, but I realise that I haven't really worked it out myself, yet.

I'm getting used to a new wheelchair, one that is slightly closer to the model I will most likely end up in, and I am happily balancing on the back wheels with ease, although I am still unable to successfully negotiate the wooden 'kerb' in wheelchair skills. The Back-Up guys look a million miles ahead, along with the prospect of ever getting off the beaten (or even tarmacked) track.

I have another goal-planning meeting, this time in my room. I lay on coffee and biscuits and I'm given a date for a weekend in a bungalow with Penny. Well, not just any bungalow, the bungalow that is used as part of the rehabilitation programme.

11

14 June 2005

Howdy doody.

Just a small ramble today. Off to table tennis in a minute. This place feels increasingly like being trapped in a bizarre holiday camp. Activities every day, and reheated food. Actually, that's not a problem these days, as the gorgeous Penny brings me lunch and dinner, and occasionally we go back to the flat to eat. I know, I'm horribly spoilt, but I'll try and make it up with late-night feeds and nappy changes. (I hope she doesn't actually read these emails ...)

I'm in a different chair now. It's a bit closer to the one my wheelchair service will provide. The wheelchair service is a government-funded scheme that provides a wheelchair to those who need them. You can either have them supply the chair, or get a voucher for the money to go towards a chair of your choice. It tends to be a postcode lottery as to what your local service will provide, but for once Hackney has come up trumps, and is prepared to supply me with the chair that I want. It's called a Quickie GPV, as I'm sure you wanted to know, and has the advantage of being very adjustable, so I can tweak it until I'm happy with the ride, before I go out in a year or two and get some super-swanky ride made to measure. I think I'll go for the alloy wheels, under-chassis lighting, spoiler and metallic paint, with a huge bass speaker set in the back-rest. It is a Hackney chair, after all ...

Finally getting some sleep these last couple of nights, although my drugs consumption has gone up somewhat.

> My nightcap now consists of 75 mg amitriptyline, 50 mg diclofenac, 600 mg gabapentin, and 20 mg temazepam. I don't snore, I rattle.

Penny picks me up and we have another fun-filled tour of the supermarket. The good burghers of Aylesbury are so used to Stoke Mandeville escapees that they treat wheelchair users as run-of-the-mill. So much so that even the kids don't stare, slack-jawed in the way we used to, at anyone with anything resembling a disability, or even so much as a large facial feature.

The other interesting discovery is that I'm a top-shelf shopper. All the stuff that I want, like Continental biscuits, Fairtrade coffee, or even Tunnock's caramel bars, are firmly established on the top shelf. My reach is such that I can just about catch the corner of an item, usually on the bottom of a stack, and flick it in the hope that one of the pile lands somewhere near my lap. All very well with biscuits and ground coffee, but try that with olive oil and you soon run into difficulties. Decide to let Penny get the high breakables.

I must confess to being slightly disappointed when nobody stares as groceries fly hither and yon, not even children. And nobody offers unnecessary help. There I am, primed and ready to scowl and assert my independence, and not so much as a sideways glance. Again, I put it down to the proximity of the spinal unit. I have been told that patients often end up settling in the area so that they are within easy access of the hospital, as one remains an outpatient of the spinal unit even after discharge. As with the support from other spinally injured people, it's like this great club that no one ever wants to become a member of.

While Penny is busy pushing the trolley, I go off on forays to find specific items that I then try to balance on my lap while pushing my way back, with varying degrees of success. On one of these missions, I bump into another 'club member'/escapee from St George's ward in the shape of Paul H.

Paul was injured in a paragliding accident on the South Downs. He is another 'delayed discharge', having been in the spinal unit for nearly a year, while trying to find some appropriate housing. His 'home' is another curtain around a bed in the same six-bed bay as my table-tennis nemesis, Eddie. Paul is intrepid, often getting the bus into Aylesbury on his own, which is probably not that much of a surprise after the best part of a year in the spinal unit. That being said, there are other patients who have been in the unit for years. Some for health reasons, but others who have nowhere to go and no motivation to try and get on with their lives. The local social services may be less motivated to find somewhere for them while the spinal unit is picking up the cost of their care. Ah, the politics of the NHS.

By contrast, Paul is trying to find his own house to rent, and he has the extra motivation of a daughter who is about to go to college whom he would like to see more of. Family and friends are such an important part of the process of 'recovery', but there's something else, something I have noticed in the past, but never really thought about. It comes back to that first day of coherence, when I met Jackie from the SIA. When I talk to another person with a spinal injury, there is a lift, almost like taking a drug, regardless of the subject matter. I notice it particularly that day, talking to Paul. The reason I notice it is because I feel a 'come down'. I roll away from the encounter feeling really jolly, but the feeling wears off once I am on my own. Now, I'm quite a gregarious person normally, and I get a lift from talking to people, especially if we have something in common, but this is somehow different. I head back to the trolley, and watching Penny filling it with every possible tomato-based foodstuff (a pregnancy craving?) fills me with warmth and I distract myself with an enthusiasm for food.

We take the spoils from our supermarket spree back to the flat, as we have our friend Gabby driving up to see us for lunch. She brings along her son Billy, who is not quite a year old. I find it quite scary watching him barrelling around, and realise how much work is involved in just keeping up with kids once they get on the move. I can only hope that I have made a comprehensive adjustment to being in a wheelchair by the time our child is that age, and I become even more determined to develop a level of agility that allows me to transfer from chair to floor to couch to floor to chair to paddling pool, etc., all with minimum effort.

After they leave, and by the time I have returned to the hospital, my low level of constant discomfort worsens. Although I manage to sleep that night it is only after taking a double dose of temazepam, which seems to work. The reason I need all of this 'help' is because once again I am kept awake by that old chestnut, the spiky neuropathic pain in my legs. This pain may fade with time, or may be a chronic condition that I have to deal with for the rest of my life. But as Dianne, my psychologist, says, you cannot deal with a lifetime of pain on one day, so it is best to just deal with that day's pain.

Earlier in the day, back at the flat, we talked of our immediate plans. Penny is due in a few weeks and she is going to have our baby in the maternity unit of Stoke Mandeville hospital, which means I can be at the birth. This is hugely important to both of us. Apart from all the normal excitement and fear about the arrival of a (first) child, it will, I'm sure, lead me to feel unconditional joy, a joy not qualified by my condition. It also means that circumstance has conspired to mean that my child will be born in the same hospital where my grandfather died.

My next encounter with Dr J is typically cryptic. We look at the recent X-rays of my spine, and the displaced L1 vertebra is very clear. It is pressing on my spinal cord, and ideally it should have been fully realigned. I suspect that had the surgery been done at Stoke, it would have been.

Dr J explains, 'It's very important that you understand

that this would have made no difference whatsoever to your functional level, or your level of recovery.'

I understand this.

And then he says, 'And as far as a cyst developing is concerned, not everyone who has this sort of pressure on their spinal cord develops a syrinx, and not everyone who develops a syrinx has pressure on their spinal cord.'

I am not relieved by this so much as puzzled. No one has mentioned a cyst before let alone a 'syrinx'.

After his departure, I go for a wander and I bump into Jackie. I ask her about a syrinx, as she is my font of all knowledge as far as spinal stuff is concerned. Her response shocks me quite deeply. Jackie was originally L1/2, and remained so for sixteen years. Then she developed a syrinx – a cavity in the spinal cord – and went from L1 to T3. The thought of going through all of this rehabilitation, learning how to balance and transfer and all the other aspects of using what you have left, only to have to do it all over again? I resolve not to think about anything further ahead than dinner ever again.

Still, before dinner comes lunch, and no ordinary lunch, oh no. Today Penny drags me screaming and kicking (ho ho) to the pub for the first time. After three months of hospital life, this feels like such a milestone adventure to be embarking on. I ask the nursing staff, and they tell me that there shouldn't be any problem with my meds and a pint, and the prospect of an ice-cold Guinness fills me with childish excitement. I am also told that Guinness often helps people who have a 'sluggish bowel'. Hurrah for justification!

The pub is a short drive from the hospital, and has a large patio and garden at the back. It comes highly recommended by the staff at the hospital, especially as it is fully wheelchair accessible. Getting from the car park to the beer garden is my first gravel path encounter, which I manage fairly well, even doing some of it on my back wheels, but once I get onto the patio there is an empty table in the middle, and I politely ask a woman by the path if she could just move her chair in a teensy bit. The entire population of the beer garden leap to their feet and embark upon a frenzy of furniture moving, until it feels as if every stick of furniture has been stacked at the sides, and I feel like I'm looking upon an IKEA re-enactment of the parting of the Red Sea. The wheelchair feels embarrassingly small.

Upon seeing me, many people may want to help, and get to their feet only to realise that I'm OK really, but having committed themselves by leaping up in public they feel slightly awkward, and in order to give their action some purpose, they busy themselves gratuitously moving random pieces of furniture in case they pose a problem to me in the future. This is an extremely uncharitable view, which I reserve the right to review upon my first encounter with people who are really unhelpful when I actually need a bit of help.

The sun shines, I hide behind my sunglasses, and Penny goes to the bar. I don't feel self-conscious at all. This is partly because the pub is obviously used to having patients from the hospital as visitors, and I can even see another patient from where I am sitting, but my lack of self-consciousness is also fuelled by the relentless openness that I seem to have developed. The same openness that has sustained me through the whole patient experience, making me comfortable with being thrown around, flopping and farting all over the place, trousers inevitably at half mast.

Penny comes back with the drinks and we sit for a few moments in contented silence. The beer drips condensation invitingly, and I savour the moment, before I break the spell with a large glug and we talk about names and going to ante-natal classes and how someone's given us a Moses basket, and I try not to think about the spinal unit for a couple of hours. It almost works, except the pain starts to flare up, and eventually we have to leave the pub and head back to the flat so that I can stretch out.

The pain seems to get worse once I've been in the chair for a few hours, and lying down eases it somewhat, although it's always there, and it makes me worry that I won't be able to be at the birth. I am making progress in other ways. I can get on and off the sofa myself now, even without the sliding board. This makes me more confident that I will be able to nail the 'floor to chair' one day. Hopefully before I nail the accidental 'chair to floor'. There is a lot of talk of falling out of the wheelchair in physio, with repeated references to the amount of paperwork that has to be submitted in the event of an accident. I am scared in a way, but I also feel like I won't really be 'in the chair' until I have fallen out of the chair, if that makes any sense at all. I think it's about boundaries or limitations or something.

The next day we hit the pub again. Good food, and great to sit around a table with friends, almost forgetting my wheels, except for the acute discomfort. I try and stay hopeful that this will get better with time, and a different chair.

Despite two days of Guinness, the next morning's challenge is the issue of constipation, and the resultant haemorrhoids. I am trying to deal with the former through my diet, rather than the unpredictability of laxatives, but the latter is a real bummer (all puns pardoned). Even though I can't feel anything directly, I can sort of feel something, even if it is just being even more uncomfortable than usual when sitting. Could this be the 'referred-pain-body-finds-a-way-of-telling-you' scenario? I can't say I'm sure, as I am pretty uncomfortable most days. When I mention this at our weekly chat, Dr J replies, 'this is not uncommon. The first time a patient who you know to have a completely severed spinal cord tells you that they get uncomfortable from sitting, you may be dismissive. But when five or six patients relate the same experience, then you have to take notice.'

It is contrary to (Western) scientific understanding of the

way that the nervous system works, but there are many mysteries surrounding the treatment of spinal-cord injury, as I am discovering. One of the mysteries surrounds bowel management (again). When we are given the bowel lecture, we get a good explanation of how the bowel works after spinal-cord injury, the ensuing risk of constipation, and the importance of eating plenty of fresh fruit and vegetables. The food in the spinal unit, with the exception of a few apples and bananas, is rather lacking in both categories, especially the fresh vegetables. On one occasion I was presented with a plate of food that included burned peas. I mean, how do you burn peas? It turns out that all the food is made in Wales and transported in large foil trays that are reheated on site in large ovens. If ever there was a case for an exception to be made, and for food to be prepared on-site, it is in a spinal unit, where diet is an essential ingredient not just for recuperation, but also for subsequent quality of life.

Incidentally, in the bowel lecture we are also introduced to the Bristol Stool Scale, which is used to identify different textures of output. Many patients find this level of involvement in things scatological to be rather distasteful, especially the notion that this will be a major topic of conversation for many years to come. The whole obsession with bowel issues can get rather tedious.

One of the other patients Cate (car accident, tetra) is more pragmatic, but she reports that her sister, in an enthusiasm to be involved and help with rehabilitation, has put the Bristol Stool Scale diagram up on the wall in her bathroom. We conceive the brilliant idea of making the subject less distasteful by devising a system based on popular chocolate confectionary, e.g.:

Type 1: Separate hard lumps, like nuts or rabbit droppings (hard to pass). (Toffee Poppets?)
Type 2: Sausage-shaped, but lumpy. (Picnic?)

Type 3: Like a sausage but with cracks on its surface. (Snickers?)

Type 4: Like a sausage or banana, smooth and soft. (A finger of fudge, naturally.)

Type 5: Soft blobs with clear-cut edges (easily passed). (Minstrels?)

Type 6: Fluffy pieces with ragged edges, a mushy stool. (Hot chocolate with marshmallows?)

Type 7: Watery, no solid pieces (entirely liquid). (Ovaltine?)

This scale also has the added advantage of being able to incorporate some of the more tricky-to-describe stools, such as the Flake, the Creme Egg, Walnut Whip or the Toblerone.

On the bodily function front, I start self intermittent catheterisation (SIC) again. This is my first time back to it since I went down with a bladder infection. Ward sister Liz comes up with a couple of boxes of a different variety of catheter that has been dropped off by a rep for one of the continence product companies who schmooze their way around the spinal unit from time to time (understandable really, get someone used to their product and they'll be using them for life, most likely – all paid for by the NHS, bless 'em), and she says that if I get on well with them, she'll grab all the boxes of samples she can find. I do find them much easier to use from the word go, and in no time the en-suite bathroom resembles a spiv's trench-coat, with boxes of illicit booty crammed into every available space. I may, perhaps, be guilty of making this sound much more exciting than it is…

The bungalow, on the other hand, now that *is* exciting. The bungalow (for no apparent reason Penny and I decided that the correct pronunciation is 'boon*gar*low', with the emphasis on the second syllable; I conclude that our attempts to make it sound exotic may be a defence mechanism, as until now it hasn't been a word we often used, but this may well be our future as far as housing options are concerned) is located in the grounds of the spinal unit, surrounded on all sides by the hospital. It is a two-bedroom house that is fully wheelchair accessible, from the wide doorways to the height-adjustable kitchen worktops. It has a hospital-specification padded toilet seat, which is important if you have no sensation in your arse, and need to sit on the loo for anything from half an hour to several hours every morning. It even has a hoist on tracks built into the ceiling that runs from the bedroom into the bathroom, so that high-level patients can be moved easily between the two. The bungalow is provided for patients to spend a couple of nights in with their partner and/or family in order to see how well they would cope at home. The hospital is about ten feet away. This means that no one who stays in the bungalow ever opens the curtains, because if you do, you are on view to everyone walking or wheeling the corridors of the hospital. This suits us, as the weekend we are in it is during the hottest weather of the year so far, and the bungalow is probably the coolest place in the hospital.

For three nights running, I don't need to take a sleeping tablet. I think this must be down to sharing a bed with Penny for the first time since my accident. What with her being heavily pregnant, and me suffering from particularly bad neuro-pathic pain in my legs, we should have sleepless nights, but having shared a bed for nine years, I'm sure that we are so used to having each other there that the familiarity and feeling of security acts in a soporific way, and we sleep soundly, only disturbed on one night by the gentle burbling sounds and smell of some annoying hospital employee smoking cigarettes, shouting into a mobile phone and thus sharing with us the intimate details her marital break-up.

We spend the days watching Wimbledon, and the evenings cooking in the adapted kitchen. Cooking has always been a passion of mine. I used to come home from work in the evenings and cook as a way of winding down. To be able to have a kitchen to ourselves and prepare food is a real boost, although I am already conscious that the kitchen in the Aylesbury flat is far from ideal, having a floor area about the same size as the wheelchair.

We also host my next goal-planning meeting and, over drinks and snacks in the warm orange glow of the curtain-filtered summer sunshine, my provisional discharge date is set as 22 July. That's one week ahead of the baby's provisional discharge date. I am excited. The staff are all very positive that I will make the most of my situation, and that I am coping well with my circumstances. After they leave, I reflect on my experience so far. As well as the obvious motivation of the upcoming new arrival, I am coming to the conclusion that my interest in and involvement with all aspects of my rehabilitation has helped me to get this far in such a short time. When I think of other patients, it seems to be those who have the same level of interest who are doing better than others. This may seem obvious, but I've also noticed that many of those who are engaging with the whole process in a positive way are people who had their accident doing something they love, whether it's paragliding, horse riding, motorcycling, mountain biking or climbing trees. I wonder whether knowing there was a risk involved makes it psychologically easier to cope with the outcome. I have nothing to base this hypothesis on other than what could be convenient coincidence, so I make a mental note never to discuss this with Dr K.

Over the next few days the pain in my legs continues to get steadily worse and, sadly, I have no more spacey side effects as the dose of my medication is increased. On the plus side, I'm getting significantly less back pain, which is a sign that the muscles are settling down and learning to live with half a box of Meccano.

We get a visit from Sarah and Jessica, and after a quick catch-up, we head in the car park to exercise their dog Queenie, a very friendly border collie, who runs up to Penny as soon as we arrive, but is slightly cautious of me, possibly because she's only seen me once before on wheels. I decide to encourage her, getting down to her level by bending forwards and resting my chest on my knees. She responds straight away with a very eager greeting, and I suddenly realise that I can't sit up in a hurry, resulting in an awful, smelly, tonguey dog snog.

I still have a feeling of foreboding about getting back to our life in London. I get strong pangs of sadness at the most unexpected times. Some friends come up from London to see us again, and during the conversation mention is made of their flat. Suddenly think about the stairs that would prevent me from moving freely about if we were to visit them now. This is a particularly ridiculous thought, as they have travelled up with a friend of theirs, Sam, who has a spinal-cord injury sustained fifteen years ago when he was fourteen. He is tetraplegic, which is obvious to me now, but I have met him briefly on a couple of previous occasions, notably in a field at the Big Chill festival, and I realise that I always assumed that he was in a wheelchair due to some kind of congenital condition.

It is difficult to acknowledge to myself that I used to make all sorts of presumptions about disabled people, and now anyone I meet for the first time could well do the same about me. I think my expectation in meeting Sam again was that we would be talking all about spinal-cord injury and rehabilitation, and indeed, I hold forth on these subjects, and Sam nods patiently, but I soon realise that for him this is very old and familiar ground. At first I feel a bit silly, but then I take encouragement from the fact that it is possible to get to a stage where you are not dominated by SCI. It's great to meet him again, and he's moved into a place just around the corner from our place in Hackney, so I'm sure we'll see more of each other in the future.

Rehab continues to go great guns, but it's obvious that my view of being ready for discharge and the hospital's view of readiness differs somewhat. Liz, the ward sister, says that if the baby comes early, then I'll be discharged. A lot of my rehab is going to go on after my discharge in the outside world, anyway. The trouble is that one gets used to being surrounded by people either with a spinal-cord injury, or an understanding of the needs of those with such an injury.

The day comes for my driving assessment, which has been booked by my occupational therapist with a local driving instructor. I manage to transfer into the car without landing on the tarmac, and the instructor tells me that many people like to fold their legs under the seat, in order to keep feet and pedals apart, especially useful if you suffer with spasm. The car has hand controls fitted, in the form of a handle alongside the steering wheel. It is automatic, and the driver simply pulls on the handle to go and pushes to stop. There is a steering ball attached to the wheel to make steering with one hand easier, and an indicator switch on the top of the hand control so that the driver can indicate without taking a hand off the controls. We head off for a drive around the grounds of the hospital initially, with the car kangarooing a little bit, but in very little time I have the feel of it, and by the end of the hour we have been out on the dual carriageway towards Oxford.

Penny arrives in my room one day accompanied by Justin, whom she met in the reception area. Justin is in a Küschall K4 wheelchair, which is one of the models being offered by the wheelchair service, and Penny asked him about it, so Justin offered to come and talk to me. We end up talking for hours about wheelchairs, life inside and outside the spinal unit. He also lets me try out his chair for a few minutes. We talk about his experience in the spinal unit about five years beforehand, and he tells us, 'Back then, the patients' and relatives' lounges were smoking areas, and patients used to drink in the hospital, too. I remember nurses opening beers for tetraplegic patients. It feels very different now.' I imagine something from *Born on the Fourth of July*.

Justin is obviously very fit, and he tells us that he goes

to the gym two or three times a week. He sits very straight and upright in his wheelchair, and he looks as I hope to look. Straight and slim and comfortable. There are other people around who look like they've almost melted, as the chair sags and they sag with it. Then there are those who look as though they are precariously balanced, perched on top of the chair, reaching nervously for the wheels in order to propel themselves, with their feet sticking out in front of them, making it almost impossible to get within reach of most things without their toes being crushed. I don't wish to sound judgemental, this is not about other people, but more about me finding a role model, and an image of a wheelchair user that I am comfortable with for myself. I decide that I will get a K4 wheelchair if at all possible.

Memory. Does one's memory get worse (it surely does) because of the spinal-cord injury, or because of the extended stay in Stoke Mandeville? Actually, I'm sure an extended stay in any hospital would probably have the same sapping effect. During working hours, I can at least find some spurious justification for going to/from the rehab gym, archery room, workshop, OT department, psychology department, old ward, even Jimmy's, at a push, but my experience of downtime at Stoke (evenings, weekends, bank holidays, etc.) is so crushingly boring. I start trying to think of positives, in order to keep my brain ticking over …

Advantages of being paraplegic.
1) Half-price season ticket at the Arsenal, for me and a 'companion'. So quarter price, really. Added boost to popularity, as companion cannot attend games alone.
2) I get to bypass queues. People seem to think that they should let me go ahead, which is strange, especially as I'm usually the only one with a chair.
3) In the event of a thunderstorm, the combination of

extra insulation from the rubber wheelchair tyres and the fact that a wheelchair user is lower than most bipeds, I am much less likely to be struck by lightning. That being said, you are less likely to be struck by lightning than you are to suffer a spinal-cord injury, but with my track record, I wouldn't exactly say luck is on my side. There are 30 to 60 people struck by lightning each year compared to over a thousand spinal injuries, which means you have about a one in twenty-one million chance of suffering a spinal-cord injury compared with, say, a one in thirteen million chance of winning the lottery. *Bon chance!*

Summer arrives in time for the tennis, and a bit of the old leather on willow coming soon, although the fun will be trying to watch that with the sound of a baby's crying and sick on shoulders. I'm starting to be able think about the whole thing again, after a couple of months with my head immersed in my own problems. I'm going be a dad. I'll be on wheels, but I'll still be a dad, and the nipper is just going to know me as I am now.

Penny comes back from the ward kitchen with a cup of hot chocolate, and sits on the end of my bed. The baby starts to wriggle about inside her, as if disturbed by the warm drink. Pen has put off the drive back to the flat in Aylesbury, as it is pissing down outside. A real summer thunderstorm. It makes me wish I could just get up and go outside and run around in the rain. There's something so simple or primal about surrendering to getting wet in the rain. I suppose if you are in a wheelchair, you have to worry about your bearings, or getting your seat cover wet, and then you have the added worry of sitting in wet clothes, which could harm your skin.

I feel as if all of my spontaneity has been taken away. Even on the previous day, when I made own way to the flat by back roads on my own for the first time, I felt as if I were on a raised platform that stretched out over green spaces inaccessible to me now. I inhabit those parts of the world that are 'wheelchair friendly', but I feel excluded from those that are not. I've never felt excluded from anywhere. Well, obviously, places with large fences around them, or guard dogs, etc., but the terrain has not restricted me in the past. If 'someone' was able to get to a place, I was fairly certain I could. This included the tops of trees of course, which is how I ended up here in the first place, so maybe it serves me right. We watch the rain, I hold Penny's tummy, and eventually I fall asleep.

12

As I spend more time away from the spinal unit, going into Aylesbury and enjoying the smooth, controlled environment of the shopping centre, I feel less rather than more confident. I am close to the end of what the hospital can offer me, but it is still a comfortable and familiar environment. Another thing that I am trying to get my head around is the whole catheter timing thing. I have discovered that every day between 8 a.m. and 12 midday, my bladder fills up like I've been binge drinking, and I have to do three catheters in that time. I can then go through the day at three-hour intervals until 11 p.m., and then leave it until 6 a.m. the next day, unless I've been at the shandy, in which case the alarm is set for a night-time fumble with tubes and bottles, which is no fun when you're half asleep, and liable to attempt to drain your bladder with the first thing that comes to hand. I have a fear of coming to, and finding myself 'impaled' on a ballpoint pen, attempting to wee into a shoe.

I sense that my physiotherapy is going very well as I now spend almost every session working with a final-year physiotherapy student. I don't mind too much, I can see how a relatively low-level paraplegic (especially a smart-arse one) is not as interesting or challenging to work with as a tetraplegic, and so doesn't command as much attention. I can also see the end of the hospital phase of my rehabilitation, and it doesn't fully tally with the intimidation I feel when I am in the outside world. The struggles I experience during my encounters with life outside leave me feeling down.

I also feel pretty tired all day, and I'm not sure why. It could be the new sleeper that I'm on instead of temazepam. My friend Neil suggested I try zopiclone instead, as it is supposed to give less of a hangover and fewer long-term dependency issues. On Dr J's ward round, I suggested this change, mistakenly saying that I thought it was some kind of new drug. They all laughed dismissively and said that of course they had been using Z for years, and Dr J said, 'Why replace one rubbish with another?' Translation (I think): 'You should be trying to get off the sleeping tablets by now, as they are not a long-term solution.'

From that night on, I am given zopiclone instead of temazepam.

I wonder if the tiredness is more a symptom of my state of mind, as I've been feeling a bit glum and also a bit tired for a couple of days. I feel a creeping sense of dread, which increases with each encounter that I have with the outside. The trips out are still bittersweet. It feels like an achievement, just going to the shops, but suddenly every shop has a doorstep. It makes sense. It keeps the rain out, but it becomes obvious that I have to get to the point where I can go up and down a step without noticing. This is something I'm going to have to learn once I'm discharged, showing the different interpretations of 'ready'. I also have a hunch that this is going to continue for quite some time. It is partly the price one pays for the security of being institutionalised and, I suspect, partly the beginning of the grieving process for my previous life. The novelty has definitely worn off. I'm just tired of all of it. Everything. I'm tired of not being able to reach things. I'm tired of not being able to move about without worrying about kerbs and rough ground and slopes. I'm tired of being dependent on other people, and needing to make sure I have enough catheters with me, and not being able to find an accessible toilet, and most of all, I'm tired of being brave. I don't want to be brave and 'you're so amazing', and 'I don't know how you do it'. I just want to be normal and boring. No I don't, I want my old life back. That wasn't normal and boring, otherwise, I wouldn't have found myself in a tree or, perhaps more importantly, out of a tree. I want my legs back. I still have my legs, I know, but they feel like someone else's legs that just lie around all day getting in the way.

I finally fall out of the chair for the first time, so that's another box ticked. I don't quite fall out, so much as over. Backwards. As I am trying to get through the outside door at the flat, I pull myself over the threshold ridge and go toes-up. I don't quite fall all of the way out, mind you. I manage to put my arms out behind me, which you're not supposed to do, because if you break your wrist, you really are fucked. Can't push yourself around, you see. No, if you tip, you tuck. This is because the greatest risk is smacking your head on the ground behind you. You're better off trying to get back into the chair from the ground than trying to stop yourself in the first place and risking serious injury. It's interesting to know that the 'arm out' is my instinctive reaction, but it's going to be a hard one to break, unless I break my wrists first. There are a couple of methods of getting back into the chair:

1) If you are over but not out, and you have help, then two people can get you back up using 'the scoop'. This is where the person in front grabs the front of the wheelchair frame, while putting their foot on the axle thus levering you back into an upright position, while the person behind helps with the lift, using the back of the chair.
2) My preferred method, because I am stubborn and bloody-minded and 'I can do it, leave me alone …' is the floor-to-chair transfer, which I have almost nailed. As usual, the technique is best explained by watching experienced patients who are back at the spinal unit for a service. The key is to tuck your feet under you, tie your knees together, and lean over your legs. If you point your head in the opposite direction to where you want your arse to go, it actually works. Your legs somehow help with the leverage. Mind you it's still bloody hard

on the arms and shoulders, and for this first occasion, I'm not confident that I'm quite there yet, and the risk of getting out of the chair is that I might not be able to get back into position to allow a 'scoop'. I instruct Pen in the art of stepping on the axle and flipping me back up, but it is asking too much of an eight-and-a-half-months pregnant woman, and so in the end I manage to shuffle over to the railings and pull myself up at the same time. Hurrah. I feel so independent.

The result of practising all of the different transfers is that even if I can't actually do them fully yet, the exercise means that I keep getting admiring comments from friends about how my arms and shoulders have got so much bigger. I counter by telling them that my arms have to do now what my legs used to do, but obviously I feel flattered and swelled by the comments. Then I wake up one day and look down at my hips and my legs. With only gravity at work on my flaccid muscles, they hang down off my legs and my hips protrude, and I am reminded of images from the *World at War* documentaries that we were shown in school history lessons. The images that come back to me are of corpses being thrown into mass graves, some naked, their muscles flaccid, and their hips protruding. It's a funny thing about body image. Just as I am being praised on my upper-body development, I become appalled at my lower limbs.

The flattery doesn't make me feel particularly tough or strong but rather, in contrast to my previous physical presence and largely due to my loss of height, I feel really vulnerable.

I have reached the end of the patient-education programme, and the final session takes the form of a visit from a former patient, so that we can ask questions about 'life on the outside'. I'm the only patient who attends, so the session is just Stuart, the former patient, and myself.

Stuart is T5, and was injured about five years ago. 'When I was discharged from hospital, I moved into my parents' living room, as it was on the ground floor of the house. I ended up living in this room for a couple of years. I got more and more depressed, and I started drinking heavily.'

This is the first time that I've heard anyone talking openly about being really unable to cope after a spinal-cord injury. He continues, 'I was out most nights getting drunk. Sometimes I would wake up in the street, or in a strange house. I developed pressure sores and had to spend days and days in bed. Not surprisingly, I fell out with my family, and the people I called friends were taking me out and getting me drunk.' He pauses, for a moment lost in a darker past.

'Then one day I was in the spinal unit and someone suggested I go along to the sports centre and have a go at wheelchair basketball.' His eyes light up. 'I really enjoyed it. Not just the game, but being around other people in wheelchairs. I wanted to play more, and that gave me a reason start looking after myself. I stopped drinking and smoking, and began to train regularly with my local team. The fitter I got, the more energy I had, and the more active I could be. I've now got my own flat, a part-time job, and I'm even teaching wheelchair skills with Back-Up.'

Stuart is open and happy to answer any questions that I put to him, and we end up talking for over an hour. It is the perfect reassurance for me, and one thing he says sticks in my mind: 'When you leave here, if you have to go to the shop for milk or whatever, don't go to the closest shop, go to the one that's a bit further away.'

His point? Push yourself. Yeah, I know, wheelchair user, push yourself, very funny. What I mean, what Stuart means, is that it's important to get out there, to drive yourself on, even when you don't feel like it. From what I have heard from several ex-patients, it seems like the first year out is definitely the hardest, and for many people, that's when they set their boundaries, and decide what they are or aren't capable of.

My physiotherapist Selina leaves to go and work in a spinal unit in Bangladesh. During our last session, we talk about what she is likely to face. She tells me how in Bangladesh, as in many poorer countries, there are very few tetraplegic patients. Anyone who suffers a broken neck is unlikely to survive, as there isn't the necessary emergency medical support available. Patients who do make it to hospital have to have their own relatives or carers to look after them while they are on bed rest. Wheelchairs are often fabricated using old bicycle parts and tubing. It is really about finding a way of getting through it, of surviving. It provides a sobering contrast to life on the NHS. I shall miss Selina, especially because in her role as my key worker she has helped to give me the confidence to set a fast pace for my rehabilitation.

I get to tick off one of the more ambitious goals from my first goal-planning meeting. The stair climb. The stairs in question are the two flights under the Jimmy Savile chandelier that was so much admired by my first visitors back in April, and it is odd to find myself at the bottom of the stairs looking up just three months later, reflecting on those first few days in the spinal unit.

The stair climb is a particularly difficult manoeuvre. It requires the wheelchair user to back up to the stairs and reach back to grab the handrail with one arm, while reaching across and grabbing the push-rim of the wheel on the same side. The fool then has to lean back, pull on the handrail and push on the rim at the same time, and thus cruise effortlessly up the stairs. In order to make it slightly easier, I have Lou going up the stairs in front to keep the chair straight, otherwise there is a tendency for the chair to twist and the occupant to pull themselves out.

After much huffing, puffing, sweating and swearing I make it to the top, exhausted but happy at my achievement.

I have reached all of the goals as far as transfers and balance are concerned, so one of the physio team makes me a pair of 'back slabs'. These are half plaster casts that are then bandaged onto the back of my legs like splints in order to keep them rigid so that I can attempt to 'walk'. For this undertaking I am under the instruction of Sue Edwards. Sue is a small, cheerful woman with short grey hair and glasses who I have occasionally seen buzzing around the gym, all energy and encouragement. Because she only comes in one day a week, I assumed that she was a helper of some kind. In fact, Sue has worked in the spinal unit since the early 1970s and I subsequently discover she is something of a legend in the physiotherapy world. She wrote many of the textbooks used in neurological physiotherapy, and is especially skilled in getting people up on their feet.

In my case, 'walking' (if I can master it) will involve me balancing on crutches, and swinging both legs forward together. I don't imagine that this is a skill that I will use very often, but if I show a talent for it, then I may go back to the hospital as an outpatient for calliper training, so I might get my Douglas Bader moment after all. It's probably not going to mean that I'll be galloping about, rather staggering like a newborn pony, but, hey, it's a change. Callipers are basically scaffolding for the legs. They lock the ankles and knees to make the legs stable. For many incomplete patients it may only be necessary to wear them, and sometimes just to give the ankle stability, but for a T12 complete such as me, the process of 'walking' is more akin to stilt walking. In other words, balancing on top of two stacks of bones. It's hard, but I miss my six-feet-two-ness especially now I get to look up everyone else's noses, instead of down mine.

After an hour of wobbling precariously in some parallel bars, I am released from the miles of bandages, and asked if there's anything else I'd like to work on in the last fifteen minutes of the session. I think about practising wedging my arms in the doorframe and screaming 'I'm not ready!', but instead, as we roll the miles of bandages back up, I pick Sue's brains a bit more, trying to learn as much as possible about the techniques necessary for calliper walking, and how realistic it is as an ambition for a T12. She is very encouraging, although by the time I leave to make my way back to my room I am in no doubt over the amount of work involved.

The next day, the news breaks of the London tube and bus bombings and I am filled with a sense of outrage and shock. I feel a weird sense of disconnection, having lived virtually all of my life in London, and yet here I am sitting in my hospital room in Aylesbury. The newsflashes are on every screen of the many televisions on the ward, but that's because the televisions are always on, and the breaking news is on every channel, and at first I am the only person who has really noticed. As I watch the details unfold of a series of deadly attacks on my home town, I am surrounded by people making beds, eating hospital food or just having a natter with staff. It almost feels like an out of body experience, especially as I am able to put myself in all of the places where the attacks took place, having passed through them many times. It serves to strengthen my sense of having been wrenched away from my life.

I find myself thinking of the injured, who are only ever really described as 'injured', sometimes with the adjective seriously attached. They are more real to me now than they were before I was seriously injured. What did I think of before when I heard the words 'seriously injured' in a news report? Did I think of people with their legs in plaster or running around clutching a piece of bloody cloth to a head wound? I'm guessing I didn't think of months of rehabilitation, or permanent disability. Not just spinal-cord injuries, but amputees, people who have become deaf or blind, brain-damaged people, disfigured people. The journey from injury to whatever can be reclaimed of an old life. This is something that I never used to think about, but now, as well as an unreasonable lack of sympathy for people who have suffered a comparatively minor trauma, I feel a pang of sadness for those who are at the beginning of a very long and painful journey.

13

16 July 2005
Subject: Almost out...

Here we go again then. I'm sitting on the bed in the flat in Aylesbury that we have rented while our local council 'ums' and 'ahs' about the grant for the renovations to our flat in London. I am out for my second weekend, and then go back for my last week in the hospital before being discharged next Friday. I have now concluded that I am ready, and in danger of being overdone, as the familiarity and security of the hospital gets ever-more enticing. I must resist the charms of enormous bathrooms with grab rails everywhere, smooth lino floors, ramps and a universal awareness of spinal-cord injuries and the needs of those who have them. Even the civvies in the hospital are relatives or friends of patients, so they have a fair idea.

We went to the Mobility Roadshow last weekend, which was my first encounter with the assembled masses of the British disabled community. I must confess that I found it crushing. It's just going to take me a while before I'm used to ticking that box. That being said, I'm sure if you took a cross-section of the able-bodied community and put them in a large tent at about 35 degrees, it would be a fairly stressed environment.

I did, however, get to look at and try a couple of groovy things. There was a wheelchair made by an American company that had the wheels on independent suspension, which I tried. It felt a smooth ride, and maybe something to think about a year or two down the line, although there is a weight penalty. The company also make a wheelchair called a Spazz (no, really – they claim it doesn't have the same meaning in the US), and a chair for going on the beach, which has big balloon tyres. I'm not making it up. Next, they'll make one with Catherine wheels for space travel.

My wheelchair service insists that I have to go to London to be assessed for a chair. It's a bit annoying, as the company that supplies the wheelchairs for Hackney also has reps at Stoke Mandeville, but I'm keen to keep them on side, as I was told today that they are intending to assess me for a couple of really good chairs, both of them very light. Sorry, I realise that this is probably boring for you 'ambulators' but it's like choosing a pair of shoes, a bicycle, an armchair, a car and a shopping trolley all rolled into one.

Penny is proper big now, with what looks like a bag of over-excited puppies for a tummy. There are legs and arms and I don't know what competing for space in there. Soon be on the outside. I can't wait to meet the little person who I'm going to spend so much time with.

Ginny is back over from Australia to supply Penny with maternal support. She's looking well, rested and ready for another round of 'Tim and Pen's crazy life' game. Playing rounds like 'fit the wheelchair in the car'. With bonus points once there's a pushchair already in there.

What's wrong with the following scene?

Penny is in the kitchen, doing the washing-up, I am in the front room, clearing the table and wiping it down, we're listening to a CD of some of our favourite songs.

What's wrong? One thing. I'm in a fucking wheelchair. During the most normal and enjoyable 'simple pleasures' moment, that's usually when it hits me. I leap out of my body, and look down upon the scene being played out, and scream, 'And what the fuck are you so happy about?'

And when this happens, I don't know the answer. I started to think I knew the answer. Perhaps more accurately, for a little while I didn't notice that there was anything wrong. Is this cognitive thinking or denial?

Having found out about the Motability scheme, we start a tour of the local car dealerships of Aylesbury. Motability is a scheme whereby someone who receives the higher rate of a state benefit called Disability Living Allowance, like me, can sign over the mobility component (about £45 a week), and use it to lease a car for a fixed period of three years. You can add a supplement to this payment and get whatever car you want. Obviously, we're looking for something family-sensible, but it's still quite fun, as I've never had a brand-new car before, or even toured the showrooms. Despite my temptation to get something totally impractical, we conclude that if I am to have any chance of getting a child into a baby seat, we are going to have to go for a car with a sliding back door to allow me to get in close enough. This narrows the field, especially as it has to be automatic as well, but it doesn't stop me from playing about, trying cars that are totally unsuitable. The tricky bit is trying to get in and out of a showroom car without smacking the super-shiny paintwork with the wheelchair. I can almost hear the sales staff clench their buttocks every time I have a go. We decide to start taking a towel with us to protect the door sills.

We meet up with some friends at the weekend. They have just come back from a week in Ibiza. It sounds like a seriously trashy week, at least for most. There is an anecdote involving two friends jumping naked from a first-floor balcony into a swimming pool. Very rock 'n' roll, only these days my first thought is that this was a spinal injury waiting to happen. This happens a lot now. For example, we drive past a superbike dealership. Penny and I look at each other, and share the same thought, although this constant picturing of spinal-cord injury in every exuberant act or 'extreme sport' is not as logical as it may seem.

While there are people in the spinal unit because they were injured paragliding, diving, horseriding, rock-climbing, climbing trees and competing at gymnastics, there are also patients who are there as a result of car accidents, falling off ladders, falling off balconies, being landed on by someone else jumping off a balcony in a nightclub, slipping in the shower, falling awkwardly on a bouncy castle, and even one patient who has the same symptoms as a spinal-cord injury, only they are caused by something called transverse myelitis, where a viral infection has caused lesions to develop in the spinal cord. SCI can happen in the most mundane circumstances, on an average day.

When people see a wheelchair, it may symbolise whatever notions they might have about disabilities, disabled people, disabled parking or any other associations. I think I am starting to have more of an understanding of what racism feels like when you're on the receiving end. Not virulent, rabid racism, but the more subtle, pernicious, unspoken kind. What I'm talking about is someone making a presumption based upon my appearance, and feeling that first I have to deal with whatever that may be, just to get to a neutral starting point.

As we continue our tour of various car dealerships, we go into one where the Motability specialist is a wheelchair user. He looks very fit and active and after we've talked cars we end up on the subject of wheelchair sport. He tells me that he used to play basketball to quite a high level, but has semi-retired now in order to get on with the rest of his life. I ask him what level he is, explaining how I'm T12 and having that 'hospital patient' conversation, and he tells me that although he is functionally T12, he didn't have a spinal-cord injury, he had spina bifida as a child. I feel myself flush with embarrassment, as I realise that because of my total immersion in the world of the spinal unit, I have made a presumption based upon his appearance. The same kind of presumption that I am so determined not to have made about me.

As my discharge date approaches, it becomes obvious that I have gained more of the skills I will need than perhaps I thought. Especially when my last wheelchair-skills session with Lou turns out to be one on one, as all the other patients due for the session are in the first of a new series of patient lectures. It reminds me a bit of school, when I see new patients who have just got out of bed for the first time, and they are pushing themselves around with a look of wide-eyed apprehension. Lou takes me out around the grounds of the hospital, and we practise kerbs and drop kerbs and even go up and down a really steep grass bank, which I suggested as a joke, but with her encouragement I am elated to find I can actually do it. For the first time I feel like I have the confidence to tackle the world outside.

However, this doesn't stop me from managing to totally fluff a 'chair to plinth' transfer in the afternoon, possibly the last one of my rehabilitation. As I launch myself from the wheelchair, the chair cushion comes loose, and as my hand is leaning on said cushion for lift, I utter a strange 'oooh' sound, thus gaining the attention of the entire population of the gym, before dropping rather ungracefully onto both knees with a loud thump. I have waited until the week of my discharge before providing the physiotherapy staff with the opportunity to fill out the extensive and much-loved accident form.

In the same session I meet another patient, M, who has come back in to train in calliper walking. He is also a T12, and was injured five years ago. The sad news is that he still suffers from pain in his legs and backside, and is still taking gabapentin years after being injured. I try not to make any comparisons, but the prospect of experiencing all this pain for years to come is an additional burden.

M is struggling with the callipers, because his hip flexors have shortened as a result of sitting in a chair for the last five years and not standing regularly. In order to use callipers, you have to be able to lean back, and 'sit' on your hip flexors, with your hips thrown forwards. If you can't do this effectively, then you run the risk of jack-knifing in the middle, and landing on your backside, which is quite a long way to go when your knees are locked. As well as leaning back, you have to keep your lateral balance using your obliques and your abdominal muscles. It's certainly not easy, and very few people end up walking in callipers regularly, but I'm determined to give it a go, as I like standing up and it could provide a less bulky alternative to a standing frame. I would also like our child to see me standing and to know how tall I am. Perhaps the fact that I find this so important is a sign that I've got a long way to go to fully accept my new physical circumstances, and that I am still trying to hold on to my previous life.

My discharge date looms ever closer and the hospital feels smaller, somehow. We head over to the maternity unit for our appointed tour and 'parentcraft' class. I am expecting to have to make a baby out of dried pasta, wool, glue and a paper plate, but sadly it's not that kind of craft. Instead we are ushered into a room to sit in a circle. This is our first 'public engagement' together in the normal world, we are the last in of about sixteen people, and as soon as the midwife has started the introductions, I lean forward to try and get myself comfortable, and in the process I release a full-blooded burst of flatulence. No one is more surprised than me, and I decide to content myself by thinking that eventually there will come a day when I hardly notice, seeing as it is so far beyond my control. Now the 'ice breaker' is out of the way, and we have all introduced ourselves, we are taken through a mini-role-playing game so that we know who all the people are who could be in attendance during the birth. I am rather relieved that I am not given a role to play, although I rather fancied myself for the part of 'instrument trolley'.

After the role-play, we have a question and answer session. 'What about MRSA?' asks one father-to-be, in a confrontational tone that suggests to me this is a subject he researched in the tabloids. I am tempted to put my hand up and say, 'I've got plenty.' But opt instead to keep it to myself. Well, I mean, I had to get my own – why can't he?

The midwife reassures us that, despite all the fuss in the papers about recent hospital-borne infections, the maternity unit is completely separate from the rest of the hospital, with no shared staff.

Next, we are taken on a tour of the maternity unit, much of which is just about wheelchair accessible, although the multi-bed bays are definitely not, which should mean that we get a side room of our own, especially once we tell them about the old MRSA. As we are leaving the maternity unit, Penny and I exchange cheerful greetings with a member of the cleaning staff who regularly works on the spinal unit, but on this occasion is obviously seconded to the maternity unit that doesn't share any staff with the rest of the hospital.

It is good to see the maternity unit, just to have an image of where we're headed, and all the staff are very friendly and sympathetic. Obviously, being in the same hospital as the spinal unit means that we are not the first SCI parents they have dealt with. But, most of all, we leave happy to have finally done something together as parents-to-be, after so many months of spinal-injury-and-spouse.

I have noticed that some of the patients have a little puff of weed every now and then, usually behind the bike sheds, which is rather quaint. I can understand why they do it, especially those who have been in hospital for almost a year, but someone tells the authorities, who have a less tolerant view.

I reflect on a suggestion from a friend that I should try using cannabis to see if it has any effect on my neuropathic pain, as many multiple sclerosis sufferers use it to cope with similar pain to good effect. The thought has crossed my mind, especially following an article in one of the Sunday news-papers about Sativex, a medication made from cannabis and licensed for use in Canada. It is used for neuropathic pain relief by MS sufferers, and is manufactured in the UK, although, understandably, the cannabis is grown in a secret location. The manufacturers have been seeking a licence from British authorities since 2003, so far without success.

I am on the way to physio. It is a hot afternoon, the sun beating down, and the courtyard too sheltered for any wind to disturb the air. I pour some water into an old bowl and watch as the family of blackbirds take it in turn to have a splash and a drink.

I spend an hour or so being assessed by a formidable Swedish physiotherapist called Ebba. She's a little over six feet tall, has a no-nonsense Scandinavian attitude and many years of experience, being a peer of Sue Edwards. We work on – and talk extensively about – walking with callipers as part of the assessment of my suitability to be put forward for three weeks of intensive training in the future. It costs the NHS around £3,000 to have full callipers, so they want to be sure that I've got the determination and the potential to make use of them. It's been interesting in the last two weeks working with a couple of the senior physiotherapists. I feel like I've learned so much in some really intensive sessions. It's also been pretty exhausting, but the experience of being back up on two legs is priceless. The decision is likely to be positive, as they have acknowledged my determination, but I also have to convince Dr J. He wants to know why I want to do it.

'If you tell me you will use them to get around every day, I don't believe you. They will not be functional for you.'

Our opinions diverge on this particular definition of 'functional'. I consider callipers to be functional because if I can make them work for me, I will not need to have a standing frame at home. While we are in Aylesbury, Dot (the head of the physiotherapy department) has agreed I can come up to the hospital to use the standing frame, but once we are back in London, I will need one of my own, and what with the space required to access the thing, it could end up taking up half the living room.

On another point of usefulness, there seems to be the definition of 'being able to carry a cup of tea'. Obviously this isn't going to be possible if I am using crutches but, frankly, I don't find it possible in a wheelchair as yet, although I have seen more seasoned wheelchair users with a cup of tea in one hand, and using the other hand to pull on door frames and the edges of tables to move themselves around Jimmy's.

The caution shown by the hospital is well founded, as most patients who start full of enthusiasm for using callipers end up with them rusting in the garage. It is a damn fool thing to do, after all. It's very hard on the shoulders, but from what I can gather, everything from here on is very hard on the shoulders. Pushing a wheelchair, playing basketball, walking with callipers, even transfers are all very hard on the shoulders. It seems that I'm going to fuck up my shoulders one way or another. It's just a question of choosing how.

Despite our differences of opinion on usefulness, Dr J gives the green light for the calliper adventure, and I am measured for them by Terry, a very dapper man with a neatly ironed short-sleeved shirt and a tie, and just a hint of Brylcreem about his hair. He measures my legs from knee to ankle around my thighs and every which way, and then draws around them on a piece of cardboard on which he makes copious notes for the technicians at the factory where the callipers are made, all in inches of course. I can picture the factory full of men in buff-coloured overalls, and women with their hair in curlers, smoking constantly.

The wheelchair service provides me with an 'interim' wheelchair while we wait for my appointment for an assessment. Unfortunately, the interim chair provided is not really suitable for someone with a spinal-cord injury, as the backrest has no adjustability and offers little support. It also has swing-out foot-plates that make me a great deal longer than I need to be, which is something of a disadvantage when it comes to manoeuvring around a small two-bedroom flat. Expressing some very colourful and derisory observations, the wheelchair technician, Andy, sets up the chair as best he can, probably as best as it can be, as he is a wheelchair user of eighteen years standing (geddit?). Andy is quite a good role model to have around, as he whizzes about the unit from his workshop, which is a bit like a cave at the back of the physiotherapy gym. His own chair is custom-made to measure, and has no adjustable elements, as these mean extra weight, which is worth losing where possible.

Seeing him working full-time in a physical and technical job is an inspiration for me, as I have always tinkered with stuff and fixed things, another parental role that I had envisaged for myself, so it is good to be able to start rebuilding that particular notion, albeit in a slightly amended form.

With two nights to go before I am discharged, I am moved from my room, which is needed in order to isolate another patient who may have a contagion of some unspecified nature. So instead of a gradual, reflective process of letting go of the last four months, I am hurriedly pulling stuff off the walls, and cramming my accumulated goods and chattels into hospital-issue grey 'patient property' carrier bags. Meanwhile, the room is undergoing a deep clean, which takes place when a room is vacated by a patient carrying any kind of infection, in my case MRSA. In this case the deep clean consists of one cleaner with a spray gun of disinfectant and a cloth, spraying and wiping as he follows me around the room. He cleans the plinth and the windowsill before I have cleared my stuff away, but this isn't a problem, he simply wipes around it, leaving little islands. At one point he even sprays some fluid on the cloth and flaps it around a bit on the curtains.

I move from my familiar home on St George's into a side room on St Joseph's. Originally I was to have been discharged directly from St George's, as I am pretty much self-caring, thanks to Alf and Liz's encouragement and making the most of my en-suite bathroom. I have even taken to making my own bed as well as my own food.

St Joseph's is different. The idea is that every patient spends at least a week on St Joseph's before they are discharged. The ward is organised differently. There are fewer staff, and patients are expected to get themselves up where possible, and undertake their own toilet and showering adventures, as well as making their own breakfast, ably assisted by Louise. Louise is much more than a cleaner or domestic helper. She also runs the kitchen, making sure that all the breakfast stuff is put out, put away, and generally tidy. The patients are supposed to do their own washing-up, and Louise makes sure. Except whenever I go near the sink, it's full of other people's washing-up, she thinks it's all mine, and I end up doing the lot. But there's more to Louise than this. She talks with all the patients, makes cups of tea for those who are unable to do it themselves, keeps a watchful maternal eye on us all, and generally creates an atmosphere that is cheerful and somehow less institutionalised than that on the other wards.

This different atmosphere is also helped by the inclusion on St Joseph's of several beds for people who are coming in for assessment, usually for physiotherapy. This is where I will stay if I come back in for calliper training. I spend a couple of nights on St Joseph's, but it feels very odd not being in my old room, and my final departure from the spinal unit feels rather spread out and disjointed.

As the desks in all of the various wards and departments are usually groaning under the weight of sweets and chocolates given as gifts by grateful patients on discharge, we decide to do something a little different, and Penny and Ginny buy a huge pile of fruit and some large foil trays, and Ginny makes up two large fruit baskets, with pineapple, strawberries, cherries, mangoes and bananas. They prove to be a big hit with the staff on St George's and in the physiotherapy department, who say that actually they much prefer fruit, but all they get is chocolate.

Feeling a bit demob happy, we pack the car and go for one final spin around the spinal unit. Having said farewell to just about everyone and completed all the paperwork, I find myself struggling to get off 'Stoke Mandeville time' and Penny, having patiently followed me around for half a day, drags me out to the car where she and Ginny shovel me in, throw the wheelchair in the boot, and off we go, past the long timber barrack-style buildings of the original spinal unit and down the road to our new, if temporary, home. I have made it out of the spinal unit with a week to spare before the baby is due. There is no doubt that the baby has forced me to engage with the process of rehabilitation sooner than many people do, as the clock was counting down regardless of what I felt about myself. I have worked hard through a lot of pain in the course of my rehab up to now.

There is a relentlessness about the spinal unit that can be overwhelming at times, and it fills me with admiration for the staff. No sooner am I out of the door, than someone else will be coming in, newly injured, to take my place. As I conducted my 'farewell tour', I could already see some of these new patients, unknown to me, starting out on the same journey.

We have a 'getting out' celebration, with lots of friends making the journey up from London. It is great seeing so many people, especially as being up in Aylesbury away from the normal support structures of friends and family feels rather isolating. It's another part of my 'alternative life' that creeps into my head, and when I hear what everyone's been up to I can put us there, as if none of this had happened. I finish the day feeling moved by the level of affection from everyone, and I wish we were back in London now, just so I could tap into this support whenever I need it, without the distance and lack of spontaneity. It's nice to see friends catching up for the first time for ages as children and careers take us in different directions, and although I feel as if I am at the centre of this, I also have a sense of being on the outside, looking in.

And now? Well now the real journey begins, as I try and work out how to pick my life back up. I've only got a week or so before another monumental change.

14

We have a week of adjusting. I have to get used to a somewhat different bathroom experience in the mornings. My transfer onto the toilet is a bit trickier, relying on a built-in shelf behind the toilet for purchase, but the real challenge starts once I've finished on the loo. I have to transfer back into the wheelchair, go out to the hall to perform a three-point turn, and re-enter the bathroom in order to transfer onto the bath-board that spans the tub underneath the shower. The transfer isn't too difficult, but once I'm on the board, I have to cross my legs in front of me in order to achieve any kind of stability.

However, all this awkwardness is counterbalanced by the pleasure of being in the flat while Penny and Ginny are busy feathering the nest, Ginny makes curtains and Penny stocks up with bottles and breast-pads and other new and occasionally puzzling baby durables.

An elaborate plan is hatched whereby Eugene will come up to Aylesbury early one morning and drive me down to London for my wheelchair-service appointment, after which our friend Gabby is to pick me up and drive back up the A41, ears finely tuned for the sound of my mobile phone. Penny is on strict instructions to keep her legs crossed until we let her know that we are past Hemel Hempstead, after which we have calculated that we could make it in time to even the quickest of births. Of course, the baby is bound to be late, on account of it being our first, and according to everyone who 'knows' (and we've met quite a few, everywhere from the spinal unit to the supermarket where one of the checkout ladies tells us what sex the baby's going to be. A boy apparently, and she's 'always right'), the first is always late. Knowing that the baby will be late takes the pressure off a bit, and I still go to London, even after Penny has been woken by a couple of contractions at five in the morning. Obviously just Braxton Hicks, and nothing to worry about.

28 July 2005
Subject: It's a ... no, nothing yet ...

I've just been for my wheelchair assessment in London, so Penny can uncross her legs now. It was weird driving into London for the first time since my accident. The most noticeable thing was that when I was injured, the trees were just budding, and now they are all resplendent in their high summer foliage. London is such a green city. It's really noticeable when you've been away for a few months.

The assessment went pretty well, but now the chair has to be ordered to spec, and the one we decided on has to come over from the US, which means a wait of six to eight weeks. Still, at least the process is under way. So in the meantime, it's a question of making the best of what I've got, and watching my feet dance around whenever I go across uneven ground. Still, at least it's dancing, I suppose.

I'm off to have a go at shooting tomorrow, assuming there's no bub locked and loaded and ready to be fired into the world. (Maybe not the best analogy, I'll grant you, but I couldn't resist.) The shooting is up at the Guttmann Centre, which is the sports centre attached to the hospital, so I'll be nearer to the maternity unit than Pen. I know that seems rather unhelpful, but seeing as I can't drive our car, it probably makes more sense to be there than here, as Ginny will have enough on her plate when things kick off, without having to pile a pregnant woman in labour AND a panicky paraplegic and a wheelchair into the car. It will be about as easy as stacking custard.

The other thing that shooting reveals is that I still have a connection with the hospital. I managed to stay away for a day or two, but it has a reassuring presence in my life, which makes the Aylesbury flat feel like a bit of a 'half-way house'. This is a great resource, and I have developed some very good relationships with many of the staff that allows me to access knowledge and support when I need it. It gets a bit scary when Jimmy Savile's around, though.

Penny's waddling around, with a lot of shuffling and rummaging for more space going on in her belly. She still looks fantastic, and only her belly gives away her condition. (Well, d'uh ... but you know what I mean.) The bag is packed, the belly's packed...

I've been practising saying 'push, push'. Trouble is, I'm saying it from a wheelchair, and so I keep getting shoved out into traffic. I probably deserve it ...

Watch this space.

And then it is upon us. As if following some pre-arranged schedule, I return from London and write the above email, only for Penny's contractions to start again at about 5 p.m. She has just come back from some mad, energised shopping frenzy with her mum Ginny, and we've all had a cup of tea, and now I'm reminding myself of the instructions for the TENS machine, the application and management of which is my designated role at this stage in the proceedings. For the uninitiated, a TENS machine can be useful in early labour, and sends electrical pulses through the skin to help prevent pain signals reaching the brain. Only trouble is, I'm shattered and rather sore from the four-and-a-half hours that I have just spent in cars going up and down the motorway. And, by the way, I fully appreciate that this is as nothing to the experience Penny is about to go through, but cut me some slack. I've been out of hospital for less than a month, and the reality of not being the centre of attention is going to take a lot of getting used to.

So, we pace (well, not me, obviously), and we listen to relaxing music, and I cover Penny's back with the sticky pads and wires of the TENS machine, and I manage to plug the right leads into the right holes, and give her the recommended amount of small electric shocks rather than one huge surge. Mind you, I do have a sneaking feeling that the TENS machine's real role isn't in pain relief, so much as distraction, for the operator as well as the wearer, especially as it gives men something technical they can get on with. This suspicion is further deepened several months later when I try a TENS machine for help with my back pain, the result being back pain plus uncomfortable irritation.

When it becomes apparent that we're not about to charge for the hospital, Ginny draws Penny a bath and we fill it with all the right potions and Penny gets in for a soak. Obviously removing the TENS machine first. I am not stupid. I read that bit.

At this point, I must confess that I sneak off to lie on my front on the bed, as my pain is becoming intolerable. I am also feeling a bit apprehensive, for while I have never been one who thinks the sky is going to fall on my head, all that changed in April when my head fell out of the sky along with the rest of me, and I have to try very hard to stop my imagination from creating awful 'what if …' scenarios.

The bath slows the pattern of contractions down quite dramatically, and the minutes between them stay pretty constant, so we lie on the bed together for a bit and the inevitable happens – the evening medication kicks in and I fall asleep. I try really hard not to, and I even wonder if it is the stress causing my brain to just shut down. But as I struggle to stay awake, lurching with a start every couple of minutes, Penny comes to my aid. 'It's likely to be a very long night and if you're going to stand any chance of getting through it and being with me through it all, you should get some rest while you can.'

'No, but I'll be all right in a minute. I'll just have a cup of tea, and …'

'Relax, Mum's here, and we won't go anywhere without you.'

Not wanting to argue with a woman in labour, I drift into semi-consciousness, thinking how soothing Penny's choice of music is.

I am woken with a gentle nudge, because it is now nearly two o'clock in the morning, and we're off!

Like a well-oiled machine, we manage to pick up Penny's bag and dressing gown, and make sure I've got my stuff too (catheters, etc.), and we all get in the car, without getting the leads from the TENS machine wrapped around everything. We are just about to pull off. Then Ginny remembers something. She gets out of the car and loads my rather forlorn-looking wheelchair into the back, and we're off!

Ginny drives cautiously down to the maternity unit of the hospital, and we disembark and head for the doors. We are welcomed with open arms into one room and then another, where Penny is examined, and told that she is only about one centimetre dilated, and that she needs to be four at least, so we're sent home. We all traipse back to the car and head home, a little deflated.

We get back, the kettle goes on again, and Penny dispatches me straight back to bed, as I am fit for little else. Four hours pass. Once again I am roused from my slumbers, and we're off!

This time, the car loading feels more rehearsed, and we make it to the maternity unit in good time, with Penny huffing and puffing, as the contractions are now only five minutes apart. She passes the initial assessment this time and we are admitted into one of the rooms we had seen in our tour earlier in the month. A trainee midwife accompanies us and stays for several hours, maintaining an atmosphere of calm. Penny does lots of pacing about and sitting on a large gym ball, as well as sitting on the bed, sitting on the armchair, more pacing about, and a fair bit huffing and puffing.

At this point, dear reader, I feel that it is important to explain that my haziness with details in not insensitivity, nor is it induced by a deep subconscious desire to block out a traumatic experience, but rather, it is due to a combination of sleep deprivation, medication and acute pain. As Penny paces, I squirm, wriggle and fidget, but I am unable to get anywhere approaching comfortable. For long periods of the time, I sit in the armchair (again, on Penny's orders), reflecting on how this is totally unlike any preconceptions I may have held of my role now we are at 'the crunch'. Thankfully, Ginny is on hand during my more self-indulgent moments, to offer words of encouragement and advice about breathing and posture. She even manages to give Penny some tips, too.

I tend to the music (everything from Nick Drake to Talvin Singh), but I can see that Penny is running out of steam. Each contraction is leaving her more and more drained, although the gas and air seems to be helping. It certainly keeps her in a good mood. I am sorely tempted to try the stuff (to be honest, it is one of the things about forthcoming parenthood I was looking forward to), but I am too concerned that if I lose it and fall out of the chair, I will never live it down.

Another member of staff comes in to check how we are doing, and suggests that Pen have an injection of the painkiller pethidine, which she does, only for it to bring everything to a grinding halt. The contractions get no closer, Penny just gets more and more knackered. The tricky subject of an epidural, an anaesthetic injected into the spine, gets raised as an option by the staff. The difficulty around the epidural is the obvious parallels that it draws with my condition, and Penny has been adamant that she didn't want one, but the trainee midwife convinces us to talk to the anaesthetist.

The anaesthetist is a Spanish woman who has an air of

utter professionalism, and tells us about the procedure, the different options, and the very small risk of something going wrong. It is true to say that the 'very small' caveat is somewhat diminished by four months of being surrounded by people whose accidents would have been in the 'very small' risk category before they happened.

But it is apparent that Penny has just run out of energy after about 32 hours without sleep and eight hours of contractions in the hospital, and she opts for the epidural. I feel a massive knot of butterflies as I sit behind her, urging her not to move and watching the anaesthetist insert a large needle into her lower back. The procedure is totally smooth, and in no time she is lying down on the bed with a small transparent tube over her right shoulder, and looking much more relaxed. She even gets to eat a banana from our bag of essentials, and drinks several bottles that were solid ice, but are now just very cold water. We all have a bit of rest and refreshment, and Penny even drops off for a few minutes.

Then suddenly we are back in the thick of it, the contractions are closer together now, and Penny tells the nurse that she feels sick, and the nurse brings a small cardboard bowl that she puts to her chin, just in time for Penny to projectile vomit all over everyone and everything except for her mother and her husband, much to the relief of both parties.

At about 3 p.m., Penny is told to start pushing during the contractions. Ginny holds her hand and mops her brow, and I am at the other end of the bed, as the room is now so full of people and trolleys that I can't get any closer, and I watch the obstetrician, who makes encouraging noises, but his hands move very quickly to and from the trolley, a blur of blood and implements, and all I can think is: I can't bear this. Is this the point when everything goes wrong? Am I witnessing the first scenes of an unimaginable tragedy? My head is spinning, these fears worsened by the gore of childbirth, which no amount of warning could have prepared me for, and then it occurs to me that Penny might see the look of fear on my face, which is an absurd thought, as Penny can't see anything at the moment on account of her being slightly distracted by giving birth and all. I become aware of the music that is on. What began as a calm, chilled CD with an Eastern flavour has turned into pounding psychedelic drum and bass, and is probably not helping anyone's stress levels, least of all mine. I turn it off, and focus on the scene unfolding before me. The staff are buzzing around and the atmosphere is one of controlled chaos. There is a sense of anticipation shared throughout the room.

And then with a swift flash of a scalpel, and a loud cry of 'Push now! Push now!' the obstetrician rummages around, and emerges with a tiny little girl. She has her eyes open, a full head of dark hair, and looks somewhat startled, which is understandable. She is whisked away briefly for a quick check over, and then presented to Penny, and we hold hands, and I cry and cry, as if all of the pain and fear and frustration of the last four months is pouring out of me, and I feel like I'll never stop.

Thankfully I do eventually, and we all share a little moment of serenity that is slightly at odds with the surroundings, as the room looks like someone has exploded in it, which is probably not a million miles from the truth. It finally dawns on me just how 'organic' the whole pregnancy/childbirth thing is – not that I was expecting to be the father pacing outside, unlit cigar in pocket, waiting for the doctor to come and shake my hand and say, 'Well done, old boy. It's a girl,' or whatever. But it is a visceral, messy, exhausting and dangerous business.

Rosalie Kate is in her mother's arms. I don't recognise her, although I was expecting to, somehow. But as much as she is a part of Penny and me, she is now herself and I have to get to know her. Her life stretches out ahead of us. She is so small. Well, having just given birth to her at just less than eight pounds, I think Penny might take issue with that, but I mean her hands and her feet are so small, and she's all curled up, wrapped in a Sunlight Laundry towel.

After a short time, Penny drops off to sleep, cradling Rosalie in her arms, and I call my parents to tell them the news. By a fortunate coincidence, my mother and Eugene are up at the hospital attending Relatives' Day, a day of lectures on various aspects of spinal-cord injury designed to help relatives to get a better understanding of what's involved and what the implications are for the future. A quick phone call to tell them the news, and they come straight over to the maternity unit to meet Rosalie within 30 minutes of her birth. The naming was easy, as we already had a girl's name decided, and although we didn't know the sex of the baby, we had been unable to come up with a boy's name.

After my parents have left, I go off in search of a cold drink, and end up doing a quick round of the spinal unit, announcing our news to anyone who will listen. It feels like the culmination of my rehab, as it was our one definite plan through it all.

Ginny and I leave Penny to get some rest, and we head back to the flat in a dazed silence. I am in a great deal of pain by now, but the emotional wave seems to have sustained me through my record-breaking wheelchair-athon, having managed longer in an upright position than ever before. We drink a toast to Penny and Rosalie, and I dash off a quick email before exhaustion overwhelms me and I stretch out on the bed. I am unconscious within minutes.

15

29 July 2005

Rosalie Kate Rushby-Smith emerged into the world at fourteen minutes past four on the 29 July 2005, with eyes open and a full head of hair.

Both mother and baby are doing well, if a little tired.

Both father and mother of mother are doing well, if a little tired.

The staff at Stoke Mandeville maternity unit did very well, and are probably now a little tired.

... she's a cracker, by the way.

Penny stays in hospital for a couple of days, exhausted and a bit beaten up by the whole thing. Ginny and I spend our time at home between visits fussing over small details, she sorting through piles of baby clothes and me acting as press officer to deal with the overwhelming calls and messages in a role reversal. It feels so strange, awaiting the arrival of a new person who will take centre stage in my life. I hope she likes me.

While we are preparing for Rosalie's homecoming, I take the opportunity to have a second run up to the spinal unit. There is a pedestrian path from the new development where our flat is that was supposed to go all the way to the Guttmann Centre, the sports centre next to the spinal unit. Unfortunately it was never completed, but at least it provides me with a good level path for about half the journey, after which I am confronted with a series of challenges straight from the bumper book of wheelchair skills. All I need is a water jump and I would have the full steeplechase. While I am undertaking this journey, I listen to music on my iPod, a pre-injury tradition.

Before my accident, I used to do quite a lot of mountain biking. From our flat in London I used to take a fifteen-minute ride over Hackney marshes and along the bank of the river Lea to arrive at the Eastway cycle track, a tarmac circuit of around a mile in length, set in a landscaped area perfect for off-road riding. There used to be a whole season of off-road races there every year. The track was originally built around 30 years ago, and was even raced by the great Eddy Merckx, hero to many a cyclist.

I didn't go to compete myself. Instead I used to go and make up my own course, haring through the undergrowth, scaring the bejesus out of rabbits on every corner, my head filled with the sound of compilation CDs made by a close friend of mine who lives in Melbourne. We made (and still do) CDs for each other, carefully timed for a good aggressive ride, and the feeling of thrashing the pedals along narrow tracks with my very own soundtrack was truly exciting. Inevitably it was punctuated with the odd crash, but as my first instinct after coming off my bike was to see if anyone saw it (which I would do even before I checked myself for life-threatening injury), the joy of having a circuit pretty much to myself was liberating. Alas, it has now disappeared under the Olympic site, another part of my old life literally disappeared.

Now I'm pushing a wheelchair along a sealed track through Aylesbury, taking a 'run' at several kerbs, and failing dismally to get up them. I blame the wheelchair each time, and convince myself that once I get my new chair, I'll be able to levitate, etc. My route takes me through a grass play area next to a housing estate, and while making my way across I pass a group of three children playing while their mothers look on. One of the children stops to watch, and then she points at me and proudly announces, 'My dad's got one of those!' Maybe I'm not the first father in a wheelchair, then.

As I push up the slight hill into the car park, I find myself thinking of the advice that I got from Stuart about going to the furthest shop whenever you need something, and that is what I am doing, in a way. Pushing up to the hospital takes a good twenty minutes of hard effort, and by the time I get to the gym, I am pretty knackered. Standing in the frame doesn't require that much effort, although the stretching out of my legs causes a degree of discomfort because even though I have no function in my hip flexors, some of them end above the level of my injury, so my brain interprets the signal as pain in my thighs, and that's what I feel.

Once I am up in the frame, I spend my time not reading the book that I have brought along, instead offering occasional encouragements to other patients, and inevitably wise-arse comments towards the staff. Word of our new arrival is all around the spinal unit, and I am congratulated by all and sundry. I also take the opportunity to talk to Dot, the head of the physiotherapy department, about the trials and tribulations of wheelchair parenting, as her husband is a wheelchair user.

We pick Penny up from the hospital, and the four of us try and establish a routine at home. At this stage, there is little that I can do as far as Rosalie is concerned, other than to have her sleep on my chest while I recline on the sofa, which is a tough job, but hey, we all have to make sacrifices. It is extremely helpful to have Ginny on hand, especially as she seems to be the only one who can placate the little one most of the time.

We construct a wheelchair-accessible change table. The main issue is having leg room underneath, and enough space in the room to enable me to get to it. But I do manage to change a nappy, and at last I am useful. Penny and Ginny go into town, leaving me at home alone with Rosalie. I wedge her on the sofa among various cushions, and rush into the other room for a rattle. On my way back, I stop to pick something else up from the hall floor, and slip forwards out of the wheelchair and onto the floor on my knees. I feel a surge of panic. Rosalie is happily burbling on the couch, and I am stranded on the hall floor. I may have damaged my knees and even more likely, I could have broken my ankles, as my feet are folded completely underneath me. After a few seconds, I manage to get a grip, and remind myself that I have been banging on about the floor-to-chair transfer since I started my rehab, so here we are, my first opportunity to put it into practice in a real-life situation. Rosalie is quite happy. She's not going anywhere.

It takes me a couple of goes, but I manage to nail the transfer, and once I have caught my breath, I get on the sofa with Rosalie, and decide not to move until the others have returned. In the evening I feel down, as the events of the day have highlighted the limitations of my situation, and I feel as if I have just seen another group of mental images of parenthood wink out of existence.

We are all having a bit of a tough time. Rosalie is three weeks old and while Ginny is really supportive, both Penny and I miss home, the casual contact and support of other friends and family. People don't – or, more accurately, can't – drop in for a quick cup of tea. If someone makes the drive up from London that takes over an hour, they understandably stay for a few hours, which means that Penny doesn't sleep during the day, as the flat is too small to 'retire' anywhere and get peace and quiet, and she's totally exhausted.

Having put an application together for a disabled facilities grant (DFG), we are still waiting on Hackney Council to start moving on it. Our occupational therapist phoned today to say that Hackney has allocated our case to a 'grant officer'. Then, when we go through the piles of paperwork that we have accumulated, we find a letter from a month ago, saying that our case had been allocated a 'grant officer'. So quite what this person has been doing since remains a mystery.

The DFG is up to £25,000 towards the cost of adaptations necessary to allow a disabled person to continue to live at home. It is a means-tested grant, and the explanatory notes and conditions consist of a stack of paper almost an inch thick.

While I was still in hospital, Penny had a meeting on site at our flat with the local occupational therapist, inevitably from a private company, as the service has been 'outsourced'. At first, the company insisted that they had to meet me on site for an assessment, but eventually conceded that this was an unreasonable demand. They have now come up with a list of required adaptations for which we have to get estimates. Most of the work is fairly straightforward. A folding platform lift to negotiate the five steps up from street level, all the internal doorways to be widened and the kitchen to be rebuilt with a space under the hob and sink for my knees. But then there is the bathroom, and this is where things get a little more complicated. In order to gain one square metre of extra space in the bathroom and make it wheelchair accessible, we have to seal up the door to the garden, and provide an alternative means of getting out to the back. This involves installing some external doors and building a balcony on the back of the house.

The OT recommends a couple of companies that specialise in adaptation work, and they come along and take a look. When we get their quotes, I am appalled. One company has suggested that instead of making the bathroom bigger, we build some kind of self-contained toilet/shower unit in the corner of our bedroom; a sort of home Portaloo. Another company quotes for the kitchen and insists that we need a height-adjustable electric 'rise and fall' unit for the sink and cooker so that we can raise and lower it depending on who's using the kitchen. This will cost around £5,000. Their quote for the kitchen cabinets comes to £7,000 alone, and this doesn't include installation costs. Perhaps most telling of all, not one of these companies has asked us what our preferences might be. The bathroom suite quoted for is basic, with quarter-turn taps, designed for people who have dexterity issues, the tiles white, the grab rails blue (included in the quote were vertical grab rails for people who can stand but need support in the shower), and no enquiry as to what kind of kitchen units we would like.

What shocks me most is the realisation that most of the DFG work these companies carry out is probably for elderly clients whose relatives arrange the adaptations while the person is still in hospital, and they are clearly used to having free rein over decisions. Plus, they are recommended by the OT company, so they already have a foot in the door when the grant application is first considered.

Suffice to say, we make other arrangements. Fortunately, my brother is a carpenter and recommends an interior designer who is more than happy to get involved. She quotes for all of the building work, except for the balcony, for which we have another friend, a metal fabricator, come and have a look.

This long and daunting process makes us reflect on our future plans. During a session of cost calculations, Penny looks up and says, 'Are we doing the right thing? Should we be thinking about selling the flat and finding somewhere more suitable?'

I'm startled by the suggestion, but I quickly see that there's sense in it. Except I can't let go.

'I need this. I just want to get back to square one, and see where we go from there.'

'I do too. It's just that we need to make sure that we have thought this through, and considered all the options. Would we be better off finding a bungalow somewhere?'

I think back to conversations with patients who were 'delayed discharge'. 'I know there is a strong emotional element to this, but after seeing other people languishing in hospital because they are unable to find somewhere accessible, what are our chances?'

For all this, Penny is right. We need to consider every option, and so we spend some time looking online at what we could get for our money. It soon becomes obvious that there is a real shortage of accessible housing, especially in London, where much of the housing stock consists of Victorian terraces.

Trying to make this decision at a distance from our home is very difficult, but we both feel like we've had enough changes in our lives for the time being, without moving (permanent) house as well, and it is with some relief that we decide together that we should concentrate all our efforts on going home.

We have our first outing with Rosalie strapped to my chest in a little papoose. She seems very happy, and I feel a sense of pride in my new role as 'pram'. Penny also expresses some milk so that I can give Rosalie a bottle feed at around 10 p.m., allowing Pen to have a full four hours uninterrupted sleep! These little contributions make me feel more involved, but they are tempered by feelings of uselessness whenever things go awry.

One night, I knock over a beer bottle. I watch it roll slowly towards the edge of the table, and I have time to catch it a dozen times. Except that I'm in a wheelchair and I can't reach it without first taking my brakes off, and wheeling myself around the table, maybe doing a five-point turn to get to the other side. So all I can do is watch it roll slowly towards the edge of the table, and then fall inevitably to the floor and explode glass and beer all over the living room. Not for the first time since the accident, I feel like a spectator. And the worst feeling of all is that there are times when I feel like I am a spectator in the life of my daughter Rosalie. But then, I guess all new dads feel a bit like that.

On another occasion, some friends come up for a visit with their two young daughters, and we head out to a small playground nearby. As one of the girls climbs the climbing frame, she gets scared, and her father comes over and plucks her from the top. I feel a huge rush of melancholy as I watch another one of my parenthood roles disappear. I decide there and then that I shall avoid playgrounds wherever possible.

16

Penny's father Leon arrives from Australia as part of the staged withdrawal of the grandparental presence. He and Ginny move into the loft that Penny and Ginny lived in when they first came up to Aylesbury while I was in the spinal unit. We go on various outings, all bundled into the car, pram and wheelchair to boot. On one visit to an old heritage site that claims to be wheelchair accessible, I am confronted with a path of large, loose stones the size of tennis balls, and very steep hills. It is a fiercely hot day, and I become more and more frustrated by the effort involved. Then, as I am trying to get up a ramp into one of the old buildings, Leon pushes me from behind. It is only out of a genuine desire to help me, but because I am not expecting it, I nearly come out of the front of the chair, and I snap at him. He apologises and explains his trying to help, but I have been totally unfair to him. There is nothing he can say or do to make things easier for me. I just can't help throwing my frustrations at those close to me.

In that moment I realise just how much everyone has had to get used to me struggling around, determined to do things for myself, and how this must be one of the most difficult things for relatives to accept. For someone like me, I need to feel independent, even if it takes longer to do something on my own than to accept help. It's this level of bloody-mindedness that has got me through the rehabilitation process so quickly, but it's hard to ask people close to you to stand there and watch as you struggle with whatever relatively minor task you may be trying to achieve. Leon has been so supportive, and is the most relentlessly positive person I know, an attribute that I should be drawing strength from instead of blindly flailing around for people to vent my frustrations at.

The next day is better, but not by much. We go on a trip to Waterperry Gardens, a stately home and gardens with a very nice plant nursery attached. We have a good lunch, with both sets of (grand)parents and baby in attendance. A great day out until we head for the nursery. I am suddenly overwhelmed with sadness, as I enter a familiar environment, the kind where Penny and I spent many days buying plants for clients as part of our garden design business. It's a painful reminder of the life we had, the outdoor and physical, the planting and nurturing.

After three weeks, departure time comes for Leon and Ginny, and we say our emotional farewells in the courtyard of the barn where they have been staying. The gradual withdrawal tactic makes their departure no easier. I watch Ginny with little Rosalie, and I feel really sad. She has been a part of every day of Rosalie's life, all six weeks of it. I'm sure she could never have imagined that her first grandchild would arrive in such circumstances, and her practical help has been invaluable. We have been through a lot, and she has been there every step of the way, busily keeping us together and helping Penny through some long nights of fretting and feeding.

And so, we are alone, we three. There is a sense of relief in a way, as this is the way it was always meant to be, and the fact that we have got here, albeit in a different town and a very different set of circumstances, makes me reflect on how things could have been so much worse. And here's an odd thing. I don't think I have really allowed the seriousness of my accident to hit home. I really could have died so very easily. If I hadn't been wearing a helmet, if I had been knocked unconscious, if I had fallen through the roof, if I had landed head first. If, if, if.

Comparisons are not helpful, but inevitable. It's hard not to think about the different outcomes as if you get some kind of choice, a form with boxes to tick.

Impaired motor function in legs?   Y/N
Impaired sensation in legs?   Y/N

Impaired hand dexterity?	Y/N
Impaired sensation in hands?	Y/N
Impaired arm function?	Y/N
Faecal incontinence?	Y/N
Urinary incontinence?	Y/N
Impotence?	Y/N
Chronic pain?	Y/N
Spasm?	Y/N
Respiratory problems?	Y/N

And this is just the form for spinal-cord injury. I'm sure the one for head injury/brain damage probably runs to several pages.

When we visit some family friends who live nearby for lunch, their eight-year-old son is transfixed by my wheelchair, especially when I pull a wheelie to get over the threshold. Within five minutes of our arrival, he starts a torrent of questions. Like a seasoned negotiator he starts with the simple stuff, but the relentlessness of his pursuit of knowledge is quite breathtaking. The highlight has to be, 'You mean to say, someone could cut your legs off and you wouldn't feel a thing? *Cool*!'

The questioning only stops after several hours, when I transfer onto the couch and let him have a go in my wheelchair. And if I'm honest, I enjoy the interrogation every bit as much as he does. Both parents look a little uncomfortable at times and are at pains to remind me of my right to silence, especially as his mother works in the legal profession, but the openness and natural curiosity of childhood is really refreshing.

The following day I find that I have a new challenge to face, when I suffer the worst night of pain since I was discharged from hospital. What starts as an uncomfortable itchy tingle develops into a pain in my left leg as if I am being stabbed with a hot knife. Penny can see the pain I am in, and we end up lying on the bed together in tears at the whole wretched business. Here we are, me in a wheelchair, she trying to come to terms with the strain of being a new mother, and we are miles away from the support of our friends and family. Meanwhile, Rosalie sleeps on, her newborn face a picture of innocent contentment and security. Finally, after I have taken two sleeping tablets, the pain is disconnected by a wave of fuzzy incoherence, and I drift off to sleep.

Things don't really improve when a few days later I meet another challenge. I am supposed to have a psychology appointment in the afternoon, a regular session where I get to sound off about everything, and the psychologist throws me a few cognitive thinking techniques and we look on the bright side. It seems to help, somehow, but on this occasion I cancel the appointment as I don't feel quite right. Just a bit off, somehow. No sooner have I finished on the phone than I feel a slight stomach ache, which is followed by a foul odour. Whatever was making me feel off colour has resulted in me 'filling my pants'. It is a pretty soul-destroying event, as I had virtually no warning. Not a helpful experience, as it will now cross my mind whenever I leave the house. It's one thing to have this kind of situation at home with a bathroom, a change of clothes and a washing machine to hand, but what if I'm in the supermarket? Or in the pub? I try and focus on the fact that I didn't feel quite right, so there was at least a small hint. I just need to store the experience, and learn how to read my body in new ways.

I finally get a positive lift in spirits when, on my way to the hospital to stand, I stop to watch some wheelchair basketball at the sports centre. Despite my earlier dismissive attitude towards the sport, I am greatly impressed by the skill and speed, and I feel inspired to have a go as soon as the opportunity presents itself. This will require the loan of a special chair, as you cannot play in a conventional wheelchair because you would spend most of the game tipping over, and then trying to get back into the damn thing. One of the most exciting aspects for me is watching the way that players are able to race around, sprinting and changing direction, because the wheelchairs are made for sport. Also inspiring in a way is how, after someone does go over, the play continues, and they try to score before they help to right the fallen, instead of stopping to hold their heads and say, 'Ohmygodohmygodohmygod. Quick, somebody do something. I've got his legs, quick, ohmygod …'

Having been so moved by the basketball, I get home and begin to watch the previous night's *Match of the Day*. All of a sudden, wheelchair basketball seems like such a shabby consolation prize. Maybe a go of it will change that. I always want a go myself, whatever I'm watching. I think this is partly to get a better insight into the skill involved. I remember how a seemingly mild tackle on the football pitch, which ruptured the posterior cruciate ligament in my knee, changed the way I viewed professional players rolling around after what looked like fairly innocuous challenges. Only now I have to find a way to stop comparing aspects of my new life with previous experience, because it will always suffer.

But there is one aspect of my new life that cannot be compared. Dadhood is all and more. When Rosalie lies asleep on my chest, the sense of utter trust and defencelessness almost makes me weep as she breathes noisily in my face. I think her acceptance of me as I am will help mine. Several people have asked how I am finding fatherhood. As I answer, I can see myself as a character in a zombie movie, the friend of the hero who goes off to get help, and is next seen scratching at the window, droning, 'Join usssss.' There I am saying all those things that I have heard before from other new parents: 'The sense of responsibility for a little life … so utterly dependent … how tiny her hands are …' etc.

We go back to the flat in London, my first visit back since I left for work on 1 April. I am really psyched up for an emotional rollercoaster, but it isn't as I imagined. There's enough pleasant familiarity to underline the homesickness we both feel living in Aylesbury. I can't get to the window to see the back garden, and there is no chance of me getting out there, so I just shut that bit out of my head somehow. We meet with various building contractors and kitchen designers, which feels like a step of progress towards making the place accessible and going home.

Unfortunately, things go a bit pear-shaped on the journey back. I'm not sure whether it is the car journey, or spending five hours in the dreadful interim wheelchair, but something has triggered off the worst type of pain. I dub this pain 'Spike', for obvious reasons. I keep trying to battle with pain in my head, but this one is off the scale, and all attempts to distract myself prove fruitless. Once we are home, Penny gets my chair out of the boot, and the baby seat out of the back, and we head inside so that I can dose myself up. Playing computer games on my laptop is quite effective as a distraction from the pain while I wait for the sleepers to kick in. It also allows me to run and jump and crouch, and carry out other leg-based activities, if only in a virtual world. I finally crash out, only for Penny to wake up in the night and find me sleeping at right angles, with my legs on the bed and my head and shoulders on the wheelchair. I don't think it has anything to do with the computer games, as there have been other occasions when she has found me contorted, my head between my feet, bent double. I think I wake up to move, but then fall asleep again halfway through my night-time manoeuvre.

Although the following day is typically 'low pain' until the afternoon, a pleasing legacy of the sleeping tablet taken the night before, by the early evening I am feeling pretty uncomfortable, and it is increasingly apparent that my pain is likely to be chronic, and therefore I need to start thinking in terms of pain management rather than cure. Although this thought has been forming for some time, acknowledging it does not help in the fight against the waves of panic which come up when I realise that the sharp stab of pain I have just felt is one of a series that occur every day. The likelihood that I will be in pain every day for the rest of my life is overwhelming, so I have to find a way of only dealing with the next ten minutes, and the last ten minutes. I have to carve out a space in order to function, and it doesn't always hold. Often something comes crashing in and I have to start all over again. I find this exhausting, and I still feel like dealing with my condition is a full-time job, which in turn accentuates the new-father-uselessness feeling.

To add to this, I manage to spill a cup of tea on myself, copping the lot in my lap. Luckily, I am by the kitchen sink, and able to slosh glasses of cold water onto myself straight away. The results of this accident are very informative. The red marks on my stomach (where I have sensation) all disappear within twelve hours. By contrast, the skin on my thighs becomes red and blistered. I am glad that I can't feel it, as some people with spinal injury have no movement, but do have sensation.

What the tea-spilling episode clearly demonstrates is the importance of being very cautious in looking after my skin, as it does not react in the same way when it is damaged. I think this may be because the body doesn't sense the burning, and therefore doesn't attempt to dissipate the heat, and the repair process is slowed down. The district nurse comes around to inspect the burns. She declares herself to be happy with the way I have treated them, and says that she isn't worried about them, which is reassuring. In the conversation that follows, I ask if she has many other patients with spinal-cord injury, what with the spinal unit being up the road, and all. She says, 'Oh yes! There's one chap who even drives a car! Well, it's one of those MPV thingies. I mean it's amazing what he does. He has special controls, and he drives. And his wife is also in a wheelchair, and she goes in the back, and they go away for the weekend, and everything!'

Well, whoopee-doo. Away for the weekend, eh? Gosh, what a life I could lead. I have to confess to being a wee bit more ambitious than that. Time will tell.

17

1 September 2005
Subject: The days go by...

And I get a little stronger, Penny gets a little sleep, and Rosalie gets a lot bigger. She has taken well to the pa-poose-style sling that attaches her to my chest. I have used it to take her out for a 'calm down' walk on a couple of occasions, to great effect. We have also been out as a family with her strapped to her dad, and all I need is a couple of shopping bags on my handles, and I make a great pushchair. I'm thinking of getting one of those rain covers made with a little transparent bit for me to look out of. A sort of wheelchair burka.

Using the boost in enthusiasm provided by the trip back to Hackney to see the flat, we wrestle with the extensive paperwork and conditions that surround the disabled facilities grant. It becomes apparent pretty quickly that the real challenge is going to be wrestling the DFG money from the vice-like little hands of Hackney Council. In their literature, they promise to 'reply' to any application within three months. I can see how it could take this long to read five sheets of A4, and I am deeply embarrassed for not having anticipated my spinal-cord injury, and lodged the application last year.

Going through the forms makes me realise that because I'm living in a sort of limbo at the moment, I have developed an unrealistic notion that when I get back to Hackney, I'll be returning to my life as it was, and this whole sorry episode will be over. How much of my life will be taken up in disabusing myself of this idea remains to be seen.

To add to my frustration, I get a call from the wheel-chair service to say that they now have my wheelchair, and would I like to come and pick it up from Hackney ... in three weeks' time. Meanwhile, I think I have found the brackets on my 'interim wheelchair' where the plough used to be attached. The constant three-point turns around the house and extensive dismantling required to get the thing into the car are really getting me down. On top of that, my feet stick out so far in front of me that I can barely reach anything in the kitchen without my feet first jamming into the cupboards, unless I come at it backwards, in which case I risk tipping out of the back of the chair. And then there is the back pain ...

Thankfully I get plenty of distraction. Rosalie is a joy. She rations the smiles, seemingly knowing that one is enough to guarantee nappy changes, feeds and sleepless nights for about three days. Ah, the nights. Yes, we are all in the same room now, and although I have heard other new parents talk about their babies, I was ill-prepared for the amount of noise R makes when she's asleep. Grunting, gurgling, farting, wheez-ing, coughing and something that sounds like 'aaaaaarghhhh', followed by a long enough silence to convince me that she's stopped breathing. As soon as I sit up in bed she emits a vic-torious huff and puff. Outwitted by a six-week-old baby. It doesn't bode well.

I manage to maintain my routine of getting up to the hospital regularly to use the standing frame in the gym. The support afforded by regular contact with other people with spinal cord injuries cannot be overstated. It is something that I suspect I will struggle to find to the same degree in London, so I'm conscious of making the most of it. The level of lift is qualified according to who I am talking to. I could almost draw a simple scale. If I talk to someone at the same level as me emotionally, then I sense that we feed each other. People who are further along, perhaps with about five years of experience, give me a tremendous lift, provided they are fairly positive. But if I meet people who are more negative, maybe less emotionally adapted to their circumstances, then I find that although I feel that I can give them a lift, it is at a cost to my own emotional equilibrium. I say things like, 'Well, you've just got to get on with it, work with what you've got,' etc. And then I leave thinking: what a crock of shit. It sucks, it's horrible, and there isn't a moment from morning till night that I don't think 'if only this hadn't happened'.

Another 'buoyancy aid' comes with visits from friends. The only trouble is, I find myself feeling emotionally reliant on such visits, and the disappointment of a cancelled visit makes me feel irrationally bitter, as if this is an outlet for my frustrations at feeling exiled from my old life.

A and M are supposed to come up to see us one Sunday, but they phone to cancel, as they have been partying at G's the previous night, and they are now knackered, and have too much to do today. My reaction is polite, but clipped, and the brief phone call is followed by a text message from M saying, 'Feel so bad about not coming today. So sorry guys!' I know that the party started on Friday night, and I feel like sending a text back saying, 'If you were bothered about coming to see us, you should have thought about it last night. Anyway, I know how you feel. The novelty has worn off for me, too.'

I feel like a petulant teenager, emotionally regressing to that time in my life when just hanging out with friends was the single most important thing in the world. And I feel left out, of course, but what makes my reaction so much worse is that A has recently lost his father, and is probably in need of a real blow-out. I have had a real blow-out in the past when I have felt the need, and these things are rarely controlled or controllable. More just a case of last one standing. And yet, I still find myself doing the truly awful weighing-up thing. You know, what's worse, losing your dad, or the use of your legs? Not only is it a deeply twisted thought, it's also academic, as A lost his dad, and I lost the use of my legs, so the blow-out for him is probably what he needs, rather than a guilt trip from a mate. I try and wind my neck back in.

All these dark thoughts make me realise that I feel pretty useless at home at the moment. In fact, more than useless, I just feel so vulnerable. I worry that I will find looking after Rosalie on my own too difficult. I worry that every other twinge or stab is the beginning of a visit by Spike. And most of all I worry that I am unable to give Penny the support that she needs. She has to look after a newborn, and by now I'd hoped that I would be completely self-caring and self-sufficient, but the battle with pain affects this ambition differently on any given day. I have to spend at least some of the time on the sofa or lying on my front on the bed. I can't really do the washing-up as I can barely reach the tap if I back into the small kitchen with the sink alongside my left shoulder. So for a significant period of every day I feel like a spectator in my own life.

And if this isn't enough, I find out that cabbage doesn't agree with me any more, when I am woken up one night by a stomach ache, only to find that I have shat the bed. I knew that this was always a possibility – I mean, incontinence is incontinence, after all. But it's still pretty soul-destroying, especially having to wake Penny so that she can strip the bed, and then trying to get myself into the shower without covering the entire flat in excrement.

All of a sudden it is time for my six-week review with my consultant. It doesn't feel like six weeks, but the distraction of Rosalie and the regular contact with the spinal unit have both contributed to days and weeks blurring into each other. I head into the meeting with Dr J clutching a list of questions, but by the end I'm still not sure which of them he actually answers. I ask him if there is any tinkering worth doing as far as pain management is concerned. He shakes his head. 'If you change any of your medication before you get home, you are likely to suffer a set-back.'

I recall a conversation I had with one of the psychology team, and I ask, 'Is it worth me trying to get an appointment with a pain-management specialist?'

He shrugs. 'You can, but there is no point. I have worked with him, and I know he won't tell you anything different from what I have told you.' Presumably meaning all the stuff about not letting it win. Well, it's certainly ahead on points at the moment. This being said, he increases my daily dose of gabapentin to 2400 mg. Then he adds, 'The pain in your back is unlikely to ease before the metalwork is taken out,' which at least helps me to be realistic in my hopes.

I ask him about the fixation.

'I will remove it in about six months' time. There is no reason why it can't be removed now, seeing as it is no longer serving any purpose.' He notices a look of concern cross my face. 'It won't be anything like the last time you had surgery, and we are in no rush.'

I am hugely relieved. I often wish that it had been Dr J who had operated on me in the first place, and that the surgery had taken place at Stoke Mandeville.

One question on my list is about fertility. It turns out that this is a field he specialises in.

'There are basically two methods,' he explains. 'The "kitchen sink" method, or the scientific method. If you can retrieve the sperm through ejaculation, then you use what I call the kitchen sink method. But if you can't, then you should go to the highest level of advanced technology, which is called ICSI. There is no point in doing anything in between.'

The fertility issue has been around off and on since I was first injured. We made enquiries at the Royal London as to whether we should have some sperm retrieved and put on ice when we were told that spinal-cord injury can quickly affect the motility of sperm, and many of the staff said this was a good idea. They even contacted a specialist to see if it would be possible, but somehow it all got forgotten. When I mention this to Dr J, he shakes his head. 'The process of freezing and defrosting sperm makes it pretty sluggish and, anyway, with ICSI, they often have to "hit the sperm on the head" in order to make it less lively, so that they are be able to put it where they want it.'

Then he smiles and waves his hand. 'But never mind this now, go home and be with your family. Go and enjoy your new baby.' He does have a point.

In the evening, I visit an acupuncturist Penny has found who is also a practising GP with experience of spinal injury, and who is interested in the treatment of chronic pain. He has worked with a German doctor who is conducting extensive studies into the pain matrix (how pain is transmitted around the nervous system), which have revealed that the way that pain is transmitted is much more complex than previously thought, through research with amputees with phantom-limb conditions, which is pretty much the same as the neurogenic pain I feel in my legs. The work has revealed that the brain can become sensitised to pain, so instead of switching off the response to the pain signal, the brain expects it, which in turn makes it more receptive, and contributes to the pain becoming chronic.

The best course of action is to intervene as early as possible to prevent the pain becoming 'hard-wired', and thus chronic. The best intervention seems to be a multidisciplinary approach, with a combination of neuropharmacology (drugs), acupuncture (needles), physiotherapy (torture) and cognitive behavioral therapy (mind-bending). The positive in all of this is that I seem to be tackling the pain with the right tools. It still bloody hurts, but it's early days yet. Unfortunately, the acupuncturist is unable to work on my lumbar region, as the two huge lumps of metal that protrude make it pretty much impossible to insert a needle anywhere near them. He does some more general, endorphin-releasing pain-management stuff, which is followed by two nights of pain, and then a really bad day.

The day starts really well, as I push myself up to the town centre with Penny's best friend Steph, who is over for a visit from Australia. The trip feels good psychologically – being out with a friend, nipping up to the shops together. All very normal, except that I start to feel acute neuropathic pain in both legs that gets so uncomfortable by the time I am on the home straight that I am wincing and swearing through gritted teeth at my old nemesis, Spike, and once home I have to drop a temazepam and retire to bed. The result of this week of pain is to further muddy the waters as to how much is brought on by physical activity, and how much is just random nastiness.

As I lie drifting in a haze of pain and medication, my mind turns to all the adjustments that I am forced to make. Most people spend most of their time living in something of a comfort zone. Occasionally we may choose to leave it, such as a ride on a rollercoaster, any sport with endurance or an adren-alin-rush involved, or even leaving creature comforts behind for a camping trip. At other times we may be pulled from it, for instance if we are the butt of a joke, embarrassed in front of people. Or perhaps we are involved in a car accident. After my injury, I find that my comfort zone has been greatly reduced, to the point that I have to leave it whenever I am forced to confront a physical barrier, such as a kerb or some steps. So I have to push myself to be more resilient and less self-conscious as I learn new skills that enable me to be more independent. This means making a complete mess of trying to get up a kerb, or having to change plans when it is apparent that there is a physical obstruction. The inevitable instinct is to play the 'well, I didn't want to go in there, anyway' game. I don't know if this is a natural reaction or the result of my heightened desire for independence.

On the social niceties front, during my rehabilitation I found myself receiving hugs and embraces from some visitors who had not normally hugged before. Some people I've always hugged, and some not, but this universal 'hugness' is perhaps a good indicator of how such a profound and major event as my accident makes social discomforts and awkwardness such as whether or not to hug seem rather trivial. However, now I am out and getting on with my life, there are some people who have abandoned the hug, perhaps out of awkwardness as the wheelchair–biped interaction can sometimes be difficult. But perhaps this is a sign, a benchmark in my recovery, that people feel comfortable enough now to revert to old awkwardness.

We finally get to pick up the new wheelchair. A long wait, but it's definitely a huge improvement. I recommend to the wheelchair service that they take my old chair out the back and shoot it, but they are planning to give it a once-over, and hand it on to some other poor sucker. At last, I have the new wheels. Suddenly I'm sitting up straight, instead of rolling around like I'm on a sun lounger. I can also get around the flat without hitting every doorframe, and having to leave the bathroom to turn around in order to get from the toilet to the shower.

After only two days in the new wheelchair my pain levels improve noticeably. The only down side is that the backrest still presses against the large lump of metal that resides in my back, so by the end of the day I feel as if I've been at the wrong end of a golf-driving range, but there is no doubt that in my overall levels of neuro and muscular pain I feel a marked improvement. The psychological effect is tremendous, too. I feel upright, alert and almost – well, to be honest – rather proud of my new toy. My appearance is closer to a comfortable self-image of 'wheelchair user'.

In the way that change seems to come in clusters, the same week that I get my new wheels we find out about a charity called Aspire, which provides equipment and opportunities for people with spinal-cord injury. We hadn't really heard much about it before, because it is based at 'the other place', by which I mean Stanmore, the spinal unit in west London that was another possible when the Royal London was looking for a spinal unit to send me to. Stanmore only has around twenty beds, compared to the hundred or so at Stoke Mandeville, and although it is a national charity, Aspire has its headquarters at Stanmore, as well as sports facilities, including a pool and gym.

Aspire has identified the problem encountered by people who have suffered a spinal-cord injury and have a home to return to eventually, but who have interim housing needs because of the severe shortage of accessible housing throughout the UK. London is particularly bad, and it is here that Aspire has most places, although it is expanding its housing programme. The housing we are told about is in Edgware, which is only just in London if you live in Hackney, but right in the heart of the seething metropolis if you live in Aylesbury. There is a bunga-low available that is provided for rent by the Guinness Trust Housing Association in conjunction with Aspire. Alarmingly, it was renovated by *Challenge Anneka* in the early 1990s, and I'm not sure if the transition in benefactors from Jimmy Savile to Anneka Rice is up, down or sideways. All I know is that both have been known for their awful taste in sportswear and I'm not sure why that unnerves me even more, but it does, somehow.

The bungalows are fully accessible (even the kitchen, hurrah!), and living there would put us in range of the odd weekday evening visit, and give us the chance to go out and about to test the wheelchair accessibility of many of our friends' homes. I am excited at the possibility of feeling more in touch with our old life.

18

Penny continues to cope admirably on sleep in one- or two-hour instalments, with Rosalie being a bit on the grizzly side. Every seasoned parent we talk to says it all tends to peak at three months, so we're past the halfway stage. Every seasoned parent doesn't say things like this *before* you have a baby. Then again, maybe you just don't listen before you have a baby, which is why you become boring to all your friends who don't have a baby after you've had a baby, when all you do is talk about how it tends to peak at three months. And you smell vaguely of sick.

Rosalie, meanwhile, becomes more alert, smiley and gurgly with every day, and she's big enough to go into a bedside cot, which enables us to put up a mobile or two. I thought these would soothe her to sleep, but all the noise, colour and movement end up making her rather overstimulated, with her legs pumping like a beatnik's hands on the bongos, and her eyes wide in wonderment. I begin to worry that we won't be able to compete for her attention without swinging from the light fittings singing 'Old MacDonald'.

In more reflective moments, I find myself thinking of all the things I wanted to be when I grow up. I also think about all the things that I have tried and thought, 'I'd like to do *this* for a living.' Funnily enough, being a paraplegic wasn't on either list. I feel like it's a full-time job, and something that forces the striking-off of most things from both lists.

I also think about the effect the changes to my physiognomy might have, especially in terms of hormone production. I remember reading that ejaculation actually increases the production of testosterone (in case you are wondering, it was in the context of sporting performance and whether abstaining from sex before a game had any effect on a player's hormone levels). This makes me wonder whether not being able to ejaculate has had an effect on my testosterone levels. I have been thinking a lot about this, as I seem to have developed something akin to acne on my forehead. Either that or the lumps on my head are the first signs of a hormonally induced sprouting of antlers, and I should expect to be clashing with the nearest hat-stand by the end of the week.

My sexual appetite is different, partly because my partner has just had a child, but also because it is not so 'climax driven'. I know that sounds like such wank, and I do miss having orgasms as much as walking, running or climbing, but there is a different process that has always been there, which now comes centre stage (oh, do stop it, that's not what I meant). The mental processes, the urge, the sensory pleasure of intimate contact, all these things are there. If anything, these feelings are stronger, more intense, but there is no final satiation. I remember watching a video in the sexuality and fertility lecture during my rehabilitation. All the people interviewed spoke very openly about their sexual experiences since injury. They talked about the importance of emptying your bladder and bowels before, and how things took a little more planning. They laughed and joked about falling off the bed and peculiar positions that sometimes have to be assumed, and they all said that after a period of adjustment, they enjoyed sex as much now as they ever did. There was mention of injections to get an erection, something that I had heard mentioned before, but without detail. That was it, as far as sex was concerned.

All they talked about after that was adjusting to spinal-cord injury, and the most memorable thing for me was that they all said that it took them about two years to come to terms with. I take comfort from this, because it means that I have some breathing space. It makes me feel more confident that things will get better with time. I fully expect to have some kind of epiphany on 1 April 2007, when I will become a qualified paraplegic. Maybe with a small badge, or a hat or something, I don't know.

Another great resource offered by the National Spinal Injuries Centre is something called SPOP (SPinal Out Patients). This is where patients go to attend outpatients appointments for a review, or to seek help for any medical problems they may be experiencing. Among the support that SPOP offers is advice and help on sexuality and fertility, and I go in to see one of the nurses who specialises in this area. We discuss many issues, from getting an erection to having a baby. Fortunately, I am quite happy to talk about any and every topic, so I don't feel uncomfortable.

Some patients with higher-level injuries do get what's called a reflex erection, which means that although they can't feel it, localised stimulation can cause an erection using pretty much the same circuit that can cause spasm. The advice given is to 'have a play in the shower' to see what happens. In my case, nothing, but at least my legs stay where I put them, rather than dancing off all over the bathroom.

To be fair, I do get the odd 'semi', but it's nothing you could work with, as it were, and it's also unpredictable. The left-testicle sensation thing gives me some sort of (dis)comfort, as it means that there are at least a couple of nerve pathways still connected, but I must confess to being keen to try anything that might 'stiffen my resolve'.

The injection method involves exactly that: an injection directly into the penis, of a drug that produces a hard erection that can last for one to two hours. I must confess that I am reluctant to start shoving needles into my cock just from a point of principle, although I know I won't feel it. To be honest, I could imagine this being a bit of a passion-killer, rather akin to pulling out a couple of resuscitation paddles and yelling, 'CLEAR!' before shocking the poor little fellow into life.

Another method is to take Viagra or a similar product, but the recommended course is to take it for the first time in the outpatients department in case it causes some kind of autonomic response. Unlikely in my case, as this is more of an issue for higher-level lesions, generally above T5/T6. For them, anything that would have been painful, uncomfortable, or physically irritating before injury has the potential to cause autonomic dysreflexia. This triggers a fight-or-flight response, increased heart rate, constriction of the vascular system, etc. Trouble is, the signal to say everything's OK doesn't get through, and so the heart rate and blood pressure can increase until it results in intracranial haemorrhage, or 'head exploding'. If someone starts having this response then it is extremely important that they get medication to reduce their blood pressure. This is a complication that I am thankfully spared, but I can understand the caution as far as Viagra is concerned. The thing is, I don't know if I want to fill my system with Viagra, especially not in the spinal unit.

There is another option … a vacuum pump can produce an erection that, for most men, is sufficient for intercourse. The penis is placed in a vacuum cylinder and air is pumped out of the cylinder, causing blood to be drawn into the erectile tissues. The erection is maintained by placing a constriction ring around the base of the penis. It is important to remove the ring after intercourse to avoid prolonged pressure and the risk of sores.

And finally, there is surgical implantation. This is often the last treatment option because it requires a permanent penile prosthesis. The procedure involves inserting an implant directly into the erectile tissues to obtain an erection. Three types of implants are available: semi-rigid or malleable rods, fully inflatable devices, and self-contained unit implants. Obviously I'm quoting a bit here, but, ding dong! Fully inflatable, eh? With what, helium? Cue several gags about oral sex and high-pitched voices.

I tell Penny about the different options.

'It's not very … well, erotic, is it?'

She has a point.

'I'm not about to start injecting myself in the penis if I can help it, and there's no way anyone's building me a bionic cock, either.'

She is relieved, but then asks, 'Unless it could enable you to walk in some way?'

I wince, and place a protective hand in my lap. 'You have no idea the level of mental pain and anguish I just suffered in just imagining such a thing.'

I opt for the pump, as it seems the least intrusive, although probably only a tad less of a passion killer than the injection. I am also slightly nervous after reading the literature, and watching the accompanying DVD made by the manufacturer, which tells me I'm not just receiving a tube and a pump. Oh no. Now I am joining the ErecAid™ community. I'm not exactly sure whether using a vacuum pump and a rubber band to get an erection provides enough social glue to create a community, but the DVD shows men in white coats waiting to answer calls to 1-800-STIFFY or whatever the helpline number was. I suspect that these same people field the calls of everyone from the flaccid masses to users of prosthetic limbs and anyone else who needs to feel that there is someone in a white coat who lives for answering their queries about quasi-medical products and accessories. I am issued with the pumpenhausen (as I have named it, for no particular reason) on prescription. Hurrah again for the NHS. I decide to practise on my own, just to make sure that the results aren't totally scary. Like all the blood rushes to my penis and my head implodes, or something.

19

13 October 2005
Subject: Basketballs, burns and bungalows

You should have seen me. Squealing down the basketball court at top speed, turning this way and that and stopping on a sixpence. Now all I've got to do is work out how to pick up the ball, pass and shoot, and I'll have it cracked. I'm also looking for funding for my latest film project, *Paraplegics Can't Jump*. I'm going to give basketball another go this week, after which I may be totally fed up at not having mastered it in the first couple of attempts, and I won't mention it again.

The new chair is a definite improvement. I have also added some tarty front wheels that flash like a mobile disco when I'm on the move. All I need is some huge speakers, and I can blast out 'Hi Ho Silver Lining' and do the wedding-reception circuit.

We went to see the interim accommodation in Edgware on Tuesday, and we've decided to take it. It will put us nearer to home when the work eventually starts on the flat, which I think is important. It also has the advantage of being near to Stanmore spinal unit, which has a gym with personal trainers experienced in working with people with spinal-cord injury, and a pool with a ramp down into it (waterproof wheelchairs are provided). There is also a wheelchair basketball team that plays there.

Enough. My daughter has expressed a desire to drool all over my shirt, and I can't resist such an offer for long.

The accommodation in Edgware is in need of redecoration and a seriously good clean, but we conclude that we will be able to make a go of things there and it feels like time to move on. The lease is coming up on the Aylesbury flat, and we also feel that it's time to let go of the hand provided by the generous support of our anonymous friends who have helped so much by paying the rent on the place. So we pack up the ridiculous amounts of stuff that we have accumulated in our exile, and prepare to move. I freely confess to having a music addiction, but my prolonged incapacity has made it worse, and it has been fuelled by internet purchasing of CDs, not to mention downloads. I speculate as to whether I can get some kind of government support to wean me off, but I conclude that I would rather be a user than someone who says, 'Yeah, well, I started on vinyl, didn't I? But that was just a gateway format, and as soon as CDs were invented, I was hooked. Off the needle and onto the laser. And then I was mixing it with MP3s, and in no time I was listening to two or three compilations before lunch, and downloading the really heavy stuff like theme tunes to obscure children's programmes. I'm clean now, though. Just the odd audiobook or motivational CD on addiction.'

Books on the other hand … I enjoy reading, and I've certainly bought my fair share, but while I was in hospital, I was given 32 books. I read three.

Retail therapy has become a big part of our life, as there's naff all else to do in Aylesbury, especially if you have a little baby. We do have a thrilling adventure when we take a trip to the Job Centre or, rather, Job Centre Plus! I'm not sure what makes a Job Centre into a Job Centre Plus, as it still looks like a Job Centre to my untrained eye. Obviously we aren't there for me to find a job, but rather to sort out the paperwork for some of my benefits. The staff are pretty helpful, but for me, the highlight of the visit comes when one of the advisers starts talking to me, pauses and, while sitting down, says, 'I'm just sitting down so that I can put myself at eye level to you.'

This is obviously the result of some kind of disability-awareness training, but I feel like saying, 'It doesn't count if you say it out loud while you're doing it.' But I haven't the heart to, as her body language and demeanour is the now familiar 'I'll make a big effort to make you feel normal', in which the nervous protagonist fusses and flaps as they try desperately to remember what it is they are supposed to do or not do.

And so, back to Stoke Mandeville for a fitting for my callipers, which have arrived from the factory, all black steel and leather. I finally have the exoskeleton my friend predicted back in the first week after my accident. This does make them sound a bit more sexy than they actually are, being less Mad Max and more reminiscent of the polio charity box kid that used to stand in shop doorways in the 1960s and 70s. They have reinforced, wide straps around my thighs, attached to steel bars that go down the side of each leg and terminate in pins that lock into the sides of the heel on specially adapted shoes. As well as these dashing sartorial accessories, I have been given a date to return to the spinal unit for two weeks of assessment and calliper training. I seem to have passed the first test, that of demonstrating sufficient bloody-mindedness and persistence.

I am back at the spinal unit again a few days later, this time to meet up with some people from the Shepherd Centre, a spinal unit in Georgia, USA, who have come over to share experiences between different spinal units around the world. The Shepherd Centre is CARF accredited. CARF stands for Commission on Accreditation of Rehabilitation Facilities, which is an international scheme designed to make sure that the rehabilitation programme is focused on the needs of the patient, in order to ensure the best possible outcome.

The idea is that every part of your treatment from injury to discharge should be treated as part of your rehabilitation, so, for example, you will be interviewed early on to find out what your normal habits were before you were injured, such as bowel function, waking times and so on, and your rehabilitation will reflect this as much as possible, so that you don't have to get used to the hospital programme first before having to adjust again when you are discharged. Stoke Mandeville is working towards becoming accredited, with a great deal of encouragement from the Spinal Injuries Association.

While I am at the hospital, I receive news that my calliper training begins on 5 December, when I'll be back in Stoke Mandeville for two weeks. I have to go back as an in-patient, and spend at least one night in three in the hospital ('bed blocking', as it's widely known) because there is a funding shortfall that means physiotherapy services for outpatients have been suspended. The training itself involves about an hour and a half each day, and is likely to be pretty painful, in the way that my original rehab was. And I'm not as strong as I was when I left the hospital, as all I've done for the last three months is sit on my arse eating pies, and changing the odd nappy.

Unfortunately, the news from Hackney is less positive, as the grant application has to be put on hold while we wait to hear if we need planning permission to move the rear access. All very tedious, as a planning application would add another eight weeks to an already indeterminate timescale.

In one of my final acts as an Aylesbury resident, I have another go at basketball. I manage to 'shoot a couple of hoops' (I even know the lingo and everything!) in practice, buoying my confidence, and allowing me the absurd delusion that I could be some kind of 'natural'. However, when it comes to the game at the end of the session, I start to work out more of what's going on around me, and it dawns on me that my first effort had involved me whizzing around in blissful ignorance, getting in everyone's way like a dog on a football pitch. Ah, the more you learn, the more you realise how little you actually know.

The basketball experience does make me feel more confident of my wheelchair skills. I get the tools out and tweak the chair a bit (the only surprise is that it's taken me this long to get around to fiddling with it), and I manage to make it more responsive by making it more 'tippy'. Success! The next morning I manage to fall out of the back of it in a battle with my old nemesis 'The Front Door' (sounds like the name of a crap wrestler). Nothing broken except my pride and, luckily, the only spectators on this occasion are the two girls in my life, and one of them is busy trying to fit the whole of her blanket into her mouth (Rosalie, obviously!), while the other just laughs. It feels like I have passed a benchmark as a wheelchair user, and yet again I am disappointed to find that there isn't even so much as a proficiency badge for me to sew onto the upholstery.

20

We get the keys to the Edgware bungalow (another dodgy wrestler?) and the day of the move is upon us in no time. I try to make myself as useful as possible, putting things in boxes that I am then unable to lift. It is frustrating to be on the receiving end of the kind of help that I have been able to offer and frequently been asked to provide for so many people for so many years, that of fetching and carrying. Yet, here I am, useless except for childminding, pointing at stuff and making smart-arsed observations on the way other people are doing things. Again, I must confess that the latter is a long-developed habit that has remained unchanged, except for the added thrill of knowing that people can no longer say to me, 'If you're so fucking clever, you show us how to do it then!'

My feeling of uselessness is compounded when we go back to clean the flat in Aylesbury, and I wrestle with the vacuum cleaner and the box from which it has recently been freed, and into which it refuses to return. Although I recognise the now familiar wheelchair-based frustration, when the box finally splits, I lose it. And then my anger spills over and ... I try to kick the box. Of course, this makes me feel a whole lot better. But it is a milestone of sorts, this being the first time since the accident that I have unconsciously tried to use my legs.

Our new home is a 1930s bungalow, with somewhat oddly proportioned rooms, half-filled with a mixture of specialist furniture and a rather oversized three-piece suite. We manage to cram the garden shed and the garage with the suite and a very expensive-looking computer table, all attachments and doohickies designed to enable even the most profoundly disabled tetraplegic to be able to use a computer.

The one piece of 'adaptive' equipment that we leave in place is an enormous height-adjustable bed with a memory-foam mattress some eight inches thick. I sit on it with Rosalie to try and stay out of the way during the move, and we play with the buttons, folding the bed almost in half, and then raising it up until it feels like we are inches from the ceiling. Rosalie loves this, breaking into fits of giggling and cooing as we are raised, dropped, folded and flattened on an enormous slab of marshmallow.

The road we have moved into is packed full of bungalows of a similar age, most of which have black taxis parked on the drive of an evening, but between two of the houses there is a 'corridor' of green space, two rows of oak trees making an avenue that runs down the hill to a park with a pond and a small brook. Once again, London surprises me with its capacity to produce these open spaces in the middle of a densely populated suburb. There is quite a hill involved, however, and the first time we go for a 'walk' in the park is no walk in the park. The hill back up is very punishing, especially as it gets quite a lot steeper near the top. I confirm to myself a suspicion that I have held for a while, that I am in worse shape than I was when I left the spinal unit, where I had daily physiotherapy, weekly swims and weight training. I have a half-baked idea that I should do this hill every day as a way of getting fitter, but this thought is swiftly abandoned after the general discomfort of the push and what it does to my neuropathic pain an hour or so later.

There is another side effect of the hill-climbing effort that is rather more worrying. I develop a heat rash and a very unpleasant prickly itchy feeling. It is probably caused by over-heating with the effort of pushing up such a steep hill with too much clothing on, and on a rather muggy day, but the problem of temperature regulation is yet another issue that people with SCI have to deal with.

In my case, as with similar injuries, I no longer sweat

below the level of injury because the signals that cause this temperature-regulation process to take place are no longer able to get through. The result is that only half of my body is attempting to regulate temperature, and the most obvious side effect of this shortcoming is the prickly feeling. This is rather a concern to me, especially as we would like to try living in Australia at some point in the future. I have to remind myself that there are already many people with spinal-cord injury living in Australia, so it must be manageable, but to have such a direct symptom that impedes physical effort is extremely frustrating.

It doesn't take long for a new routine to be established. I get free membership for the Aspire gym and swimming pool at Stanmore, and I start with enthusiasm. I have stayed in touch with Justin, the man with good posture whom we met at the hospital, and we meet up at the gym and compare our different experiences after leaving hospital.

Justin was injured in a motorcycle accident. He was in his late twenties, owned his own flat and worked for a large public-transport company based in London. He was knocked off his bike when a driver turned behind him, and clipped the back of his bike, causing him to lose control and hit a lamppost before breaking his back on a garden wall. Justin received no compensation (although the car driver was compensated for the post-traumatic stress that he suffered in paralysing Justin), and lost his job. His union also managed to miss the deadline to apply for an industrial tribunal to appeal against unfair dismissal.

So he gradually used up his savings, money he had put by throughout his twenties by not going out all the time having fun with his mates or buying a flashy car. His game plan was to save hard and invest the money so that by the time he was 30 he would already have built a good financial future and could then get on with the serious business of having fun. By the time he was 30, he was paralysed from the waist down.

Justin is a good example of how quickly and easily spinal-cord injury can dismantle someone's life. Having a sense of losing mental images and dreams of one's life ahead can also be accompanied by a very real practical loss of money, property, and in some cases even family. I do know of people whose relationships have not been able to withstand the trauma of trying to come to terms with SCI. It really is like being hit by a freight train. After the shock and the immediate danger, you have to look around you and see what is left of your life. Justin has had the determination to get his life back together and look after himself, stay fit, and even go to college. Many people never really get past the shock of loss.

I have been lucky. While I will freely admit to being determined – although that usually manifests itself as bloody-mindedness, especially if it means I can snap at people who offer me help – what really keeps me pushing on is the close support of family and friends. But there are times when I just don't have the energy to fight any more. Times when I just want a day off, especially from the pain. Sometimes this relentless pain and discomfort leads to me thinking very dark thoughts.

In some ways, suicide can seem like a brave decision. By this, I don't mean 'throwing yourself on the grenade' type of suicide, but more the 'not going on' type. I find myself thinking about suicide as a concept when I am in a lot of pain and all I can see is a lot of pain in the future. I don't consider suicide as a participation exercise, primarily because there are people I love and I would never dream of reducing the time I get to be with them, let alone inflicting my loss upon their lives, but also because I would be too scared to take my own life. This fear can be hard, because it means that in my darkest hours, I cannot retreat into idle fantasy to make me feel a bit of relief. Suicide seems brave in that it is an action, a deliberate act. Just living with spinal-cord injury doesn't make me brave. I can do this by doing nothing, just by existing. I am brave, though. Fucking brave. You betcha.

Then Rosalie cuts herself reaching for a stick in the back garden. It's a tiny little cut, but I see her blood for the first time, and the surge of upset and protectiveness makes me feel sick. I have had Rosalie in my life for four months. I am 37, and I think of my parents seeing me strapped to a backboard, in a neck brace, or in tears despite all the morphine I've been shot full of because I'm so terrified. Suddenly all the self-indulgent and abstract thoughts of suicide seem incredibly selfish.

Despite this sense of responsibility, other things come into focus on the dark days, as if the depression causes clarity of thought. One night, as well as Spike, I feel an additional jolt from the realisation that this is permanent. Even if there are sufficient advances in medicine to enable surgery to regain feeling and movement, I doubt that I will get back much more than an ability to shuffle along with crutches or a frame, at best. And this is what I hope to be able to achieve with callipers. All the talk of stem-cell therapies is only really a significant hope for incomplete injuries.

In another moment of clarity I realise that the sinking, 'blue' feeling that tempers much of my day-to-day experience is actually the same feeling as the sense of utter screaming panic that I felt for the first three weeks after the accident. All that has happened is that I have somehow learned how to 'live with it', in other words I am able to suppress it sufficiently to be able to function.

So, I've died and, like all devout atheists, I go straight down to hell to suffer damnation for all eternity. As the fiery daemons are busily nailing me to a pentangle or whatever, I start to scream at the overwhelming horror of my fate, stretching out for all eternity, when I notice the man nailed up next to me on the adjoining plot of nastiness, and he looks quite calm. Bored, even. He smiles politely.

'How can you be so calm?' I cry. 'Is this not the worst torment for all eternity?'

'Yeah,' says he. 'But you adjust.'

Of course, it's not just pain that triggers this kind of introspective melancholy. Sometimes it's as obvious as a song on the radio. One afternoon, Dobie Gray's 'Out On The Floor' comes on, and suddenly I'm thinking back to all-nighters at the 100 Club. The idea of dancing is a difficult one to deal with, as it is the embodiment of the whole concept of spontaneous movement, the loss that I feel most sharply.

There are other occasions when I find it difficult to fully immerse myself in films, books or music when certain 'tragedies' or causes of heartbreak just seem so trivial by comparison to what I have to deal with every waking moment.

Other causes for an emotional crash can be cumulative. Sometimes I skirt around the whole issue in order to function and stay relatively cheerful. Only what happens is that I almost convince myself that there's a way around, and when I remember that there isn't I come down very hard. I feel emasculated, vulnerable and dependent. But pain is the most common trigger for dark thoughts, and the least predictable. The randomness is very demoralising. Rather than good day, bad day, it seems to be good week, bad week, and I am unable to link cause and effect so I have to just plough on and stay as active as I can on any given day.

21

A new distraction arrives in the form of a shiny new car, a Renault Kangoo. On the day of collection we have hand controls fitted, thanks to my dad, who has been very enthusiastic about the whole car thing. I think he has been pleased to have something practical and positive to do, as there has been a real shortage of things that people can actually do to help.

So now I have wheels. I am mobile, the world is my oyster, etc. It feels wonderful to have such a dramatic increase in my range, no longer having to rely on other people to drive me around. I go up to the pool for a swim on one day, and take myself to the gym on the next. With all the car use, I have to learn a new skill, that of dismantling a wheelchair and getting it into the car. I had some instruction in this at Stoke, where they have a car body in the archery gym to practise in.

The days pass, and I listen in wonder as Rosalie gets more and more vocal each day with an expanding vocabulary of screams, squeals and giggles. Penny says she's worried that Rosalie has a lisp, and then realises that of course she'd have a lisp, as she has no teeth. I'm not even sure how she could hear a lisp, as there's no way of knowing what sound Rosalie is trying to make. If she says 'Ga ga ga,' should we worry that she has a stutter?

And so to calliper training. After an emotional farewell to Penny and Rosalie, I leave London for two weeks of training in the spinal unit at the beginning of December, where I quickly realise that this skill will take a while to master. If I hope to get some further training at Stoke Mandeville in the future, I have to convince them of my determination all the way down the line, especially as it is a damn fool thing to do in the first place.

Yes, it is good for my bone density and circulation, but it does put a lot of strain on the shoulders.

Being back in the hospital is a bittersweet experience. Even St Joseph's ward feels very institutional. It all serves as a reminder of just how far I have come, and how much I have learned since my discharge from hospital. The first two nights in the unit are dominated by particularly bad pain in my legs, triggered by the excessive stretch involved in standing in callipers for a couple of hours each day. I dose myself with the usual Z to try and knock myself out, but I end up spending several hours tossing and turning, in a state of semi-conscious agony. And I miss Penny and Rosalie extremely. It is my first time away from them since Rosalie was born, and I am struck by a sudden understanding of the parent–child bond, even when the child involved is only four months old.

On the third afternoon, I race home after the physiotherapy session to spend the night in the arms/under the dribble of my loving family. Rosalie greets me with a smile so warm that it guarantees my undying loyalty for at least thirteen years, and I wonder what the hell I'm doing going away in the first place.

I return to Stoke and manage to get a session with Sue Edwards, doyenne of the world of neuro-physiotherapy, who recommends that I move out of the parallel bars and start trying to do more with a walking frame. She also changes the technique I am using, and encourages me to take more risks. It makes me realise that what I am trying to do is inherently risky, and certainly outside of the 'risk assessment' procedures that exist in the physiotherapy world as much as in any workplace. Spinal physios have to undertake 'manual handling' that is very demanding and awkward, as much of it involves a transition from reliance on help to independence for the patient. There is a lot of what to the untrained eye looks like all-in wrestling, but is in fact the patient and physio trying to untangle themselves rather than get the upper hand (or leg).

Along with Sue's advice, we also get advice from a number of other, more senior staff. I say 'we' because I sense that the learning process involves both Kara, the physiotherapist I am working with, and me. It is not that she is inexperienced, but there are very few patients with my level of injury that go on to try and walk in callipers – certainly fewer than there used to be – and the variety of different techniques involved seem almost never-ending, especially as the subtlest of changes in positioning can have a massive effect on whether I am able to stay upright, let alone propel myself in a controlled fashion.

The time passes pretty quickly with me doing the drive to and from Edgware several times, making slow progress in the callipers, and realising that they look a whole lot better under my clothes rather than over, which means that a considerable proportion of each day involves me lying on my hospital bed, wrestling with a tangled mass of steel, leather, Velcro and tracksuit.

Once I'm back, we get on with planning Christmas, going on trips to Brent Cross shopping centre, or the local shops in Edgware, visiting friends, or having people over for tea and cakes. Just days before Christmas, we receive an early present with news from Hackney Council that we have been awarded the full disabled facilities grant, which means we're halfway to getting the money together, so all we are waiting for is planning permission. At last it feels like things are moving towards getting back to where we started.

We spend Christmas day with my parents in Finsbury Park, where I am able to access the large kitchen/dining room via a pair of wooden ramps that Eugene has constructed down the side of the house. I go through the garden before re-entering the house through the French doors at the back. Toilet facilities consist of me finding a corner, turning my back and fiddling around with a catheter. My family have to take it in turns to carry a bag of my wee through the house and up to the toilet, before trying to empty it without getting it everywhere. Now that emptying my bladder is such a process, I prefer wine to beer, as the volume of fluid compared to its 'mood altering' qualities make wine lower maintenance.

In the evening we check into a hotel in Islington so that we don't have to face the journey back to Edgware. It felt like such a luxury when we booked it, but it turns out to be rather anonymous, although we have a couple of quiet drinks with some friends in our room as Rosalie gets more and more restless, and after our guests leave we end up sitting in silence in the dark, sucking a bag of crisps and drinking wine from paper cups while she fusses and farts and grunts and snores in the travel cot in the corner of the room. Our first Christmas as parents, and already I can see the focus has shifted inexorably onto the new generation.

22

10 January 2006
Subject: So this is Christmas ...

And what have you done? Well, I'VE fallen out of a tree, been paralysed, spent four months in hospital, become a dad, moved house (twice), been given a new wheel-chair, a new car (and a new set of callipers), and been overwhelmed by the support and generosity of family and friends.

I also became a paraplegic, although there was no in-vestiture ceremony, and I didn't even get a certificate.

And, yes I know it is not Christmas any more, but it was such a good intro, and it has taken me this long to get back to writing this message, so please accept my apologies.

Christmas was a quiet affair, with a lovely calm day, but we missed my brother Chris, his partner Sarah, their two daughters (and their dog) charging around, chasing sticks (the dog, mainly). I found myself thinking about future Christmas celebrations as Rosalie gets older and discovers the magic of Christmas, only to have it smashed by her cynical git of a father, who is hardly about to dress as Santa as it would be a bit of a giveaway, all things con-sidered.

New Year was ushered in with our friends Matthew, Kirsten and their daughter Evelyn, who is eighteen months old and a study in perpetual motion (as all children are at that age) and has a wonderful line in unintelligible almost-speak. I am increasingly aware of the strange look in the eye of parents as they talk to you, while simultaneously trying to watch their nipper busily sticking everything in the bin, the DVD player, or up their nose. I also have the added joy of watching them trying to take my wheelchair apart and it won't be long before one of the little cherubs succeeds, and I take off, only to leave a pile of wheels, brakes and dignity behind.

Right, I'm off to be chewed and slobbered over by our daughter. Teeth may be on the horizon ...

New Year's resolutions? It's not something that I normally do, but on this occasion, and a few days late, I come up with one. I decide that I shall master the art of bum-shuffling. In particular, bum-shuffling up and down stairs. This resolution is made following the first night of a trip to stay at my father's, or more accurately, a stay at a B&B near to my father's, as my dad's place is on two floors with the bathrooms and all the bedrooms on the first floor. The B&B is 'wheelchair accessible', except that it is extremely difficult to get the door closed with the twin beds, a cot and a wheelchair in the room, and the fold-down shower seat in the wheel-in shower is on the opposite wall from the taps and nozzle, thus making a solo shower impossible for me. This, combined with the churning of the refrigeration unit in the cold room next door and the feeling of anonymity, makes me determined to master the technique required to overcome stairs so that I may reduce the number of places that are off-limits.

While I was at the spinal unit, I did have one session on the stairs. There is a special cushion available that has a strap to go around the waist and one for each thigh, thus protecting the wearer's bony arse from damage. Having struggled into this thing, I got out of the chair and onto the first step. I was instructed on the official technique, which involves the same principle as any transfer, that of pointing your head in the opposite place to where you want your backside to go. However, when this method is applied to stair-climbing, it meant sitting on a flight of stairs, putting my hands on the step behind my back and shoving my head between my legs, pointing face down the staircase. However hard I tried, my self-preservation instinct kicked in and refused the challenge. When I pointed this out to the physio at the time, she tried it herself and did concede that it was pretty scary, even for an able-bodied person, let alone for someone who feels totally top heavy and precariously balanced at the best of times. I decided then that I would come back to this particular 'challenge' at a later date.

That later date arrives, and I go online to find someone who stocks the strap-on (cushion, obviously), only to find that the one that I used in the hospital is no longer being sold in the UK as the manufacturer is American, and has decided that going for the CE mark required to sell the product in Europe wasn't worth the effort. Fortunately, there is an alternative in the shape of a Dutch company that makes a similar product called the Academy All-Rounder, the main difference being that this one has no gel in it. Instead it is ingeniously filled with small, pyramid-shaped separate air pockets, known as tea bags because of their passing resemblance to a certain well-known pyramid-shaped tea bag. These air pockets are made of a slippery nylon fabric, which means they slide effortlessly against each other, thus spreading the weight of the wearer evenly around, and protecting any bony bits from damage.

There is another difference in my latest attempt at stair-climbing. Penny discovers a website called Crip College, belonging to a Canadian, Christian Bagg, a T8 who was injured snowboarding, and even has a clip of the accident on the site. More valuable and less shudder-inducing are 'tricks of the trade', which include clips of himself and others showing ways of getting up and down kerbs, flights of stairs, getting in and out of the wheelchair, going up and down ramps, even taking a wheel off while staying in the chair. There are also a couple of clips showing a different technique for going up and down stairs, one that looks a lot less terrifying, and one that I find actually works rather well.

This is a very good demonstration of how useful the internet can be when you are disabled. Trying to find specialist equipment may be disheartening at first, as the first sites you hit are usually selling walk-in baths and incontinence pyjamas. But after about ten minutes, I generally find something of use, and then I think how hard it must have been to find this kind of stuff before the www.

The other great resource to be found online is advice and information from other people who are tackling similar difficulties in their everyday experience. There are some excellent forums for disseminating information as well as support. Often people who hit these sites are friends or relatives of people who have just been injured and who are struggling to understand what has happened and want to be of help.

So, with practice first on the four steps down to the garden, I conquer stairs with some difficulty, in the way that everything I try these days turns out to be more difficult than I think it will be. But stairs can be done, and knowing this makes me feel freer somehow. If I need to, I can get up them without being carried in the chair by a bunch of enthusiastic but untrained volunteers. This has been the alternative in the past and, to be frank, it was pretty terrifying. Now I have the choice to go it alone, providing there's someone to bring the chair, or I have a rope to attach to it to drag it up/lower it down the stairs.

Still, as per usual, for every little feeling of independence gained, there is a reminder of my limitations. I head off to meet up with friends at a 'gastro-pub' in Islington one afternoon. The friend who booked the place phoned me the day before to say that, although the listing in a restaurant guide says that the pub has a disabled toilet, when she phoned them, they told her that they didn't. She asked me if this was a problem, or would it be OK if I went to her place first to use the toilet. I said that was fine, and I do feel genuinely pleased that she has considered me in this way, but on arrival I decide that I am going to be a bit more fussy from now on. The pub has a step up, a two-part door with one part bolted, and no disabled toilet. I think that that's pretty poor for a venue that probably has a very healthy turnover and is listed as being accessible.

The whole afternoon leaves me feeling pretty down, as once more the similarities to my old life merely serve to highlight the differences. I would like to be able to go out with friends without having my bladder capacity as a time constraint. I have run out of enthusiasm for making do. I started out with an attitude of defiant determination that my disability would not exclude me from anywhere, but I have run out of steam. I just want to feel 'normal', and be able to go out for lunch and have a relaxing time, without having to psych myself up for an assault on the summit of Mount Gastropub. The novelty has worn off. Knowing that I can get anywhere doesn't make the effort worth the reward. I can feel the transition from enthusiastic amateur wheelchair user to professional arsey cripple.

This change is partly forced upon me with the realisation that now when people meet me for the first time I'm no longer just Tim, tall Tim or, if I may be so bold, tall and very attractive Tim. To many people I am now 'disabled people'. As in, 'There was this guy trying to get his wheelchair out of the car, and I offered to help, but he just said he could manage. I mean, disabled people are so ungrateful.'

I would like to point out at this juncture that when people offer me help to get in or out of the car, I always decline with a smile and a thank you, although some people are rather taken aback, and look rather puzzled. I mean, what do they think? I just sit around by the car in the hope that someone will come and put the chair in for me? How did I get to the supermarket in the first place? Etc. In truth, as I have perfected a technique where I take the wheels off first and then throw the whole chair on the back seat, it is quicker for me to do it myself than it is to explain to someone what needs doing.

Even old ladies ask me if I 'need a hand, dear?' Does this mean I am now ahead of them on the perceived feebleness scale? And what is the standard unit of measure for feebleness? Why do some people seem so offended if I just want to get on with things on my own? I'm always profusely polite in declining their offer of help, but the fact that I'm in a wheelchair seems to make me open season as far as assistance is concerned, and any attempt to mind my own business is treated by some in the same way as if I had set fire to their dog or something. Really, all I want is for people not to let go of doors in my face or push me without me asking. And yet, I think back to my attitudes before I was injured, and how I would sometimes shy away from offering help because I was intimidated by the possibility that I might cause offence. While it might seem obvious to me which things may be difficult to manage unaided, it wasn't obvious to me before.

There are occasions when I find myself rather guiltily enjoying people's discomfort and awkwardness, especially when it is caused by a terror of saying the wrong thing. The time comes for me to renew my season ticket with Arsenal, and to choose a seat location in the new stadium, so I go along with my friend James, who I have been going to the football with for 23 years, and four other guys who all know each other from the Arsenal where we all sat as neighbours. They are keen for us all to still be seated in the same area, even though I will now be in a wheelchair space. Once in the offices of Arsenal, a man who looks as if he is about fourteen greets us, all spots, hair gel and crisp white shirt, and I can see a look of confusion in his eyes. We get to his desk, and I explain that I have been a season-ticket holder for seventeen years, only my circumstances have recently changed, and I would now like a wheelchair-accessible 'seat'. I watch the confusion turn to fear.

'We can do that, sir, but, um, you'll have to go on a waiting list for the disabled seats, as there are other people who have been waiting for a long time, and we're not allocating those seats for a few months yet.'

This is close to what I was expecting. 'I'm very sorry,' I explain, 'but I'm not going on any waiting list. I am an existing season-ticket holder, and I wish to renew my ticket as I have been invited here to do. My circumstances have changed, I admit, but I would hate to feel that my disability was the reason why my ticket cannot be renewed.'

He blanches visibly, and sets about making several frantic telephone calls, before he gets the nod, and explains that it 'shouldn't be a problem', and I choose a disabled space, with my friends choosing a bank of seats immediately in front of me. That done, we all adjourn to celebrate our victory over lunch in a French restaurant. *Santé*, Arsene!

Meanwhile, things plod along slowly on the home front. We are still waiting on planning permission before the work can begin. On a more positive note, we meet with Rachel, our project manager on site, and she is such a whirlwind of energy and enthusiasm that she makes it feel as if we have simply decided to renovate our flat, which is usually the case with her other clients.

The days go by. My routine involves Penny pouring very strong coffee down my neck until I am able to shake off the groggy feeling caused by all the pain medication. It is a real struggle most mornings, and I am still in pain for the rest of the day, so I am unsure if the medication is having any effect, but I'm terrified of even attempting to reduce it, as I just can't face the possibility of the pain getting worse. I remind myself that it can take a couple of years for things to settle down. I am conscious that the pain isn't just affecting me. I can see Penny's frustration at being unable to do anything to ease my suffering.

23

1 February 2006
Subject: Ouch

Well, things pootle along here at bungalow central, nothing moving particularly fast. I have been doing a bit of 'stay-at-home dad'. Jeez, that's a crap expression. Mind you, so is 'house husband'. Or housewife, come to that. Penny has been getting out on site to a garden that she is working on, and I've been getting covered in mushed apple/broccoli/pumpkin/baby sick. After the first time, when I managed to clonk Rosalie on the head with a piece of furniture within ten minutes of Penny leaving the house, and spending the day crying at each other, we now get on like a house on fire. (We haven't actually set the house on fire, so no worries there, as yet.)

She really is a cheerful little soul, with a huge gurgly laugh, and an endless supply of ticklish bits. The whole picking-up-baby-from-wheelchair thing has been made easier with the introduction of a lap-strap that attaches me to the chair, and makes me much more stable. Moving her around is getting a bit more difficult though, as she is now too fat/big-boned for the 'papoose' that we had been using. Last time we tried, it took both of us to pull her out of it.

Pen has got a very bad cold/flu at the moment, and as I did the breakfast routine for Rosalie this a.m. I found a popular new toy for her. Typically, you can surround her with the most sophisticated toys that have been designed by developmental psychologists and hand-made in Bolivia using organic llama parts etc., but nothing

gets the same response as ... an inflated rubber glove.
Maybe it's a booby thing.

Right, I'm going to look after the missus. Keep the cold/
sun from your toes, depending which hemisphere you're
in. And do us a favour. Go for a brisk walk, think of me and
ENJOY it!

I have developed a sense of dread at the prospect of meeting
old acquaintances for the first time post-injury. I think it's like
another window into my 'old' life. My first realisation of the
pit-of-the-stomach dread comes when we are shopping in
Brent Cross one day and I see someone I used to play football
with. I find myself hiding, hovering in a doorway, as I know
that we would both feel uncomfortable. Eventually, I will have
seen everyone I knew before, and anyone new will not be a
problem, although of course I still feel a need to explain to new
acquaintances that I was injured recently, almost as if what I
am trying to say is, 'I'm not normally like this.'

At last we receive notification that our planning permission has been granted, and that work can begin in earnest.
Now all we have to do is get the platform lift installed, the
balcony constructed and fitted, the back door bricked up, all
the doors replaced, the kitchen and bathroom stripped out and
refitted, our studio converted into a bedroom, and one of those
amusing little pictures of a boy taking a pee into a potty for the
bathroom door.

The studio to be converted was our, well, studio. Both
Penny and I paint. In fact, that is how we met, when mutual
friends stuck us in the corner together, saying something like,
'You're both arty types. You should talk to each other,' the
subtext being, 'Yeah, and spare us any of your "deep and mean-
ingful" outpourings.'

Our first 'date' was a trip to an art-supplies shop, and back
to my place so that I could show Penny my work. I know this

sounds like, 'Would you like to come back and see my etchings?' But I did, in fact, show her all of my work, play her all of my music and show her all of my books before we got it on. Just nerves, I guess.

Now our beloved studio (which was, in truth, part-painting studio/part-landscaping tools and materials store) is to become our bedroom. Fortunately, in a wonderful piece of serendipity, we manage to find a small studio space in a warehouse just off the bottom of our street in Stoke Newington, and we take it on to use first as temporary storage while we get sorted, and then as a painting space. The prospect of having a painting space again fills me with excitement at the idea of getting back to something creative, something other than finding ways of doing everyday things from a wheelchair.

We reach another milestone when we decide to go on our first post-injury flight, a trip to Holland to visit some friends for their daughter's second birthday, and to meet their new baby for the first time. It is a daunting prospect, especially as the internet and the Spinal Injuries Association magazines are awash with nightmare tales of people having their wheelchairs destroyed by baggage handlers, waiting for hours while their wheelchair does laps on the baggage carousel, or being man-handled onto the aeroplane in front of all the other passengers and crew.

In our case, the big achievement comes in getting our travelling circus on a flight. This exercise is made easier by flying from London City to Rotterdam, where the advantage of small, friendly airports is made clear by the cheerful way the ground crew lift me onto the plane and into my seat. It turns out to be an interesting experience, especially when it comes to the 'aisle chair', which is a very narrow, small-wheeled chair into which I am strapped on the tarmac. I'm then lifted up the steps into the aircraft with my knees by my ears, flapping like windscreen wipers. All the flight staff are very helpful, friendly and keen to chat, making an effort to ensure that I don't feel too awkward, as I have to be put on the aircraft first and taken off last. I can understand why some disabled people feel uncomfortable with the 'piece of freight' feeling, but if that's what it takes for me to go where I want again, then so be it. Especially if it means I am the centre of attention.

As we are getting ready for take-off and the flight crew began their well-rehearsed emergency instructions mime, I sense a slight sideways glance from the stewardess, as if to say, 'Really, don't bother. If it comes to this, you're fucked, mate.'

On landing in Rotterdam, the rest of the passengers get off the plane, and we chat with the flight attendants and the pilot while we wait for the ground crew, who then get me off the plane and back into my wheelchair before we go together into the airport building. All the time Rosalie is being cooed to and fussed over, much to her delight. I am reminded yet again of the advantage that having a small child can give if you wish to be out of the limelight.

We have a lovely child-centric weekend with our friends in a village just outside Rotterdam, and I even manage to 'shufflebum' my way up their stairs, which is a real achievement, considering they are typically Dutch stairs, and as such they are at the most precipitous gradient possible, which is surely a cultural compensation for the lack of hills or mountains in Holland. Anyway, I spend a good hour sitting on the floor playing with giggly babies, and having conquered stairs in a 'real' situation, I feel a sense of achievement. I even manage to have a shower in the upstairs bathroom, and it feels good as I spend the rest of the time wedging myself into the downstairs toilet when needed, which is particularly challenging as I can't close the door fully, and the house is full of curious toddlers.

By the time we get home, we both feel much more confident about the prospect of travelling in future, and I can really feel my boundaries expanding as I mentally tick another box in my bumper book of rehabilitation. We even start to consider the possibility of going to Australia again. First Rotterdam, then the world!

In the week that follows our return, I feel those boundaries being constricted again, this time by pain. I have one of the worst nights that I can remember. Yes, Spike is back, and this time even two sleeping tablets take several hours to overcome the pain and my consciousness. After such a night in the past, I have enjoyed a period of several days of relatively low levels of pain. Not this time. This time I am worn down by a series of bad days, when I feel really unwell, and find myself constantly wincing and recoiling from the pain. Some days I am just too tired, unable to find the energy to face the day, the pain, the frustration, the emotional anguish. But I'm also aware that inaction will only make things worse, and so I never get a break.

Before my accident, I just got up and went about the day. OK, sometimes I was tired, grouchy, hung-over or whatever, but the getting up, the act of getting out of bed and throwing myself at the shower, that was something I could do on auto-pilot. Now, even rolling over in bed is a conscious effort, and I miss all those not-thinking things. Sitting on a sofa with the Sunday papers and being comfortable. Wrapping Penny in my arms and legs. Walking barefoot into the garden, and feeling first the rounded discomfort of gravel underfoot, followed by the cold freshness of dew-covered grass. If this may seem somewhat romantic, that's because these things become so when they are denied you.

I do eventually bounce back, or at least find the energy to fight, and just in time, as the next big event is soon upon us, when I go back to Stoke Mandeville for X-rays, and an appointment with 'the Enigmatic Dr J©'. Penny and Rosalie also come up to Aylesbury to catch up with friends who have recently moved to the area, and so we arrive in the spinal unit as a family of three, much to the joy of the nursing staff, who are very pleased to see Rosalie and Penny again. When Dr J arrives, he sternly orders me into a side room before disappearing around the corner to talk to Penny. I go to the door, only for him to order me back into the room with a mock-stern voice, 'Where are you going? I told you to go in there.' Penny tells me later that he then has a 'hold' of Rosalie and gives her a kiss, while she gleefully dribbles down his tie.

I am at the hospital so Dr J can make a decision as to when to take the large and frankly fucking uncomfortable pieces of titanium out of my back. The idea is that my spine, having been immobilised at the point of damage, fuses together to make some kind of überspine, thus giving me special powers. The ability to go through low doorways or under low branches without having to duck, and making me invisible to people selling credit cards or cable TV in supermarkets. Powers I have already noticed I possess, of course. Although sadly, I will always be undone by my nemesis, the dreaded Pedal Bin, who always seems to hide out in disabled toilets, with his side-kick Tiny Sink, as all disabled people must have tiny hands. Bizarrely, pedal bins even populate all the toilets in the spinal unit. Someone in the hospital cleaning department clearly has a twisted sense of humour. I applaud them.

I am somewhat apprehensive at the prospect of further surgery and the recovery thereafter, but I have learned how important it is to try and project ahead and remember the long term. Just the thought that all of this will be a part of my history one day helps me to cope, somehow. After all, there was a time when I was flat on my back, unable to even lift my head, whacked out on morphine and eating Ready Brek through a straw. Here's to progress.

Back to Edgware and, having been referred by the team at the spinal unit, I begin regular physiotherapy with the neurological physiotherapy department at Barnet General in order to progress with calliper training before my next trip up to Stoke Mandeville. My physiotherapist turns out to be from Sydney, of course, which is a good contact in terms of finding out about life with a spinal-cord injury in Australia. She is very enthusiastic, and while she is very knowledgeable about SCI, she does not really have any experience of calliper walking, certainly not by a T12 complete injury. This further illustrates just what a foolhardy activity it is.

24

23 March 2006
Subject: I've got a screw loose ...

Well, snapped, really. Yes, I met with the enigmatic Dr J at Stoke Mandeville, had a couple of X-rays and a consultation, which revealed that I have broken one of the titanium screws that secures the fixation bars to my spine. Too much of something, I guess, but I'm not sure what. Apparently, it's not that uncommon for people to break the fixing in the back, and it does demonstrate that I still have flexibility in my spine at the level of the injury, which is good, and the Doc is confident that my spine has healed pretty well. All this means that he is keen to whip all the metalwork out as soon as, and reckons that I'll probably be going in just after Easter.

While up at Stoke, I met up with another patient who was in at the same time as me, and has really got on with his life. M was working in Thailand as a scuba-diving instructor when he fell from a balcony and suffered a spinal-cord injury. He was brought back to Stoke Mandeville for treatment, and discharged in June of last year. Since then, he has gone back to Thailand, and gone back to work as a scuba-diving instructor, only now he's paraplegic, and takes other disabled people out diving.

I found this really inspiring. Not because of the diving, as that has never appealed to me. Frankly, I'd rather stick my head in a fish tank, where at least I can come up for air as and when I want to. And I wouldn't need to struggle into a wetsuit. I imagine that getting paralysed legs into a wetsuit is something akin to trying to get live eels into a duffel bag. No, the reason I found it inspiring was partly the adventurous outdoor lifestyle that he has returned to, which pushes the boundaries of what can be done following SCI, but also because he has returned to doing something that he loves.

I have put myself down as a competitor at the Inter-Spinal Games, which takes place at the end of April in the sports centre adjoining Stoke Mandeville. It's a competition between all the spinal units in the UK, and is really about showcasing wheelchair sport, and encouraging people who have been injured in the last twelve months to get involved. I shall be competing in the swimming, archery, table tennis and shooting as part of the Stoke Mandeville team (not all at once; although ... now there's an exciting idea for a new sport ...). Except, I shall probably not be doing any of this, as it's got to be even money that my operation will be that week.

God speed until next we meet upon this most digital of highways...

The three of us go down with a gastro-bug. Yeeuuch! Rosalie bounces back the quickest, and me the slowest. This may have something to do with the way in which my digestive system works now. As everything takes a bit longer, that includes getting rid of bacterial infections. It may also reflect Penny's resilient soldiering on through adversity, compared to my traditional male conviction that I am the most ill of anyone anywhere ever, and may even be dying, etc.

After two days of hideous nausea and vomiting, I finally get to a point where I can at least consider eating something, which is a big relief. I am, however, left feeling pretty washed out, and if I didn't know better, I'd swear that Rosalie has spent the time pogo-ing on my stomach while I was asleep. The resulting exhaustion has implications that are quite worrying. I struggle to get from the bed into my wheelchair, my balance when I am on the seat in the shower is poor, and had we still been struggling with the bathroom in Aylesbury, I would have been back to bed baths. I feel vulnerable when I think of the implications, if this is what I feel like after only two days in bed.

In spinal injury terms I have been fortunate in that my injury is relatively low, I am fit and strong, with no other underlying health conditions. Obviously, if I had a high-level injury, I would be dependent on other people, but my experience makes me realise that this would also be the case if I were overweight or particularly unfit, or if I had shoulder, elbow or wrist problems. For many people, the ideal of being 'self-caring' is unachievable, and I find it difficult to imagine my life without being independent, at least at home, or out in the car.

That being said, before my accident and rehabilitation, I certainly couldn't have imagined a life in a wheelchair. Even now it's not often that the full magnitude of what I'm up against fills my mind all at once. It's more piecemeal. I might be struggling with something basic, like opening a window, or hanging out some washing, and I become frustrated because in my mind I still expect to carry out tasks like these with relative ease. Then I find myself struggling to keep my balance when I reach for something, and then I get a twinge of pain in my legs and the whole world I have created to be able to function (and even have moments of happiness) comes crashing down, demolished by a flood of everything that has changed or is now denied me.

Pain is still the most common trigger for this deluge, and I rebuild afterwards, of course. But where the next flood is coming from I never can tell. On one occasion I get together with friends, including a couple I haven't met before. The encounter starts along the lines of, 'So *you're* Tim.' I suppose the wheelchair rather gives the game away. 'I've heard so much about you,' etc.

Then the conversation takes a familiar turn. The one

where they ask how I'm coping, and this time another friend interjects that I am coping brilliantly, many other people would have 'given up and died' (sic).

I soldier on with the 'you've just got to get on with it' speech, including such classics as 'parenthood has given me a great focus', and 'higher-level injuries must be so much worse', and I can sense everyone's relief. But it costs. For every action there is an equal and opposite reaction. I have moved from my base level of low, reluctant acceptance and distraction-seeking, up to a philosophical, 'You only go around once', 'What can you do?' 'You've just got to make the best of things.' And I'm not sure why I'm up here. Because I want to make other people feel a bit less uncomfortable? Or maybe it's just a desire not to be totally overshadowed by my injury.

The payback comes as I leave, and the reaction kicks in, taking me into a deep sense of frustration and some resentment. The truth? The truth is that it's a fucking miserable state of affairs. When I wake up in the morning, I'm in pain. For most of the day I'm in pain. I get frustrated that I can't reach things, climb things, negotiate stairs, step over things, bounce my daughter on my knee or carry her on my shoulders. The truth? At the end of every day I am filled with a mixture of rage and utter debilitating terror, as I struggle to accept that it is me this is happening to, and that I will never get back my life as I knew it. There's a part of me that's still screaming like I did when I first fell from the tree. It's never stopped. I just try and find ways to drown it out.

Keep busy. That can be hard when you don't have deadlines or the routine of a workplace. I've never been one for the whole Protestant work ethic, but I do know from the experience of producing work for exhibitions that a deadline seems to sharpen the mind, so I have to scale down my expectations, and I set myself to more modest routines. The first challenge is to be up, showered and dressed by 10.30 a.m. I don't always manage this. Some days I'll be on the toilet for nearly an hour, and that's quick compared to some SCIs – I have heard tales of two hours and more.

In a couple of more private moments, i.e. when Penny is out with Rosalie, I even remember the ErecAid™, and the 'community' that I will be joining just by using the thing. Self-conscious doesn't even begin to describe my feelings towards this one, but I am determined to give it a try on my own, to see what I can make of it, or indeed it of me. To use the thing it has to be first primed with a thick rubber band that gets slipped onto the base of the penis once an erection has been created using only the magic of a vacuum. The whole device is then slathered in lubricant, and put over the penis. As the pump is operated, it draws blood into the penis. Unfortunately, it also has a tendency to draw the testicles into the tube if you're not careful, and as that is the one area of sensation I do have below the waist, it comes as something of a shock the first time it happens, made worse by the loud 'schloop' sound.

I try the kit out on a couple of occasions with limited success, especially because, though it does create an erection, it, er, lacks a foundation, as it were. It also looks a bit angry, what with the elastic band choking it off. In case you are wondering what I am doing with this thing on my own, I just want to make sure that I can work the thing before introducing it to the boudoir. The third time I try it out, I apply a bit too much suction, and although I diligently hold onto my testes, I end up with little burst blood vessels all over my penis. Spotted dick. The suction kit is banished to a bottom drawer, never to return. Thankfully, the red spots also disappear in a day or two.

The next challenge is to make sure to get out of the house every day, if not up the big hill to the park, then at least around the block. Rosalie enjoys this, as she sits on my lap, and I have a strap that joins her to me. This is how I spend the morning of 1 April – the anniversary of my accident. We roll along and I point out trees and birds and cars and flowers, and she burbles contentedly, enjoying the way that her voice wobbles whenever we go over the cracks in the pavement. Every now and then she turns her head so that she can look up at me, and when she does I just want to squeeze her and never let go.

Gradually, parts of my old life are slotted back in wherever they can fit. On a more ambitious day I finally make it back to the swimming pool at the Aspire centre in Stanmore. I feel a sense of achievement at just being in the water, although, inevitably, I am not allowed to enjoy this, because having just completed eight lengths of the pool, an exhausting effort having not been swimming for months, I have to cross the adjoining lane in order to get back to the shower chair and out of the pool. There are three people swimming in the lane, so I wait for all of them to complete the length, and they all pause at the end of the pool. Seeing my opportunity, I swim under the rope and strike out for the other side. However, I haven't managed more than two strokes, before one of the three swimmers decides to launch into me in a quite deliberate and aggressive way. I stop. He stops and tells me off for swimming across the lane.

'I waited until you had all stopped and you just deliberately swam into me.'

'Well,' says he, 'you were swimming across the lane.'

'I know,' me, again. 'I'm trying to get out of the pool.'

'You should use the ladder on your side.'

'I can't. I'm paraplegic.'

He pauses, and then says, 'I could have hurt you.'

I lose my temper. 'NO, YOU COULDN'T HAVE FUCKING HURT ME. YOU COULD HAVE SWUM INTO ME, AND YOU DID.'

He swims off, and I leave the pool fuming. He wasn't concerned about hurting me until he found out that I was paraplegic. Paraplegic, not made of porcelain. I am becoming aware of a small, freshly dug potato, which has taken up residence on my shoulder, and it will not take too many more events like this for it to be scrubbed, peeled, chipped and dropped into hot fat.

I am now regularly looking after Rosalie while Penny returns to her gardening work, which is a learning experience for all of us, as we discover new techniques to overcome difficult challenges with the creative use of any available equipment. For instance, I now appreciate the value of a strong pair of dungarees. No, not for me, although thinking about it, it might prevent my trousers from sliding down to my knees every time I transfer to and from my wheelchair. The dungarees are on Rosalie, and the straps provide a great set of handles for lifting her and shifting her around. In fact, we have perfected 'the grab', whereby I lower her with one hand, and she picks up objects from the floor. I'm sure once she's crawling she'll be towing me around the bungalow.

After one such exhausting day, Penny returns home and administers food to our daughter, while I lie on the small patch of grass in front of the bungalow. It is surrounded by a large hedge, and catches the evening sun. When I am outside, I feel compelled to lie on the ground wherever possible. It's an attempt to feel connected, somehow. To actually be a part of outside, rather than a spectator, insulated by the wheelchair. My moment of Zen is interrupted by the discordant melody of an ice-cream van outside, which triggers some kind of subconscious childhood urge, and I heave myself back into the wheelchair and rush across the road to buy two 99s with flakes and nuts and chocolate sauce, with the intention of presenting one to Penny as a surprise. Purchase successful, I find myself in a wheelchair holding two rapidly melting ice creams. I put both cones in one hand and began to push myself around in a circle with the other. The ice-cream man promptly drives off, mainly, I suspect, because of a distinctly uncomfortable sense of embarrassment caused by watching the circling fool in a wheelchair with ice cream running down to his elbow. Now alone in the street, I attempt to push with the heel of the ice-cream hand, which causes the two ice creams to become one, which lurches precariously on the edge of the cones. I quickly right the one big ice cream, losing my battle with the camber of the road, and roll back to the gutter. Just as I am contemplating eating both of the damn things, and probably feeling sick for the rest of the day, my saviour(s) arrives in the form of Penny holding Rosalie, and we celebrate by all covering our faces in ice cream as the sun comes out, and it is good. Proving again, if proof was needed, there are few things in life that don't benefit from a pause for ice cream.

I am allocated a date for surgery to have the fixation removed from my back. It is the week of the Inter-Spinal Unit Games, and I am forced to withdraw from the team, as I am impatient to get the metalwork removed. For the next few weeks, I try and keep myself distracted, and convince myself that my next post-op experience will be nothing like the previous one at the Royal London.

After persistent requests to the disability liaison officer at Arsenal, he comes up trumps, sending me a ticket for the Champions' League match between Arsenal and Villarreal. There is no charge for these tickets and a high demand, so I am very pleased to be able to go to one of the last games at Highbury. I suspect that the policy of free tickets for disabled supporters harks back to the days when football teams were not expected to make any money, but were more of a way for successful businessmen to give something back to the local community, and I'm sure that the first disabled supporters to be offered free entry were probably ex-soldiers.

I go to the match with James as my 'carer', because the ticket is for me plus one. I can feel the excitement building, and even though I can't see much past the backside of the person in front of me, joining the crowd around the stadium gives me a real buzz, as I return to another part of my old life, and the chance to have one last visit to Highbury, a place I know intimately from so many visits over more than twenty years. We make our way to the disabled entrance and into the stadium, surrounded by other disabled supporters, who all seem to know each other pretty well.

Once in the ground, my initial excitement subsides, and I feel a bit deflated. I realise that, however illogically, I was thinking that it would feel like old times. But we are on the opposite side to our old seats, pitch-side instead of halfway up the West Stand Lower, and because I am sitting down, coupled with the camber on the pitch, my eye level isn't much above the grass, and when players are on the opposite wing I can't really see below their knees. Still, we get through the game, laughing and joking with our usual peculiar and frankly rather silly banter. And James points out that by being in the disabled section, we have now watched from every part of the ground.

My experience at Arsenal reminds me of what my friend Richard said on one of his visits. For starters, he was the first person to really take the piss out of me after my accident, and I remember thinking that he was very at ease with me being in a wheelchair. The only thing that changed was that he gave me a hug instead of a handshake. When we talked a bit about coming to terms with my disability, he compared the process to grieving: 'When you're grieving, you have to go and visit all the places that you used to go and do all the things you used to do with the loved one you have lost, and once you have done that, then you can move on.'

It's a true comparison in a way. I do have to do all the things that I used to do, or at least try those that are still open to me in some form, and in the process, I will perhaps learn how to come to terms with all of this.

The other good thing about the trip to Highbury is that when we leave the stadium, I am struck by how it makes a nice change not to be the only person in a reflective mood. There are about 40,000 others around me, and by the time I get back to Edgware, my sense of sadness is tempered with a feeling of achievement at going to a football match barely a year after my accident.

Another change to adjust to is the public outbursts of flatulence by what can perhaps best be described as my 'random wind generator'. We meet Matt and Kirsten for lunch one day, and upon finishing our meal together, Matt goes off to the toilet while Kirsten goes outside with their fidgety daughter and Penny with Rosalie. This leaves me alone in the restaurant, except for a couple sitting at the table behind me, holding hands and cooing softly to each other. Once I have paid the bill, I bend forwards to put my wallet back into the zip-up bag that hangs under my wheelchair. In doing so, I let out a long and extremely raucous fart. This is obviously not deliberate, as I now have no control over such things, but I cannot say for certain that other people are aware of this and it was certainly loud enough to drown out their sweet nothings.

Quick switch: I now imagine the same scene for the couple behind me. There we are, minding our own business and having a romantic coffee together. Man in wheelchair, sitting with his back to us finishes lunch, pays, and then waits for his fellow diners to leave before pointing bum towards us, bending over and farting uproariously in our general direction. Nice.

25

20 April 2006
Subject: No time like the present

Word on the street is that there's a blade with my name on it. Turns out that Dr J (for it is he) is after me, and plans to drug me on Tuesday of next week before stealing my valuable titanium core. On the plus side, it doesn't give me long to build my levels of anxiety and it won't be on my birthday. The downside, which I'm sure you've all worked out by now, is that Tuesday is when Arsenal takes on Villarreal in the second leg of the semi-final in the Champions' League. A match that I will attempt to watch, but will no doubt be too dopey from the operation to know what's really going on. Then again, depending on the result, that could be a blessing.

I am a little nervous about the forthcoming week's adventure, but I'm hopeful that it will result in less pain on a day-to-day level, so... bring it on. DOSE ME, DR J!

Back soon. I hope.

Off we go to Stoke Mandeville to have the Meccano removed. I check in the day before my surgery, waiting until the last possible moment before leaving home. I am nervous; in fact, with a little bit of work, I could build 'nervous' up to 'terrified' quite easily, but if I have learned anything in the last twelve months, it is how to stop my thoughts from wandering/wondering down certain corridors. It's as if my brain has developed its own crack team of stroppy security guards who patrol my subconscious, demanding authorisation from any idle thought that might be drifting aimlessly around.

My MRSA privileges are upheld, I get a side room just inside the entrance to St Patrick's, and I find myself on the readmissions ward for the first time. St P's is populated with old patients coming back in for repairs and, going on totally uncharitable first impressions, it seems to be full of fat people and smells of poo. Of course, this is an awful thought, and I'm sure people will have first impressions of me that I would rather not know. Hopefully I don't smell of poo, although I may have done when I was in the hospital before, and probably will again at some point in the future.

My bloods are taken by one of Dr J's team, who manages to liberally spray the red stuff around the room, some on the sheet, and a few decent-sized blobs on the floor and, while, continuing our conversation, he casually rubs them with the sole of his shoe. He leaves me marvelling once more at meticulous infection-control methods, and the inconsistencies in the NHS.

I unpack my few belongings, put my family picture on the bedside table, and go and run myself a bath in my allocated MRSA bathroom, which contains one of only three baths in the unit. Well, to be frank, a bath is pretty useless to most spinal patients, especially recently injured ones, as they are very unlikely to be able to get in and completely unable to get out. I have a lavender shower gel with me that makes for a very relaxing bath full of bubbles, and clutching a book, I settle in for a soak. This is a real luxury for me, especially as we don't have a bath in the bungalow, but also because this bath is about seven feet long, which means that I can get fully stretched out. By the time I struggle out, dry off and get myself back to my room, I am feeling distinctly relaxed – serene, even, and I settle into the foam mattress and feather pillow (brought from home, one thing that I have learned from my frequent visits to hospital). Without thinking about anything very much, I drift off to sleep.

At 8.30 a.m. the following day, I feel like I am dealing with a mechanic.

Dr J (sharp intake of breath): 'Who done this lot then? Royal London, eh? Well, that's yer problem right there. See, for this stuff you need a special tool. Got to order one in. Gonna take a couple of weeks easy, that will,' etc.

In truth, there is an air of gravitas and genuine regret as the news is broken to me that Dr J only realised this morning at 6 a.m. that because my fixation was done at the Royal London, he would need to hire in special equipment to facilitate a swift removal. This is despite our consultation over a month ago, and the conversation I had with one of his team yesterday when I was signing consent to be drugged up, cut open, rummaged around in and stapled shut. Miffed? Moi? You betcha.

The best bit comes with the discovery that the next available date means that I will be going under the knife on my birthday after all. Actually, I must make a correction here. The really best bit comes immediately after I am told the news in the morning, and while struggling with the mixture of frustration generated by my desire to get the surgery over with, relief generated by my desire never to have surgery ever again, and clumsiness generated by my desire to have breakfast, I manage to drop my mobile down the toilet. Hurrah.

Still, all this does mean that after a quick telephone call (from the ward phone) to the archery gym, I'm back on the team for the Spinal Games, and then in the afternoon I get the chance to go to the shooting range for a spot of air-rifle target practice, and I find out that I'm a bit of a dab hand at shooting. It seems that all I have to do is imagine a face. That of a consultant, perhaps?

After a night at home, I go back to the spinal unit as a

competitor in the 2006 Inter-Spinal Unit Games. Obviously, I am taking the competition extremely seriously, having trained hard for my surgery, and having been nowhere near a table-tennis table or bow and arrow in the last five or six months. I have been swimming twice in that time, of course, so I am quietly confident. These three, and the shooting, which I tried for the first time the day before the games, make up my personal quadrathlon.

There is a good spirit in the team, especially when we are issued with our lurid blue Stoke Mandeville polo shirts and hoodies, with 'try something different' written on the back in bright orange, courtesy of our sponsor. I'm not sure if this is supposed to refer to the sport or the wheelchairs. The team is a mixture of former patients I have met before, and current patients who are far enough along in their rehabilitation to take part. It feels funny being the 'old hand', as I have been out for the longest. We have a range of injuries, both complete and incomplete, and looking around at the other competitors, I do not envy the organisers their task.

P, the former jockey, who I knew from my in-patient days, is in the team, along with D, who was enjoying a family lunch on the balcony when the wind slammed the door. He climbed over the railings and lowered himself down, as he had done many times before, only this time as he let go, his foot caught the down-pipe and, instead of landing on his feet, he landed on his neck, leaving him an incomplete tetraplegic. We also have an ex-gymnast who broke his neck in competition when a tumbling move went wrong. Then there's A (paraplegic following a snowboarding accident in Japan), E (mountain-biking accident in Cambodia), D (a paraplegic who was injured in a motorbike accident), M (another para of about sixteen, who was injured in a BMX accident) and, finally, A, who has Brown-Séquard syndrome, a condition I was totally unfamiliar with until I met A. He was stabbed in the back during a robbery at his girlfriend's apartment in Sweden, causing an incomplete spinal-cord injury. Now, here's where it gets a bit freaky; because of the way that the various nerve bundles leave the spinal cord, damage caused by a puncture wound, such as a gunshot or stabbing, can cause the victim to suffer impaired movement down one side of the body and impaired sensation on the other. So if A wants to know how warm something is, he has to pick it up with his right hand, and hold it to his left.

In some sports there are different categories for complete or incomplete lesions, and in all there are different categories for paraplegia and tetraplegia. My first competition comes in the table tennis, and I take to the table relaxed and confident, until the warm-up, when I realise just how long it has been since I last hit a ping-pong ball in anger. Or in any other way, come to that.

I start well enough, but I suffer a mid-game lack of form, caused by a lack of concentration. This is something that I have always suffered with whenever doing anything competitive, especially in front of an audience. All will be going swimmingly, and then I suddenly feel detached, and think, 'Wow! It's me, and I'm playing in a serious, proper, competitive thing. And people are watching, and stuff. I mean, how silly is this, it's only a game,' etc.

Luckily, I regain my composure, and manage to finish off my opponent who, to be fair, looked rather overawed before we even started. Success! I move through to the next round, and head off to watch my team-mates in competition.

This is where it all starts to get a bit difficult. I am full of the Corinthian spirit and all that, until I see anything that could be even slightly construed as 'unfair', at which point all my magnanimity gets hoofed out of the window, and I start to grumble, gripe and moan to anyone who will listen, and often to people who won't.

My second game in the table tennis brings me up against a player who is widely tipped as being 'very good'. Before the game, we shake hands, and his gaze dances here and there as he retains a rather serious expression, and I realise that I have met my match. He is clearly taking it all *very* seriously, and my competitive streak shrinks shyly away and cowers behind my jaunty sense of humour, which gallantly takes up the baton, and I try a few little jovial witticisms during the warm-up, with no response. We start, and he takes an early lead, but then a funny thing happens. I take a few points off him, and he starts to look nervous, really nervous. He misses a few shots, and I can see in his eyes that he has been told that I am 'very good', and he believes it of me more than I of him. I press home my advantage, and move through to the semi-final.

I know this is all a bit Sun Tzu, but I can't help myself. Here is a 'tournament', the primary purpose of which is to introduce people who have recently suffered a spinal-cord injury to the joy of participating in sport of any kind, and yet I can't control the disproportionate development of a competitive streak in me that threatens to get totally out of control. Although we were briefed in our lectures about bladder, bowel and skin, etc., there wasn't one mention of the risk of developing an enlarged competitive streak.

Interestingly, all this cod sports psychology bullshit has only emerged in me since my injury, as the role that sport plays becomes much more emotionally important. For years I quite rightly took my physical abilities for granted. Now just having the opportunity to participate in any sport is of huge psychological importance to me, and I am more competitive, but this is because I still have benchmarks of personal expectation that were set before my accident.

The following day is the table-tennis semi-final, and I manage to keep my pseudo-psychobabble at bay long enough to play a good game and get through to the final. This time there is a more sizeable crowd watching, and it feels like a proper competition. The crowd of which I speak is comprised of other competitors, as well as physiotherapists and carers, many of whom are attending as volunteers. It is an impressive show of commitment to the event, and a part of the legacy of Dr Guttmann, also reflected in the number of organisers and officials who attend from the various Paralympic disciplines, all busy looking for the talent of the future, and as soon as anyone shows a degree of ability in any event, the whisper of Beijing 2008, or even London 2012 can be heard.

At 37 years old, I have to be realistic about my Olympic expectations, but I must confess that it is a real boost to the ego. It also reminds me of my first post-injury conversation with my nine-year-old niece Scarlett, who was emphatic about my competing at the Paralympics in the future. I could almost see her young mind casting around for a positive image of wheelchair users, latching onto the Paralympics and thinking, 'That'll do. We'll go with that.'

The swimming is pretty chaotic, as all the lanes are being used for different races in order to get all of the races in all of the categories completed in time. However, this has not been made clear to the competitors and spectators, and so we are left to rail against the blatantly unfair competition, as three swimmers bedecked in various buoyancy aids, helpers in the water with them, swim a length of the pool using only limited arm movement, while in the next lane a man puts his walking stick to one side, dives into the pool, swims a length of front crawl, and then climbs out of the other end before walking the length of the pool to retrieve his walking stick, the purpose of which I am unsure of. To be fair, he does have a six-inch scar along his spine, but as an incomplete, I can only assume that he has made a very good recovery in the last year. Now, I can see how inclusiveness is important to an event of this nature, but if I have a beef (and let's be honest, I do), it is with the spinal unit that he is representing for putting him in their team, as it is pretty demoralising for those he is competing against. Perhaps they could have said to him. 'I'm afraid we have decided not to pick you to represent us at the Inter-Spinal Unit Games. We are sorry. But on the plus side, you *can* walk.'

And then my race is next, and I find myself transferring onto the edge of the pool and sliding into the water. I am ready for this event, having practised extensively for two half-hour sessions in the last three months, and I have a cunning plan. It is clear to me that I can swim faster under water than on the surface, so when the gun goes, I swim the first half of the pool underwater, and then bob up to drive home my superior turn of pace, only to find myself last in the heat. Staying on the surface for the rest of the length, I manage to make up most of the lost ground, and I swim up to a close second. After a review of the race from my poolside team-mates, I discover my fatal tactical error. I may feel like I'm swimming faster underwater, but it turns out that I'm not at all. I'm considerably slower. So I might have won, had I not been brainwashed by too many episodes of *The Man From Atlantis* during my impressionable youth. Curse you, Patrick Duffy, with your webbed hands and peculiar dolphinesque swimming style!

Having snatched defeat from the jaws of victory, my crest is somewhat fallen as I return home after the second day of competition, but I drive down the A41 safe in the knowledge that my 'Joker' event is yet to come, and the welcome home makes the Games seem remote and unimportant.

So, the final day of competition and I'm focused, relaxed and confident. I arrive at the centre in time for a late breakfast with the team, some of whom appear to be rather jaded after a night on the beer. So much for the discipline and focus of the finely honed athlete.

My competitive day begins with the shooting. Shooting? Well, air rifle, and although I don't manage to shoot as well as I did the first time I ever tried it which was only three days ago, of course, I manage eighth out of a field of 44. I head back to the main hall for my main event, archery. Now this is something that I am pretty good at, and I rather enjoy. Lou arrives with the bow that I used when I was in the hospital, complete with the sight, which she assures me hasn't been touched since, and the organisers let me have a few arrows to remind myself what I am supposed to be doing after such a long absence. I have a sense of joining in with something that is very much a part of the Paralympic movement, as archery was the sport chosen to inaugurate the first Games at Stoke Mandeville in 1948.

I win. I shoot 338 out of 360. That's with 36 arrows. And the highest score anyone can remember being scored in the Inter-Spinal Games. There, my trumpet parps happily as I blow. I am approached by various people from the British Wheelchair Archery Association, who obviously feel that I have some potential. I think I may give it more of a go.

Riding high after my fine performance in the archery, I come to the table-tennis final full of confidence, only to be told before the match that the other finalist played for England before his accident, and I know already that I have lost. My opponent turns out to be the swimmer with the walking stick, who has borrowed a wheelchair in order to take part in the table tennis. He is cautioned for putting his feet down on several occasions, but it is clear that he has much better balance than me. To make it worse, he is terribly magnanimous throughout the game, praising my good shots, and commiserating with me on my misses. It is all over very quickly, and I am back down on terra firma after the dizzy heights of my archery win.

The hall is cleared of sporting equipment in preparation for the dinner and presentations, but in one corner a new sport is invented; two on two basketball with a flat football. Myself and two other former patients, accompanied by the ever-enthusiastic Sean from Back-Up, who is at the games to encourage people to get involved, spend a very amusing half-hour clowning around and generally having a laugh. It is during this simple, spontaneous bit of playground lunacy that I find myself thinking of the quote writ large on the wall by the door of the sports centre, by Dr Ludwig Guttmann, 'If I ever did one good thing in my medical career, it was to introduce sport into the treatment and rehabilitation of disabled people.'

In the evening I am awarded the archery trophy, only to find that, unlike the Cup Final, they don't have an engraver on standby, and it's actually down to me to get my name added to the shield. The hung-over drive home the next day is enough for the euphoria of the last few days to drain away, but is replaced by excitement at seeing Penny and Rosalie after a night away. I also make a promise to myself that I will go on the multi-activity course with the Back-Up Trust as soon as possible. All in all, and despite a pretty lousy start, this week turned out to be a good one. And I get a big baby-smile when I get home.

26

5 May 2006

I've managed to ensure that there is to be no surgery on my birthday. My clever ruse was to burn my knee so badly that it would be impossible for me to lie on my front for any length of time. Clever, huh? There I was, showering in much the same way as I have for the last six months or so, only this time, I thought I'd be a bit radical, and tilt my left knee at a slightly different angle, placing it neatly under the hot pipe. The hot pipe feeds into a special thermostatic mixer, which is set to ensure that the water stays at a safe temperature. The hot water pipe also leaks. The water it leaks is not at a safe temperature, as it has not been through the mixer. Normally, one would yell, 'Ouch, me knee hurts!' and move the knee. Not me, oh no. I just leave it there for a few minutes so that I can grow a blister the size of a cricket ball.

Off I go to hospital. I explain to the doctor that I am a complete paraplegic. 'OK,' says the doctor, nodding sagely, followed by yelling to a nurse, 'Quickly! Get this man some painkillers!' I now appreciate the outpatient support from Stoke, as I realise that there isn't as much knowledge of SCI out there as I thought.

At the end of May I'm back at Stoke Mandeville for what I am informed is three weeks of calliper training rather than the two I was expecting, which dovetails rather neatly into my next scheduled surgery date, 13 June. Up at the spinal unit, rumour has it that they've laid their hands on the right set of spanners this time, so hopefully I'll be stripped down, stitched up and ready to roll by the end of June.

In the spinal unit my burn, now healing, attracts attention, and is photographed by the outpatient team, no doubt to be shown in some PowerPoint horror show intended to shock patients into only taking cold showers, thus saving the hospital the cost of heating the water. The burn itself is quite strange to look at, as it gradually tapers and becomes less severe where it travels down my calf. The water was so hot that if I had felt it, I would only have been able to take a few drops before it became unbearable, but as my knee was under it for about five minutes, most of it suffered a second-degree burn.

Despite my best efforts at distraction, I think a lot about the forthcoming surgery. I am very nervous after my last experience, and the resulting pain and drug nightmares. I miss both Penny and Rosalie an incredible amount, and I realise that it's worse now than when I was first in, as Penny isn't just down the road any more, and there are two of them. I'm also steeling myself for the distinct possibility that the surgery will not bring an end to all the neurogenic pain I suffer.

Physiotherapy is a good focus to keep my mind off the surgery, and while I am 'staggering' around the gym (and believe me, even that is an optimistic description of my reeling and swaying), I meet another patient, Harry. Harry is a former Army captain who was injured while on a night-time orienteering training session in Wales. It was one o'clock in the morning in freezing fog, when he stepped off a 30-metre cliff that wasn't marked on the map. As a result of his fall he broke both his back and his neck.

Harry is not so much stoical, as downright cheerful. We share a sharp sense of humour and he has a practical approach to his situation, which is immediately uplifting. We talk tactics on how to get in and out of cars, pros and cons of different wheelchair designs and the frustrations of Stoke life. He, too, is a patient of the eminent, enigmatic Dr J, and we compare notes on our fiendishly clever consultant over toast and Marmite and a cup of tea in the afternoons.

Harry invites me to join him and his wife Abbie for dinner with some of their friends at a pub in Wendover. I jump at the chance to get away from the unit, and I feel myself to be very welcome, but rather like a fish out of water, as my only connection to Harry is my spinal injury. I have a very good night, a real night off in many ways. The only reminder of what I've got to look forward to is when I turn to reach for my glass, and there is a loud 'pop!', which definitely emanates from my lower back. I am not the only one to hear it. Harry thought it came from the table or my wheelchair, but I know where it came from, although not what it was. I have a quick wriggle and there is a new grinding sensation when I arch my back but, thankfully, I have no new pain to add to the usual ones.

My efforts to contribute to the cost of the meal are politely rebuffed, and I throw myself in the car, and pootle back to the hospital tired, but in good spirits.

Dr J himself comes to visit me on the day before the operation, and we joke about the difficulty in getting the right tools for the job, and then he assures me that I am to be the first op in the morning, which is what I had hoped for, as it means less time spent awake, thinking about what is to come and getting an increasingly dry mouth without being able to drink anything. I also receive a visit from the anaesthetist and I voice my concerns over anything even remotely nausea-esque, and he tells me that he will make sure to use something that doesn't make me feel sick. It is only afterwards that I wonder why they would use something that *does* make patients sick if there is an alternative.

Penny comes in to see me with our delightful, heart-melting daughter, and we have a nice 'last meal' together. I am feeling pretty relaxed, as I have tapped back into the part of my brain that remembers how to be institutionalised on 'Stoke

Mandeville time'. There is a sense that although I will always be a patient here, this should be the last major procedure for a long time, touch wood (although, perhaps this isn't the luckiest choice of phrase for me, as it was the last thing I touched before my accident).

When I wake up after the op, there is a member of the anaesthesia team looking over me, and I come around fairly quickly, although obviously I make no attempt to move. Everything has gone very smoothly, and I am taken back up to the ward. The whole event has been unimaginably calm and cheerful, an atmosphere that has only been accentuated by my reacquaintance with morphine and the PCA machine. This one works, too.

I arrive back up on the ward to be greeted by Penny and Rosalie, who get to see me drug-fucked, and happy to have finally had the surgery. I feel a warm wave of affection sweep over me, and a sense of relief that I have woken up again, because however much I tried not to think of the risk of something going disastrously wrong, it was still lurking there, waiting for an unguarded moment. Especially as I am now a person to whom the unthinkable can happen.

Penny and I talk about what we have coming up in the future. As well as the battle to get the building work completed, we have some friends getting married in Australia in October and we plan to be there. Now that I have had the surgery, we decide to just get on with it and book our flights. It is time to start making plans again.

But just as the future comes into view, the present demands my attention as I begin to get a few twinges of pain, and I hit the button to good effect in terms of analgesia, less so as far as any kind of coherent conversation is concerned, and time is getting on, so Penny heads off with Rosalie, leaving me holding forth to my poor room-mate on any and every topic.

Dr J pays me a visit at the end of the day, and tells me that the operation went very smoothly, although it turns out that I have snapped two of the titanium screws, not one, and I immediately think back to the popping noise I heard when I was out for dinner with Harry and Abbie. Dr J explains that although he could have removed the broken screws, the amount of bone that would have had to be drilled out would have weakened the vertebra. I am really not worried about having them left in, as long as the 'lumps' have gone. It is a reassuring conversation, and I am left feeling grateful to him for his skill and professionalism. As I lie there, I remember a tale told to me by a former patient. He required a surgical procedure to be carried out on a part of his body where he has no sensation, and when discussing the procedure, he suggested to Dr J that he be allowed to remain conscious rather than receive an anaesthetic. Dr J refused, explaining that the anaesthesia wasn't just for the patient's benefit: 'It is for me, too. I couldn't even cut the throat of a chicken. But when I enter the operating theatre, there is a window open in the sheet, and I focus only on what needs to be done.'

In order to be able to carry out a task with such profound implications to someone else's life, it becomes necessary to disengage emotionally, and treat it as a purely intellectual and technical exercise. This can go some way towards explaining the apparent insensitivity of some consultants, and also the gallows humour that is prevalent in so many professions that deal with life-changing circumstances.

I have a couple of drains emanating from my back on either side of the wound, which draw away any fluid that may gather at the site, thus speeding up the healing process. I am extremely hungry after a night and a day without food, but I am not even allowed to drink anything until I have 'good bowel sounds'. If the bowel is functioning normally, it makes rather a lot of noise when heard through a stethoscope. In my case, the nursing staff check every hour to see if my bowel has woken up, following the general anaesthetic. My appetite has certainly woken up, but there is real caution about eating before things are moving again, and in view of the morphine in my 'diet' I am happy to wait. To be honest, with the morphine, I am happy to do pretty much anything. Or nothing. It's all fine. No trouble.

I do eventually get to eat a few small bits and pieces that Penny brought in for me, and then drift off to sleep.

In the afternoon of the next day, I have the drains removed from my back, and I get a visit from the pain-management team. I tell them of a few twinges here and there, and they tell me that I can have the PCA machine for a few more days if I would like, and that there's no reason why I should have any pain, and that I should press the button before the pain becomes at all acute. I agree warmly with all these sentiments.

Chris and Sarah come up for a visit, and I get to watch Jessica play peek-a-boo between my toes. It alarms me to think how many of her memories of me must be hospital-based. During the visit I try and move a little in bed, and the movement is met with a twinge of pain and a pulling sensation that feels deeply unpleasant. I hit the button. The rest of the day follows a similar pattern of wiggle, twinge, press the button. I sleep well again. The morphine machine is working smoothly. A bit too smoothly. Makes everything feel distant. Pain, hunger, coherent conversation, digestive function ... Then POP! The bubble bursts as in walks Dr J.

'What are you doing still on the heavy stuff? You should be off that rubbish, and just on paracetamol and diclofenac by now.'

All of a sudden I feel foolish, as if I have been caught doing something I know I shouldn't.

'And mobilise straight away, as pain allows.'

This is only the second day after surgery. As pain allows. Good one that. What exactly does pain allow, anyway? Pain surely prevents, rather than allowing anything. I know that when I have tried to move, even the slightest twist or effort to sit up causes a very unpleasant hot twinge in my back. Still, he has a point. In the evening I get the nurse to remove the knitting needle from my arm (I'm not kidding – the thing she pulls out of my wrist is the size of a drinking straw), and after a less comfortable night, I start to mobilise the next day.

The first attempt to sit up is very stiff and painful. I get up on my elbows before conceding defeat and lying back down to rest. I think nostalgically of the PCA machine and its cute little reassuring beep, as if to say, 'Don't worry, here's something to make you feel much better.'

The second attempt I push a bit further, and to my surprise the pain remains the same but no worse as I push up into a seated position. I do feel pretty light-headed, which serves to remind me how, yet again, Dr J is right. The longer I stay in bed taking hits on the pipe of inner peace, the further I get from recovery. I think of the mindset that I needed to adopt in order to get through my rehabilitation, an almost ascetic self-discipline whereby everything I did had to be judged as to whether it moved me along or set me back. At the time, my focus was on Penny's due date and my desire to be with her at the birth. Now my focus is on getting back home to be with her and Rosalie. I struggle into my wheelchair and instantly regret it when the backrest and the sausage-shaped wound area come into contact with each other. Once I've stopped weeping, I struggle back into bed with relief, and vow to not be quite so stupid in future. Still, it is progress.

With Friday looming (remember, folks, Friday is bed-meeting day!) and me having struggled into an upright position, I am booted downstairs to continue my rehab with old friends on St George's, and thus make way for a new admission on the acute ward.

Having freed myself of the stigma of MRSA positive, I

no longer get to be housed in a side room. Instead I am put in a four-bed bay opposite the nurses' station, which is noisy and bright all day and night, and surrounds me with other patients, whether I wish to be sociable or not. All this makes me even more determined to get out of hospital as soon as possible, and I drop a sleeper on the first night, before putting on a mask and earplugs. All I need is a dustbin to sleep in, and I could be Top Cat.

By the time Monday comes around, I am getting myself washed, dressed and breakfasted, and the only purpose to being in hospital any more is to pick up an infection. I am sore as all hell, mind you. And the pain isn't allowing a great deal more than mooching around. I have 33 staples that will be removed by the district nurse after a few more days. I am sent home with a special pair of staple removers for the job. And that's not all. After repeated enquiries, I go in person to pick up the metalwork that was removed. Well, I had grown rather attached to it. Literally, in a rather icky way. The fixation is pretty chunky, although very light, being made of titanium. Two bars about five inches long, two screws and four clever little connectors that look like miniature scaffolding couplers.

Before leaving, I also get the wound site checked out, as it is still very puffy. I can feel it whenever I lean back, as if I am growing a dorsal fin. Perhaps I have said something out of place in the spinal unit, and Dr J has actually sewn a dorsal fin on my back? Perhaps not.

I am assured that everything is as it should be, and I check out of the unit, tender, but excited at the prospect of being home with my family again. On the drive, I think about the phrase 'my family', and I realise that it's the first time that I've fully grasped this change in my life. My family, even after meeting and marrying Penny, was the way I referred to my parents and brother. But now, well, my family means first and foremost my wife and our daughter.

It feels as though my hospital visits may be over for a while. I always knew that I would have to go under the knife again to take out what was left in, and now I can concentrate on getting back home. My family's home. And I don't mean Edgware.

27

15 August 2006
Subject: Pith and vinegar

Car park rant: one day, God forbid, you might suffer a spinal-cord injury, because it can happen to anyone, at any time, doing anything. It could be a sports injury, a car accident, a slip in the shower. You could have a spinal stroke. A sharp pain, and you lose the use of your legs. If that day comes and you find yourself in a wheelchair, you may look back and wish you had revelled in, celebrated the use of your legs, maybe even parked a little further away, just to enjoy the walk. Instead, you park your lazy behind in a disabled bay. What a waste.

Yet to be delivered, and probably too well thought out, so that I would end up stumbling over the words, and in frustration descend into a torrent of sour 'urban vernacular'. Still, it's nice to dream.

Rosalie is close to standing, and talkative as ever. It is alarming how often she holds objects to her ear and chatters excitedly. It makes us realise how much time we spend on the phone. I'm thinking of switching back to old methods. If we reinstate semaphore, at least she'll get some exercise. And arguments would be quieter. Station announcers and news presenters would need to have really big arms/flags for extra 'volume', and handcuffs would be an infringement of the right to free speech. I'm rambling again.

ta ta

On the home front things are coming together at last. The balcony is fitted, and when we 'step' out onto it, the mesh flexes quite alarmingly, but the materials are all well within their tolerances, so there's no danger of suddenly ending up in the garden. With that in mind, I resolve to start working on some kind of Heath Robinson-like designs for equipment to get me into (and, ideally, back out of) the garden. There's no way that we can afford to have a lift fitted at the back as well, and it was enough of a battle to get the balcony passed by the planning office, so it's down to a bit of ingenuity and brute strength. And hopefully I'll get down to the ground at a more leisurely pace than I have done in the past.

As everything essential has been finished, we decide to start a phased withdrawal from Edgware over the course of the following week.

While work nears completion on our flat in Hackney, we get busy planning our trip to Oz in October and dealing with the challenges involved in finding accessible accommodation. We are planning a stopover for one night, but a bit of internet research reveals that it's not totally straightforward. For instance, we have discovered from several online disability forums that in Singapore people tend to say yes to enquiries, regardless of whether they have the right facilities or not, as they have a culture of not wanting to disappoint customers. Tales abound of pre-booked wheelchair-user guests arriving at the bottom of a grand staircase entrance to the hotel.

The internet forums are a really useful resource, and one that up to now I haven't put to best use, but it makes good sense as there is one spinally injured person for every fifteen hundred people in the UK, and it's obviously easier to interact and share information and support online. One of the forums I join is international, and I end up spending several hours on it every time I take a look, distracted by some side topic, and finding out all sorts of stuff from people who have been injured for years. When I think of the resources the internet can provide, or even the freedom of communication access Bluetooth head-sets provide, as used by many tetraplegics in hospital, it makes me wonder what life must have been like with SCI before all this kind of technology was available.

My continued involvement with the spinal unit takes on a more formal role as I join the Service Users Committee, a body that allows the patients (service users) to have some input into the way the unit is run. Despite my initial reservations, it turns out that the Trust does take this committee seriously, which is to their credit, and reassuring, as I will be an outpatient of the spinal unit for many years to come. It also feels good to contribute to the unit in some capacity, as it is a place that has a huge significance in my life and my ability to cope with the life-changing event of 1 April 2005.

I finally have my first visit to the pain-management clinic at the neurological hospital in Queen Square, a year after I was referred by the psychology team up at Stoke Mandeville and a couple of months after my second operation. While the sausagey lump on my back finally went away, as did the inden-tations where the metalwork used to be, the pain didn't. I am given a bunch of forms to fill out, lots of 'on a scale of one to ten' questions, and shading the areas where I get pain, and then I go to the waiting area. I sit for about half an hour staring at a dead weeping fig with desiccated leaves in a flaky terracotta pot that sits forlornly on a round stain on the carpet, suggest-ing that the plant may have received water once, but it was long ago. If the forms had asked me to draw chronic pain, I would certainly have considered this scene as an option.

I am called for my appointment and I speak at some length with the consultant, who takes copious notes, and I leave over an hour later, feeling encouraged that there are certainly other approaches to try, both in terms of medica-tion and cognitive behavioural therapy. It's good to talk to a pain-management specialist before going to see Dr J again at the end of the month. Considering all he has told me is that 'you mustn't let it win,' I feel this is maybe not his area of real expertise. Unless, of course, when I go and see the psychologist at Queen Square they tell me, 'You mustn't let it win.'

My other pain relief comes through sport. Strenuous physical activity used to be thought to release endorphins, the so called 'runner's high', but recent research suggests that it actually triggers production of another body chemical called anandamide, which is similar to THC, the psychoactive chemical in cannabis. After a three-hour wheelchair-basketball training session, I find that I am virtually pain-free for much of the rest of the day.

I start playing much more regularly, and find that as well as the pain benefits, I enjoy it more than I could ever have imagined. The sprit of the team at Stanmore is really agreeable, with a combination of good humour and competitiveness that is very much to my taste. I help to provide humour by accidentally flipping my chair over two or three times a session, but I soon decide that I must learn to lose this habit, especially as I'm strapped in, so the whole experience is, well, 'uncomfortable'. I rediscover the added pleasure of playing a team sport over something like archery. I think it's something to do with making a contribution to a bigger common objective.

I find other challenges, too. One in particular sort of finds me, and also finds me challenging Penny's stress levels. I set off in the car on my way up to Stoke Mandeville to speak at Relatives' Day, an event organised to provide information to the relatives of recently injured patients and to give them the opportunity to meet former patients who are 'getting on with their lives'. After two hours, Penny receives a call from me.

'Er ... Hi, Pen ... I'm absolutely fine, but ...'

'But what?'

'Well, I've kind of written off the car.'

Pause. Heavy sigh. 'What happened?'

My journey starts routinely, and I am in good spirits, listening to a Beethoven violin concerto on Radio 3 as I drive in the outside lane of the A41 at about 70-ish miles per hour. Three miles short of Aylesbury, I hear, 'Thud! Flappa flappa flappa.'

'Mmmm. That can't be good.' (My inner voice again).

I know that a tyre has burst, but what happens next is so sudden that I have no other warning. I barely feel a tug on the steering wheel, and the view of the road and the surrounding scenery is replaced by a close-up view of the tarmac. In turn, the tarmac is replaced by the sky, more tarmac, a bit of grass, a lot of glass, sky again, and finally the lighter-coloured tarmac of the hard shoulder. I brace myself for something really nasty to happen and wait for the violent kick of whiplash. Nothing. I try and get my bearings. I can smell petrol quite strongly, and the inside of the roof of the car is full of broken glass. I am upside down. I do a quick mental check to see if there is any pain or new numbness, but everything seems to be as it was a few minutes ago.

Holding the steering wheel, I release my seat belt, slide my legs out from over the wheel, and turn myself right way up. Through the side window/hole, I can see that a car and a lorry have stopped, and a group of three or four people are looking over at the car, but they seem reluctant to get too close, despite my shouted requests for 'a hand'. I reach for an old blanket on the roof behind me, and lay it over the broken glass where the mangled doorframe meets the road. By the time I have slid myself out onto the hard shoulder, the onlookers have gathered to offer assistance. Looking at the state of the car, I conclude that their reluctance to approach was probably due to the inevitable scene of carnage that should have greeted them. For a fraction of a second I consider pulling the hilarious, 'I can't feel my legs!' routine, but I quickly decide that it would be most unfair. My wheelchair is salvaged unharmed from the rear of the car, and I manage to get into it before we move back up the hard shoulder away from the car.

So this is where I sit, blanket around my shoulders, when I call Penny to let her know where I am. I even take a picture of the car with my mobile phone, which one of my 'assistants' retrieves unharmed from the wreckage. There is only one panel on the car that isn't totally smashed in. From the gouges in the road and the grass verge, it is clear that the car has gone from the outside lane, across the inside lane and hard shoulder and onto the grass, rolling over three times or so, before the crash barrier brought it to a standstill.

I survey the scene and the state of the car, yet I feel completely calm. Serene, almost. I am at a loss as to why I feel like this. Either:

a) In my head I am still braced for the impact, which never came because the rolling-over dissipated the car's momentum without a jarring, whiplash-inducing impact. Or,

b) My brain has been through such a traumatic time of late that when anything serious happens it just says, 'Aw, fuck it,' and switches off for a while.

The first emergency service to arrive some fifteen minutes after the accident is the fire brigade, who cone off the crash site and insist on putting a neck brace on me, in case I have a neck injury or delayed whiplash. Next on the scene is an ambulance from Stoke Mandeville hospital. The crew are obviously well versed on spinal-cord injury, but as a precaution they insist that I lie on a backboard for a full neurological exam, and make sure that I don't have any internal injuries. So, like a bizarre flashback, I am immobilised on a gurney, and we drive off to the A & E department. It is not how I intended to arrive at the hospital, but once I am given the all-clear, I decide that I might as well go to the Relatives' Day anyway. I arrive slightly late, but the session goes pretty well – thankfully none of the relatives are here because their loved one was injured in a car accident. At one point I slide my fingers through my hair. Bits of broken glass tinkle onto the table in front of me.

Penny drives up to Aylesbury to rescue me, and we head home at a cautious speed. On reflection, I have had an unbelievably lucky escape, having rolled a car at 70 miles per hour, but it all feels rather surreal. The only thing that concerns me is the inconvenience of being without the car. Maybe I am becoming complacent about my obvious invincibility.

Rosalie is turning into a little girl at an alarming rate. Her language continues to develop onomatopoeically, with 'oof-oof' now joined by 'cack-cack' for duck (and any other bird), and a new and rather alarming grunting sound that we conclude is for pig, but could just be a sinus infection. She pulls herself up into a standing position quite often, but then gets a bit apprehensive about how to get back down to the ground. I wonder if I am in part to blame for not giving her a more positive role model in the field of walking.

Penny still finds the energy to keep both Rosalie and me going somehow, coping with the chaos and still laughing along the way. She even manages to continue to get the odd day of work done, too, although I'm sure digging holes and shovelling compost is probably a nice break from food fights, nappy changes and a cantankerous git in a wheelchair ranting about all and sundry. That's when he's not out wrapping cars around all and sundry.

To add to the stress and excitement of car accidents and moving house again, I book onto an activity course with the Back-Up Trust in Exmoor. As it looms ever larger on the horizon, I feel increasingly nervous at the prospect. The week of outdoor adventure is all about pushing one's expectations and the realisation that you can do more than you think. My biggest fear is that I may discover that I can actually do less than I think. I'm not good at accepting help, and I'm not good at admitting defeat. I imagine myself in a field with a flat tyre on my wheelchair, ploughing circles for three days. On the plus side, the course also includes advanced wheelchair skills, so by the end of the week I expect to be able to go up ladders and under water and stuff. Not unrealistic, I think.

The move goes fairly smoothly, although it is frightening just how much stuff we have accumulated over sixteen months. Actually, it's all Rosalie's fault. I really don't know why she needs so many paintings, art materials and wheelchairs. And as for all her CDs ...

And then we're home. I don't know what I was expecting to feel on coming home. Nostalgia? Sadness, I suppose. But our lives have changed so much in the last year and a half that our previous life is almost unrecognisable – as is the flat, in many ways. We have a new kitchen, a new bathroom, a new bedroom, and a new child, obviously. Seeing Rosalie exploring the flat feels very strange, and it's through watching her that I start to feel emotional about our return. This will be her third home and she's only fourteen months old. I think back to when we were last here, when Penny was pregnant and we had breakfast together on a bright spring morning before heading out to a job that it has taken us eighteen months to come home from.

28

The drive down to Exmoor – in my replacement car on the Motability scheme – isn't as arduous as I expect, although it probably helps that I have company. I give a lift to H, a carer who is on the course to help out, having been on several other Back-Up courses in the past. We arrive just in time to join the end of the first day's briefing, where everyone writes down their hopes and fears for the week ahead. Next, we head over to the sports hall, where David Ball – the same David who ran the Back-Up course at Stoke Mandeville when I was still on the spinal unit – runs the first session of advanced wheelchair skills.

As well as seven wheelchair users, there are eight able-bodied 'buddies', including group leader Larnie, who used to work for Back-Up. Of the wheelchair users, or wheelies (an abbreviation that I really hate for some reason – probably due to a TV show when I was a child called *Chorlton and the Wheelies*), Phil is the other group leader. He has been paraplegic for about ten years. The idea of the group leaders is that they provide support and encouragement from a position of experience. Among the other wheelchair users is Paul, the paraglider from Stoke Mandeville. Although I have stayed in occasional telephone contact with him, it is a welcome surprise to find him here, especially participating with Back-Up, which I consider to be really positive.

It becomes apparent in the wheelchair-skills session that many of the able-bodied participants (ABs from now on) are really nervous about saying or doing the wrong thing, and that they seem intimidated by us. We perform a series of icebreakers, the best of which is putting the ABs into wheelchairs, as there are spare chairs at the centre for just this purpose. The idea is that they also participate in all the wheelchair-skills sessions to give them a better idea of just what's involved in getting around in a wheelchair. I am struck by the smiles that spread across their faces as they each get their wheelchairs. There is a sort of simple pleasure in having a go on any kind of self-propelled machine that is immediately apparent when children make a beeline for my wheelchair whenever I get out of it. The difference is that adults feel some kind of social taboo, which would make it seem unacceptable in normal circumstances, but here they are given the green light to have fun in a wheelchair, and the childlike enthusiasm soon bubbles up to the surface, especially when we end the session with an impromptu basketball match.

Over the course of the week, we take part in a number of different activities, and I do push my boundaries. I get in a rope and harness for the first time since my accident when we take on the climbing wall. I manage to climb the wall using just my arms with someone belaying me so that they can take the weight and allow me to take frequent rests. I feel a huge sense of achievement when I get to the top, but I quickly conclude that the strain on my shoulders would deter me from taking up climbing as a pastime. When rock-climbing, I was always taught that where possible you should climb with your legs and hold on with your hands. Trying to do it all with just my arms feels like a particularly cruel punishment.

Kayaking is very satisfying when I discover very quickly that I have enough strength in my core muscles to keep myself balanced without needing specialist seating. This is a big boost to my hopes of going kayaking with Leon in Australia, as they have a two-seat kayak. It is wonderful to be out on water because once I'm in a kayak I can forget all about the paraplegia, as I'm on a level playing field (well, not literally; frankly if I *was* on a level playing field in a kayak I would feel totally immobile – and extremely stupid). In fact, I have an advantage over the AB paddlers, as my shoulders are now much stronger.

We go out on a day trip on hand-bikes, which is also a very useful experience, and are offered the opportunity to try getting onto a horse. The problem is, the only horse that they have who is brave/foolish enough to stand under the hoist while someone is lowered onto his back is not strong enough to take a big lump like me. Undeterred, I head over to the stables, and up the ramp alongside a large and very patient horse with the nickname Wonky Donkey. Parking alongside the horse, the pommel is at my eye level, but after the climbing wall, I feel like I can conquer anything, and I manage to pull myself out of the chair and onto the saddle. While I am, technically, 'in the saddle', I am in the 'stomach-down' position usually occupied by an outlaw who has just been caught by the bounty hunter in a cowboy movie. I shift my weight to allow one of the four brave helpers to swing one of my legs over the saddle, and the subsequent shift in pressure causes me to fire off a sustained and polyphonic flatulent outburst. The worst thing is not the embarrassment, but that I miss the golden opportunity to blame the horse. Still, after a bit more grunting and hefting of limbs, I am up. On the back of a horse. I am holding the pommel for dear life, but I am on a horse for the first time ever.

We head around the dressage ring, one person on either side, ready to grab a leg if I start to slide off. We even manage to trot, and the experience is much more profound than I was expecting. Without getting too mystical, it is the interaction with an animal, the idea of cross-species collaboration, I suppose. It also makes me feel like an all-terrain vehicle once again.

The evenings are spent having a few drinks in the bar, an opportunity to talk and find out a bit more about each other. It is interesting watching the ABs start to think what having a spinal-cord injury would be like, which is part of what a Back-Up course invites them to do. The evenings also provide the opportunity to make a bunch of able-bodied 'buddies' with no experience of spinal injury feel extremely uncomfortable. Especially when we start to take the piss out of each other. Not literally. It isn't some kind of catheter-swap initiation or anything, but simply a bit of light-hearted joshing. It seems to happen when a few SCI people get together, especially if they are on a bit of an adventure. I am the lowest-level injury of all of us, so I am the 'flesh wound' for the week, thus commanding no respect for any physical accomplishments. But as the only one who doesn't suffer from spasm, I am able to mock the stiff legs or dancing feet. On this course there are no 'incompletes'. They usually sit at the bottom of the pecking order. Part-timers, I call them.

I do have one bad night during the week. It comes after a whole day spent kayaking, and Spike drops in for a holiday visit while we are on the bus on the way back to the centre. I let Larnie know that I need to bail straight away, in case people think I am ducking out of unpacking the kit from the bus. She's very understanding and supportive, and I head back to my room, drop a Z and try and read a book. The day's effort works in my favour, and I conk out fairly quickly. I have the room to myself rather than sharing, as I warned the organisers at the beginning of the week that I often have disturbed nights that could be disruptive for any room-mate, and they were very accommodating. I can't imagine what it would be like to go through one of these pain 'episodes' without somewhere to go in order to be alone.

On the penultimate night, we spend a night under canvas at a local Scout campsite, which we have all to ourselves. In the evening we set up the tents, or rather, everyone else sets up the tents, and I set up the cooker and cook the food that has been provided by the chef at the centre. After dinner, we sit in a circle round a large fire and work our way through a considerable quantity of alcohol. By midnight, too much red wine and the warmth of the bonfire take their toll, and feeling a little 'overdone', I make my apologies and leave without a torch, striking out defiantly for the tents in a kind of 'reverse Captain Oates': 'I am just going inside and may be some time.'

However, this gesture of self-serving gallantry, coupled with the dark and a degree of geographical confusion, sees me speed off over a lip and down a steep grass slope, the footplate at the front of the chair digs in, and as I give the distress signal by muttering, 'Oh, bollocks,' I am jettisoned face first down the slope to land in a heap at the bottom. Now it is often said that drunks don't hurt themselves when they fall, because they are relaxed. Luckily, this counts double for me on this occasion, as half of me is permanently relaxed. Unfortunately, the relaxed nature of the rest of me makes any prospect of getting myself back in the wheelchair impossible, and I am grateful when several of the 'professional' members of our party fetch the fabric sling from the minibus and haul me back into my chair, accompany me back to the campsite, and make sure that I am coherent enough to get into my sleeping bag before leaving me to sleep it off.

Morning comes and, remarkably, my excesses are only rewarded with a red-faced ask-around to see if anyone has found my dignity, and a slightly fuzzy feeling over breakfast, which is a fairly swift affair before we pack up and head back to the centre, as the toilet facilities at the campsite are just not equipped to deal with the morning routines of so many SCI campers.

On the final afternoon, we have a debrief, and it quickly becomes clear that we have all had a pretty special week. The chemistry seems to have been right, and we all feel as if we are leaving having achieved something. For myself, I head home with new wheelchair skills and a new confidence to tackle some more challenging obstacles. I also leave having ridden a horse, climbed a wall, learned a bit more about hand-cycling and 'reclaimed' camping, as well as a number of other outdoor activities.

* * *

So, back to London, exhausted, but brimming with newly found confidence. I arrive home to a rapturous welcome from Penny and Rosalie. The week away has made being back in our own flat feel strange. I don't feel home yet, somehow. The hall is narrower than Edgware, which means that I need to develop a greater decisiveness when moving from room to room, and an ability to carry more things. I also need to improve my reversing skills, the easiest way of tipping out of the chair.

It is already apparent that the skirting boards, doors, doorframes, wall and kitchen units are destined to be covered in scuff marks and scratches. Penny's frustrations often bubble over as I defile our pristine home. When making tea in the kitchen, I pick the cups up before realising that I don't have the brakes on. Both hands full, I brace myself for impact as I glide backwards down the hill that is the Victorian floor, and stop with a clunk, wheelchair against new kitchen cupboard.

'Can't you be more careful, instead of crashing into everything all the time? The doors and skirting boards are already ruined.'

'I can't help it. The slopes, the narrow hall, trying to reach things at the back of cupboards …'

But she's right. I'm just never good at admitting my clumsiness. I should use the brakes more, and I don't know why or when I subconsciously decided not to, especially as I have now discovered that just about every house I go in is on some kind of slope. I have become a human spirit level. At home it is also a choice for me between either feeling mobile, unimpaired and relatively relaxed, or having clean, chip-free paintwork.

Soon we begin packing for the trip to Australia. Fortunately we now have the best GP practice on the planet. They are knowledgeable, proactive, understanding and very supportive. I am given prescriptions aplenty so I have a suitcase full of medication to take with me, and the catheter supplier even sends a month's supply of catheters to Australia ahead of our trip so that I don't have to take up my whole luggage allowance with continence products.

My GP also prescribes Viagra for me to try, confident after having checked my blood pressure and looked through my notes that I am unlikely to have any side effects more serious than a headache. I try it. My God, but that's astonishing. The wonders of modern medicine, etc. Although I still can't feel anything below the waist, the psychological boost from this most mechanical of physical reactions is huge. Titter, titter. It is unfair to expect anyone to be able to imagine what sex feels like when you have no feeling below the waist. But somehow, there is still an intensity of emotion and sensation that is profound and surprising. I am sure that the Viagra-induced ability to have sexual intercourse satiates some psychological aspect of my masculinity, perhaps alleviates some sense of emasculation, but that does not come close to explaining how pleasurable it is. And how sharing that intimate pleasure with Penny, having those moments lost to passion, connect us to our old life together, makes the before and the after into a whole, single experience.

Applying my newfound awareness of my body is also useful when preparing for the flight. A bit of 'local knowledge' helps, and a couple of days before departure I eat some cabbage. The predictable effect of this choice of foodstuff is that within a few hours I get a mild stomach ache, head to the toilet and have a total clear out. Now, I'm sure you are probably thinking that this much detail is gratuitous, but imagine the prospect of two long-haul flights when you have very little warning and no control of your bowels, your wheelchair is in the hold and you are in an airline seat. The result of my 'cabbage clear-out' is that I won't need to go to the toilet again for several days. These are the kind of things that I am learning when it comes to managing my body.

On the subject of 'ones and twos', I have also taken delivery of a few indwelling catheters, and an L-shaped leg bag that straps to the inside of the knee and has a capacity approaching two litres, rather than the standard 750 ml. If that isn't big enough, then our plan is to siphon off a bit of wee into a water bottle, and Penny will go and empty it in the toilet. Simple. Well, in theory, but still extremely daunting, having not done this before. It's one thing dealing with continence issues on the ground, when I can always excuse myself and find a toilet, but strapped to a seat on a packed flight with no wheelchair makes it all quite terrifying. It is also a sign of my rehabilitation that I have learned how to feel embarrassed about this kind of stuff again.

On the recommendation of a couple of wheelchair travellers, I buy some 'luggage racks' for my wheelchair, which consist of two fold-down plastic blades that make the wheelchair look a bit like a forklift truck, enabling me to stand a suitcase on them, resting against my knees. They could also be used for 'shin-boning' my way through crowded public places, but I'll keep that one for emergencies.

Even though I am perhaps over-prepared, and the anticipation of the flight is stressful, I find myself more daunted by the prospect of returning home. Up to now we have had future plans. Being discharged from the spinal unit, having a baby, moving back to London, having the flat adapted, applying for grants and means-tested benefits, moving home, going to Exmoor and preparing for the trip to Australia. But when we get back, then what?

The 'incredible journey' begins early in the morning for a lunchtime flight. After showering I do battle with the indwelling catheter. I have left this to the last minute, of course, because I am less than excited at the prospect of having an indweller again, and the increased risk of getting a bladder infection. Finally I manage to get everything where it should be, the pipe held in place with Velcro straps and the yet-to-be-inflated blimp attached to my leg. We finish the last forgotten bits of packing and check our passports and tickets for the seventeenth time. Penny stops just short of slapping me about the face, and manages to talk me down to panicky from hysterical.

Eugene drives our little travelling circus to the airport. As soon as a member of staff spots us in the check-in queue, we are ushered to the first-class check-in desk ahead of the hoi polloi. My first suspicion is that we have been identified as 'secret shoppers' sent to test the staff's helpfulness, as no one in their right minds would travel with both a small child and a wheelchair user. But the airport staff are all friendly and extremely helpful, as is Rosalie, who bats her big blue eyes at all and sundry, ensuring that if we don't get the pity vote, at least we're guaranteed winners in the cute stakes.

The official queue-jumping continues through security. I am led through the metal detector, which goes off (surprise), and then I am patted down. I suddenly think of all the media coverage of the new extra-tight security measures at airports, with particularly stringent rules over liquids being taken on board. Tales of mothers having to drink some of their babies' bottled milk to demonstrate it's not some kind of gelignite. I brace myself for a difficult encounter, but am determined to remain defiant. There's no way anyone is going to make me drink a single drop of urine from my leg zeppelin. I have a bit of a rule that I only drink liquids once. Luckily, there are no such demands made upon me, and we breeze through the departure lounge.

At the departure gate, we meet another wheelchair user and his wife. We nod acknowledgement to each other and I notice that he has callipers on and is equipped with crutches, so that he can make his own way from the wheelchair onto the plane and into his seat. I explain to a member of the ground staff that I cannot do the same, and he tells me that they are still waiting for the people who are supposed to put me on the plane. Eventually, the rest of the passengers are told to board while we wait, with Rosalie getting ever more restless.

At last we are joined by two less well known of Snow White's friends, Surly and Awkward. They unfurl an aisle chair that has certainly seen some action. There is not only no padding on it, but there are two screws sticking through the webbing seat. I just want to get on the aeroplane so I say nothing. I transfer onto the aisle chair and clutch my knees as we approach the plane. My generous and charming hosts have the air of a couple of old hand(ler)s who are on a cushy number, but don't know how to switch the 'grumble' off. They complain about the step onto the plane. One step, mind. Not the whole flight of steep stairs two cheerful guys at London City took me up, oh no. One. And I can tell that they are thinking of refusing to get me on board, so while they shake their heads and huff, I speak up: 'Oh, well, you'd better just leave me here, then,' with a big and hopefully slightly menacing smile on my face.

They relent, and I am taken through to my seat.

Just as they are about to grab me, I say, 'It's all right, I can get into the seat by myself, thanks.'

More grumbles and tuts, as one of them says, "E's gotta do it on 'is own ain't 'e,' in an extremely sarcastic voice.

I admit that I may have turned the 'Dick van Dyke in *Mary Poppins*' up a bit, but there is definitely an overbearing manner, coupled with an assumption that I'm deaf. Undeterred, I manage the transfer fairly effortlessly and I am free of the miserable (baggage) tossers.

Finally we are under the care of the cabin crew, who are particularly helpful, and even explain to me that there is an aisle chair on board the aircraft, and an accessible toilet. We are sat next to the couple that we nodded to in the departure lounge, who have made the journey to Australia several times before. It turns out that he had a spinal stroke twenty years ago, leaving him L1 incomplete. And his consultant at Stoke Mandeville is ... Dr J. Spooky, huh? They are a really positive example of how far you can go in a wheelchair if you are a little intrepid, having travelled extensively in the Far East as well as Australasia. They are also very understanding of Rosalie's squirming and whining, which finally abates after several hours, and she conks out in the bassinet – a sort of travel cot – provided, which barely holds her.

On arrival at Kuala Lumpur, the other passengers disembark before we are joined by two diminutive female ground crew members, who allow me to transfer into the brand-new aisle chair on my own, before cheerfully wheeling me to the exit, and lifting me down the step to where my wheelchair is waiting. I am certainly relieved to see it there, as I have spent weeks fretting over those tales of wheelchairs (or the damaged remains thereof) doing the rounds on the baggage carousel, or even getting reports that it is in another airport elsewhere in the world.

We collect our luggage, and head to the hotel that adjoins Kuala Lumpur airport. We check in, and spend most of the next twenty-four hours in the enormous double bed in our room. It's even big enough for all three of us to sleep in at once, which means it can accommodate Rosalie sleeping sideways in the middle.

The following day there's more queue-jumping and efficient embarkation. A few hours into the flight, curiosity gets the better of me, and I ask to use the toilet on the plane. The cabin crew cheerfully oblige, reaching into the recesses of a stowage area, and sliding out a flat-pack aisle chair which, once assembled, resembles a milk crate with two pop-up handles on the top, and four tiny casters on the bottom. The chair proves quite a challenge to steer, and also to stay on top of (literally), but the real challenge comes when we meet the 3-mm-high threshold strip separating us from the toilet cubicle. The minute casters struggle with the obstruction, and there is much pulling and pushing before we make it into the cubicle. All four of us. An elaborate dance ensues, culminating in me having the cubicle to myself at last.

I hoist my foot onto the rim of the toilet and rummage up my trouser leg for the valve on the leg bag. Unfortunately, in the ensuing struggle, my elbow hits the flush button and, although I am not sucked out of the aircraft, I do end up with damp trousers. I dry them off with the hand towels as best I can, and decide that it is likely that the flight crew are hanging on my every noise, so I let go of my leg in order to squeeze the bag and speed up the emptying process. As the bag is draining, my foot slips, and gets wedged under the toilet seat. I finish the job in hand, all the time sliding back and forth on the brake-free milk crate. I then spend several minutes trying to get my foot out of the toilet seat and my arm out of the sink, where my cuff has caught the tap and my sleeve is filling with water. I finally recover my posture, go through another half a dozen paper towels, and press the call button before being manoeuvred back to my seat a little wiser and a lot damper.

We eventually arrive in Sydney to be greeted by Penny's parents, and I bask in the warmth of the welcome, the warm air, the smell of eucalyptus and the feeling I always get on arrival in Australia. It feels exotic. It feels like I'm on the other side of the world.

29

In the weeks that follow, I get to do the 'first time since the accident' meeting thing with some of the last remaining friends. Most people seem a bit nervous. They don't know what to expect, which is understandable. Sadly though, I miss the opportunity to comb flour through my hair, rub black pencil around my eyes, dress in grey and cough consumptively, while occasionally pointing over the victim's shoulder and moaning softly 'please don't take me yet' or ' I must go into the light', etc. Instead of which, the most common reaction by people is that I 'look well'. I think that the slight tinge of disappointment in their voices is in my imagination.

One night we catch up with a group of friends, including one that I'd only met for the first time during our last visit to Australia the week before my accident. I can sense his nervousness, especially as the rest of us have been friends for about ten years. Unfortunately, he ends up getting steaming drunk, and asking me lots of questions, including several about how my sex life has been affected, before pausing mid-conversation, and proffering his hand to shake as a gesture of his admiration at how well I am coping with everything. I don't want admiring handshakes. They are patronising and rather embarrassing. And they are usually only 'awarded' by drunk people.

When it comes to farewells at the end of the night, one girl launches herself on me for an affectionate hug, only I don't have my brakes on and her enthusiasm takes me by surprise. As her heartfelt embrace starts to tip me over backwards, she cries, 'Oh no! Oh my God! Oh, I'm so sorry!' To make matters worse, in an attempt to help she keeps me in a headlock, thus preventing me from being able to correct my balance, and we go over together. The panic continues, much to Penny and my amusement, especially when the poor girl's husband tries to help me back into the wheelchair. By picking my legs up. It's not his fault. It's a very common response from people who haven't got used to being around me since my accident. Most panic as soon as I'm out of the chair, whereas those who are used to the whole business treat it much the same as if I had tripped over when I was able-bodied. On this occasion, I end up sliding all the way out of my chair so that I can demonstrate to our friends that getting back into the chair is no big deal, and, by the way, nor is being out of it. I mean the chair, of course.

I had been told by one of the basketball team who was at the Sydney Paralympics that the city is very wheelchair-friendly, and that is my overall experience, especially in the centre of town, although the tropical volume of rain that can fall means that many kerbs are unsurmountable, and shops often have stepped access, especially a bit further out of the centre. However, the main challenge is an unavoidable geographical one, as the city is built around a huge natural harbour, which means most suburbs slope down to the water. Steeply down.

While in Sydney, we stay in some self-catering accommodation that wasn't specifically advertised as wheelchair accessible, but as my chair fits through a standard width door-frame and my transfers are fairly intrepid, we opted for the place, especially as there is ramped access at the front of the building, although this turns out to be a bit misleading. The foyer of the building is at the top of a dozen steps and there is a ground-floor car park, which is accessed via an electric roller shutter and a steep slope. To go anywhere 'on foot', Penny takes Rosalie through the front, and I hit the button for the roller shutter, before hurtling down the slope and turning sharply into the middle of the road. Fortunately it is a quiet cul-de-sac, but I still wish I had a siren and flashing lights.

As well as catching up with friends and meeting the newest members of our extended family, we get out and about a bit. Up in the Blue Mountains for the wedding that was the impetus to visit now, we drive out to a lookout on the bluff that has been made wheelchair accessible. It is a rather unnerving experience, following a black tarmac path as it snakes through the bush, all smooth and ordered, while all around is an organic chaos of leaf matter, ground cover and a myriad of insects. Yet again I miss the spontaneity of movement that allows exploration of the great outdoors. Although there are opportunities such as this, where a real effort has been made to create wheelchair access, it's just not the same, and I feel divorced from my surroundings.

While we are in Sydney, I take the opportunity and telephone the Moolong spinal rehabilitation unit to see if I can blag a visit. I speak to Gillian, the nurse manager who happens to be from the UK, and she invites me to come in and take a look. The majority of the patients are tetraplegic, as many paras get discharged straight from the acute unit. I trade information with the nurse manager, which is informative for me and, I hope, for her. The most sobering aspects of spinal-cord injury in Australia are to do with support from the health service. I discover that as well as scans such as MRIs being relatively rare, spinal physicians frequently have to make clinical decisions that are often based on the patient's ability to pay for medication. Then there's the cost of catheters and other continence products, a wheelchair, and maybe even the cost of MRI scans and CT scans, all of which I have provided by the state, and it makes the prospect of living in Australia quite intimidating.

As we leave the rehab unit I think about the NHS, and how, for all its imperfections and frustrating inefficiencies, the principle of free healthcare provision at the point of delivery is one of the truly great ideas of the twentieth century. In the clamour for, and obsession with, lower taxes, many people in the UK expect to have a fully functioning and efficient health service, but don't expect to have to pay for it. In many Scandinavian countries people pay more tax, but get better services and have a higher standard of living. I have been told that if you intend to have a spinal-cord injury, Sweden is about the best place to do it. Worth bearing in mind.

After doing the 'spinal Sydney' tour, we decamp to Penny's parents' place on the south coast of New South Wales, and hold court while friends come and visit. Leon has made all sorts of adjustments, including ramps and grab rails in the bathroom to enable me to feel at home there, and it feels nice to be back, although, inevitably, I end up reflecting on the last time I was here, a week before my accident.

We have major sleep disruption, with Rosalie profoundly confused by jet lag and unfamiliar surroundings, and inevitably ending up in our bed. I start having increasingly peculiar dreams. One night I have a dream in which I know that I am supposed to be disabled, so I make an effort to walk slowly and affect a limp. I have great fun walking over sharp gravel, feeling every tiny point against the soles of my feet. I try carpet next, all furry and soft, and I run my toes across it and feel them heat up with the friction, until I am woken by a snuffling sound and a small finger wandering up my nose. It takes me a while to realise that I have been dreaming, and that the limp in the dream has been replaced with the all too real and familiar paraplegia. But that gravel felt good.

The next morning is a slow start after a much needed lie in. 'Poppa' Leon has taken enthusiastically to his grandfatherly duties, rising at half-past five in the morning and taking a wide-awake Rosalie for a walk to show her his workshop. As I am getting dressed, Penny says, 'I wish you weren't paralysed. Does that mean that I haven't come to terms with it yet?' I am glad that Penny still wishes I wasn't paralysed, and long may it continue, this connection to our old life. But I do reflect on the times on this trip when those same feelings of loss have been at their most acute. When I've looked from the balcony at the view down the valley, huge eucalyptus trees disappearing off into the distance, the morning mist hanging in the foliage, and I have missed being able to wander cross-country. I think of Leon's workshop, and how all the machines are set up to be used from a standing position, how the tracks in the bush would be great on a mountain bike. How good the view would be from this or that hill or escarpment. Then I think how these are all things that Penny could still do, but she doesn't because I can't. I don't know if this wish or regret gets any less with time, or whether we have to try and fill our lives with the things that we can still do together so that we don't have space for the things we can't.

In my more negative moments, the pain of loss allows a darker side to come through again. As is often the case, when someone fills the glass half full, I feel compelled to empty it. Especially if they are able-bodied. I seem to have created a very narrow margin in which to expect people to operate. If they are at all negative or pessimistic, then I feel as if I am being made to attend my own funeral, and I hate the way that they can effectively write off my life post-SCI. But if they are optimistic then I am consumed with a wave of cynicism and I feel like asking, 'You think it's all OK? Just what do you actually know about living with spinal-cord injury?' Both responses are totally unfair and destructive, but sometimes I struggle to keep the lid on.

On a more positive day, I go with Leon to the local tip and we buy an old mountain bike. We take it back to the workshop, cut it down, and with the aid of several cups of tea, some lateral thinking, a bit of plywood and a couple of bedsprings, we convert my boring wheelchair into a downhill racer. Basically, we add a front wheel with a brake on it. There is also a safety feature, in the form of a red rope attached to the back. Leon's thinking is that we can drive in the truck up to the top of the hill, and then he and I can 'stroll' back down, enjoying the scenery and having a chat, as we used to before my accident.

Our friends Jonathan and Bettina have driven all the way down from Queensland with their two young daughters who are six and four. The girls have the disarming honesty and curiosity of youth, so I am under constant pressure to relinquish my wheelchair. Sometimes I find it difficult watching the two girls running around, climbing in the playground, racing here and there, digging holes on the beach and generally being full of youthful exuberance. I can see Rosalie doing the same at their age, and my sadness at not being able to participate is amplified by feeling that if I hadn't fallen from the tree, we would be living in Australia by now, surrounded by beaches and wilderness to explore.

The house is full, with thirteen adults, three kids and a dog. It is generously proportioned, which is just as well, as we have quite a lot of rain, and we spend long afternoons all playing hide the tantrum. Two friends, Brent and Rachel, take off for a cross-country walk down to the creek, a walk that Penny and I have made in the past, and I am filled with a mixture of claustrophobia and deep regret. Penny comes into the room and reveals how she envies them the most, as their interests and love of the great outdoors is closest to ours. The surrounding hills and the torrential rain makes leaving the house feel like an impossibility. We do manage to keep things relatively cheerful, as the children are happy to play games, especially if they get to use my wheelchair.

One morning I make it up the stairs on my backside, and heave myself from the floor into my chair. As I sit getting my breath back, I realise that the girls, Marla and Leni, are standing next to me.

'Tim, can we have a go in your wheelchair?'

'Well, no, not really, because then I will have to get out of it, and I will be stuck on the sofa. Maybe later in the day when I have a bit of a rest.'

They both sigh. 'OK.'

Ten minutes go by.

'Tim, can we have a go in your wheelchair now?'

'No, later.'

'Tim, how about now?' etc.

And I am glad. I'm glad that they like to have a go in my wheelchair, and they like to try and push me around in it because it shows that they are relaxed about the whole thing. But these are kids that I used to put on my shoulders so that they could touch the ceiling, and it feels as if they have adjusted to my disability a damn sight better than me.

When the weather finally does break, we all board Leon's truck and head to the top of the hill so that we can try our first test of the special front-wheel modification to my wheelchair, and we all set off gently down the hill. But try as I might, I just can't keep to walking pace, especially as the rims are so rusty and rough that the brake pads are disappearing before my eyes, so I let gravity take the upper hand and the chair goes like the clappers, as I clutch the handlebars, wondering if it will all hold together. It does, even stopping without dumping me in the bushes.

The red rope safety feature is attached to an eager volunteer, so that if the brakes do fail, the momentum will pull him over and the friction caused by his being dragged face down along the track will eventually slow me down. On the second run, this safety feature is removed. The second run is also made possible by Brent pushing me back up the hill, and this leads me to conclude that all I need is someone to push me up over the up and overs. And maybe a four-wheel rig. And disc brakes. Independent suspension would be nice. And a helmet. And some body armour. You see, here's the problem. I really want to get outdoors and go for long walks and all, but once I get behind a set of handlebars, I end up trying to go as fast as possible, as if I'm back on a bicycle.

As the weather is much improved, we head down to the coast and I have my first attempt at sand. I have been told that sand and wheelchairs just don't ... well, just don't. But I'm sure it's just a question of strength and determination, so we head over a small bridge that has a ramp down onto the sand, and I hit the ramp at a reasonable speed, flick the front casters up, breeze down onto the sand and stop dead. I knew it was going to be hard, but it turns out to be downright impossible. It takes a full five minutes of lung-bursting effort to make a circle of about ten feet in diameter. I leave the chair, lie on my back on the sand, and look up at the sky, trying to work out what I am going to have to invent that will enable me to take to the beach again one day.

The next sand encounter is more positive. It is Leon's birthday, and the two of us head down to the beach again, this time with the kayak. I roll onto the sand from the boat ramp, where the sand is firm enough for me to push on, so I head down to the water's edge where the river meets the sea. I sit there, looking worldly wise in my outdoor adventurer's hat (Leon prefers that I don't wear the pith helmet I've just bought in town, as he thinks it a little too 'British Colonial'). As I work on my tan and my thousand-yard stare, I fail to notice as a wave comes up the river and I sink rapidly, the sand up to my axle in no time. Much huffing and puffing later, I manage to free myself, and I vow not to think about what the sea and sand may have done to the bearings. My next challenge is to get into the kayak, but as I have already done this on the Back-Up course, I know what to expect and I drop elegantly into the front seat. The wheelchair safely on the truck, we take the next surge wave and head off up the creek, paddles at the ready. I tell Leon all about the Back-Up week, and as we paddle along it feels great to be doing something that allows me to forget my paraplegia.

Back on the balcony later, exhausted but happy, especially as my pain hasn't flared up following my exertions, I sit stroking Ben the dog, with whom I am bonding extremely well. He is a friendly and tolerant dog, despite Rosalie's best attempts to wag his tail, suck his nose, and generally pat him with vigour. As I sit taking in the view, he comes up and nuzzles me before sitting, world wearily, at my side. I do, however, hold a sneaking suspicion that one day I will look down to find him innocently chewing on one of my feet.

A green parrot lands on the handrail and looks on quizzically, as the sun sinks lower in the sky and the intricate shadows of the eucalyptus trees reach out across the grass. I sit sipping a cold beer, Penny in the house playing with Rosalie, squeals and giggles ringing out past me and down the valley, and I look back eighteen months. If I had been offered this when I was lying on my back in hospital, I think I'd have taken it. With both hands.

Acknowledgements

First thank you, of course, to Penny for allowing me to tell our story, and to Rosalie for inspiring me every day.

I would like to thank our family: Mum, Eugene, Leon, Ginny, Dad, Margaret, Chris, Sarah, Scarlett, Jessica, Simon, Cathy, Derek and Sally for all of their invaluable support, love, patience and understanding.

Also heartfelt thanks to everyone who helped us financially: the fund-raisers and contributors, the anonymous friends. Your help and support made the difference.

I am indebted to Jackie Bailey and all the staff of the National Spinal Injuries Centre at Stoke Mandeville, the London Air Ambulance, Jill Ayres, Scott Cairns, Ruth and Cal, Tanja Howarth, Jo Kobyluch, Harry Long, Marianne, Jason Naidoo, Brendan Smith, Stuart Wheeler and everyone at Aspire and Back-Up.

Special thanks to Graham Hishmurgh, Elaine Padmore, Neil Randhawa, Nigel Whitfield, and of course our many supportive, brave and loving friends without whom we would not have managed to cope. We know who you are.

Finally, thanks to KT, Ed, Davina, and everyone at Virgin Books.

Resources

In the UK
National Spinal Injuries Centre (Stoke Mandeville)

www.spinal.org.uk
01296 315000
The work of the NSIC consists of diagnosis, treatment and reha-bilitation of patients, both with acute spinal cord injuries and with non-traumatic spinal cord lesions of acute onset. Patients are referred from all over the world.

Spinal Injuries Association

www.spinal.co.uk
0845 678 6633
The Spinal Injuries Association (SIA) was set up in 1974 in order to support people with spinal cord injury (SCI). The founders them-selves had SCI and, to this day, SIA is run by a board of trustees who live with spinal cord injury.

Aspire

www.aspire.org.uk
020 8954 5759
Aspire offers practical support to the 40,000 people living with spinal cord injury in the UK so that they can lead fulfilling and independent lives in their homes, with their families, in workplaces and leisure time.

Back Up Trust

www.backuptrust.org.uk

020 8875 1805

Back Up is a small, dynamic and professional charity that runs a range of services for people with SCI as well as their friends, family and volunteers to encourage independence, self-confidence and motivation following a life-changing injury.

Apparelyzed

www.apparelyzed.com

This web site was first created to sell t-shirts and other apparel featuring SCI humour, but has grown into much more, providing information and a forum for discussion. It now aims to raise disability awareness and share life experiences between disabled people and their carers.

British Wheelchair Sport

www.wheelpower.org.uk

01296 395995

WheelPower is the national charity for wheelchair sport and aims to help people with disabilities achieve their sporting dreams. They provide accessible facilities including an Athletics Arena, as well as on-site accommodation, at the Stoke Mandeville Stadium.

Spinal Research

www.spinal-research.org

01483 898786

One of the leading international charitable organisations in the field of spinal cord injury research, their pioneering work has achieved a number of ground-breaking changes in the field.

In Australia and New Zealand
Spinal Cord Injuries Australia

www.scia.org.au

02 9661 8855; 1800 819 775 (people with disabilities and their carers outside Sydney)

Spinal Cord Injuries Australia provides consumer-based support and rehabilitation services to people with physical disabilities. Offices are located in every state of Australia and in the Northern Territory. Contact the Sydney office for information about your nearest representative.

SpinalCure Australia

www.spinalcure.org.au
02 9660 1040
SpinalCure Australia aims to end the permanence of spinal cord injury by promoting and funding research and fostering cooperation between researchers into the central nervous system and regeneration.

ANZSCIN

www.anzscin.org
1800 774 625 (for callers within Australia)
ANZSCIN aims to advance research and clinical trials into spinal cord injury and disease. Supported by the NSW Government, the network draws together leading researchers, clinicians and key stakeholders from Australia and New Zealand.

International
D-ability

www.d-ability.org
Disability leisure, arts, sports and lifestyle web guide. Provides direct links to the websites of organisations from across the world, and people with a multitude of backgrounds and abilities.

Crip College

www.cripcollege.com
Christian Bagg's web site was created to share some of his stories about life in a chair, as well as to help spread the knowledge gathered in his everyday life. Intended to be a useful resource centre for the aspiring wheelchair user.